LEAVING CERT

LESS STRESS MORE SUCCESS

Business Revision

John F. O'Sullivan

g GILL EDUCATION

Gill Education
Hume Avenue
Park West
Dublin 12
www.gilleducation.ie

Gill Education is an imprint of M.H. Gill & Co.

978 07171 4702 1

Design by Liz White Designs
Artwork and print origination by MPS Limited, a Macmillan Company

The paper used in this book is made from the wood pulp of managed forests. For every tree felled, at least one tree is planted, thereby renewing natural resources.

For permission to reproduce photographs, the author and publisher gratefully acknowledge the following:

© Alamy: 120, 148, 152, 164, 178B, 189, 208B, 223, 247, 255, 260; © Getty Images: 4B, 63, 112, 177, 198; © Photocall Ireland!: 199, 208T; © Photolibrary: 16, 178T; Courtesy of Airtricity: 254L; Courtesy of ASTI: 21TR; Courtesy of CIF: 4TR; Courtesy of Energia: 254R, Courtesy of Enterprise Ireland: 213; Courtesy of IBEC: 3; Courtesy of ICTU: 4TL; Courtesy of INTO: 21BL; Courtesy of NCA: 17; Courtesy of SIPTU: 21TL, Courtesy of TUI: 21BR; Courtesy of VHI: 98; Courtesy of Zurich: 100.

The authors and publisher have made every effort to trace all copyright holders, but if any has been inadvertently overlooked we would be pleased to make the necessary arrangement at the first opportunity.

CONTENTS

Introduction

General Examination Advice
Higher Level

 Note: Material that is to be studied only by those taking Higher Level is indicated in the text.

Section 1 Short answer questions

1. Short answer questions only have four lines of space for writing answers, so keep your answers short and to the point.
2. Write two points of information for each answer (unless told otherwise in the question). The first point should be a definition; then you can use an advantage/disadvantage or an explained example as a second point.
3. Answer all ten short questions if you have time. The examiner will mark you on your eight best answers.

Section 2 Applied Business Question (ABQ)

1. The applied business question describes a business situation facing a company or business person.
2. It usually contains three paragraphs of text with three questions based on the information given.
3. It is a compulsory question and carries 20% of the total marks. You must answer all three questions in the ABQ. There is no choice.
4. The ABQ each year is based on three different units of the course.

Advice for answering Applied Business Question

1. Read the questions first. This will tell you what to look out for when you read the question.
2. Read the information in the ABQ. Highlight or underline relevant points as you read the text of the question.
3. Answer each question as follows:

(A) State the point.

(B) Explain and develop the point.

If the question says 'describe', 'analyse' or 'evaluate' you must give more detailed information. 'Evaluation' means you must give your opinion on the topic. ('I think it is good (or bad) because . . .') Give a reason why (maybe advantage or disadvantage).

(C) Quote from the text to back up your point.

You must quote from the text for every point you make in your answer even if not asked to do so in the question. Use a red pen to highlight your quotes.

Section 3 – Long answer questions

1. Answer the required number of questions from part 1 and part 2.
2. Read the questions carefully and ensure you give the required information in your answers.
3. Divide the marks by 5 to see approximately how many points you are expected to make in your answer.
4. Answer in point form (no essays).

Number each point clearly. For each point in your answer:

- State the point.
- Explain and develop the point.
- Give an explained example if possible.

Key verbs in the questions that regularly appear at Higher Level

- **Analyse:**
  - State the point
  - Explain the point
  - Make a comment on it, state an advantage or disadvantage.
- **Apply:** Use knowledge or skill for a particular purpose.
- **Compare:** Examine two or more things so as to discover their similarities or differences.
- **Calculate:** Find out or ascertain by using numerical data.
- **Contrast/differentiate/distinguish:**
  - Show the differences between the two things mentioned in the question.
  - If the differences are obvious you could use the word 'whereas' to link the differences, otherwise you can show the differences by stating a number of points about each topic.
- **Define:**
  - State the precise meaning of the topic
  - Give at least two points of information.
- **Describe:** Give an account of person, event, institution, etc.
- **Discuss:** Give a detailed explanation, debating both side of the issue.
- **Draft:** Draw up what ever document is requested – business letter, report, memo, agenda, business plan – or sketch diagram or chart.
- **Evaluate:**
  - State the point
  - Explain and develop the point
  - Evaluate: Give your opinion on the topic (assess or judge something).

State whether it is a good thing or a bad thing and back it up with a reason (advantage or disadvantage).

- **Explain:** Make clear in a detailed manner.
- **Identify:** Show that you recognise something.
- **Illustrate:**
  - State the point
  - Explain and develop the point
  - Give an example for each point (make clear by means of examples, charts, diagrams, graphs, etc.).
- **List:** Write down a number of names or things that have something in common.
- **Outline:** Give a short summary of the chief elements, omitting details.

Legislation on the course

The following are the seven laws in the course:

- Sale of Goods and Supply of Services Act 1980
- Consumer Protection Act 2007
- Industrial Relations Act 1990
- Employment Equality Act 1998
- Unfair Dismissals Acts 1977 to 2007
- Data Protection Acts 1988 and 2003
- Companies Act 1990 (as it relates to the formation of private companies only)

Practise calculation-type questions

- Ratio analysis (profitability, liquidity, debt–equity ratio)
- Tax calculation
- Average clause (insurance)
- Balance of trade/balance of payments
- Break-even point/margin of safety
- Be able to analyse a cash flow forecast

Practise essential diagrams

- Maslow's hierarchy of needs
- Break-even chart
- Bar chart, pie chart
- Product life cycle
- Organisational chart (functional/matrix)
- Span of control
- Channels of distribution

Drafting documents

- Business letter
- Business report
- Notice, agenda and minutes of meeting
- Memorandum (memo)
- Business plan

Higher Level examination layout – 400 marks – 3 hours (180 minutes)

Section	Questions	Answer	Marks (%)	Areas covered	Timing
1	Ten short answer questions	Eight questions	80/400 (20%)	All parts of course.	30 minutes (approx. 4 minutes per question).
2	Applied business questions (ABQ)	All three parts (compulsory question)	80/400 (20%)	The ABQ each year is based on three different units of the course as follows: 2012 units 4 5 6 2013 units 5 6 7 2014 units 1 2 3 2015 units 2 3 4 2016 units 3 4 5	40 minutes
3	Seven Questions. Part 1 contains **three** questions. Part 2 contains **four** questions.	Four Questions Part 1: Answer **one** question; Part 2: Answer **two** questions; Answer fourth question from either Part 1 or Part 2.	240/400 60% Each question is worth 60 marks.	Part 1 questions are taken from units 1, 6, 7 Part 2 questions are taken from units 2, 3, 4, 5.	100 minutes (approx. 25 minutes per question)

Timing above allows five minutes for reading examination paper and selecting questions and five minutes for reading over your answers and checking work at the end of the exam.

Past exam paper analysis Higher Level

	2012	2011	2010	2009	2008	2007	2006	2005	2004	2003	2002	2001	2000	1999
Unit 1														
Relationships in business			Q1(C)	Q1(AB)	Q1(A)	Q1(C)	Q1(AC)	Q1(AB)	Q1(A)	Q1(AB)	Q1(AB)	Q1(AB)		Q1(AB)
Consumer/Retailer			Q1(B)					Q1(C)				Q1(C)		
Employer/Employee			Q1(A)	Q1(C)	Q1(C)	Q1(A)	Q1(B)		Q1(BC)	Q1(C)	Q1(C)		Q1(ABC)	Q1(C)
Unit 2														
Enterprise					Q4(A)	Q4(A)	Q4(C)			Q4(ABC)				
Unit 3														
Management											Q4(B)			
Leading–Motivating				Q4(AB)			Q4(AB)	Q4(C)		Q5(ABC)		Q4(B)		
Communication				Q4(C)J6(A)	Q4(B)	Q4(BC)		Q4(AB)	Q4(C)	Q5(ABC)	Q4(A)	Q4(A)	Q4(ABC)	Q4(AB)
Planning/Organising/Controlling			Q4(ABC)		Q4(C)				Q4(AB)		Q4(C)	Q4(C)		Q4(C)

	1999	2000	2001	2002	2003	2004	2005	2006	2007	2008	2009	2010	2011	2012
Unit 4														
Household and Business: Finance	Q5(AC)		Q5(A)	Q5(AC)					Q6(B)	Q6(A)	Q6(C)	Q5(A)		
Household and Business: Insurance	Q5(AB)		Q5(B)	Q5(AB)				Q5(A)		Q6(B)	Q6(B)			
Household and Business: Taxation	Q5(AB)		Q5(C)	Q5(A)					Q5(AB)	Q6(A)	Q5(C)			
Human Resource Management					Q6 (ABC)	Q5(B)				Q5(AB)		Q5(A)		
Changing Role of Management		Q5 (ABC)				Q5(AC)			Q5(C)	Q5 (C) 6 (C)	Q6(B)			
Monitoring the Business	Q6(AB)		Q6(AB)			Q6(AB)		Q5(B)	Q6(C)			Q5(BC)		
Unit 5														
Identifying Opportunities	Q7(A)	Q6 (ABC)	Q7(A)	Q7(A)	Q7(A)	Q7(AB)	Q6(A)			Q7(C)	Q7(A)	Q7(A)		
Marketing	Q7(BC)		Q7(B)	Q7(BC)	Q7(B)	Q7(C)	Q6 (B) Q7(ABC)	Q7 (ABC)	Q6 (A) Q7(ABC)	Q7(B)	Q7(BC)	Q7(BC)		
Getting Started				Q6(AB)			Q5(A)	Q6(A)		Q7(A)		Q6(BC)		
Business Expansion		Q7 (ABC)					Q5(BC)	Q6(B)			Q5(AB)	Q6(A)		

Unit 6												
Categories of Industry	Q2(B)	Q2(A)		Q2(A)	Q2(A)		Q2(A)	Q2(BC)	Q2(A)	Q2(A)	Q2(B)	Q2(B)
												Q2(A)
Type of Business Organisations		Q2(A)					Q2(B)		Q2(B)	Q2(B)			
Community Development				Q2(B)			Q2(B)		Q2(B)				
Business and the Economy					Q2(B)			Q2 (B) (I)	Q2(C)	Q2(C)			Q2(C)
Government and Business	Q2(C)	Q2(C)	Q2(C)	Q2(C)		Q2(A)						Q2(C)	
Social Responsibility of Business	Q2(A)	Q2(B)	Q2(B)	Q2(C)	Q2(C)			Q2 (B) (I)		Q2(A)		Q2(A)	Q2(B)
Unit 7												
International Trading	Q3(AB)			Q3(A)	Q3(C)	Q3(C)	Q3(AB)	Q3(A)	Q3(A)	Q3(A)	Q3(C)	Q3(C)	Q3(A)
European Union	Q3(C)	Q3(A)	Q3 (ABC)	Q3(C)	Q3(AB)	Q3(AB)	Q3(C)	Q3(AB)		Q3(B)	Q3(B)	Q3(B)	Q3(B)
Global Marketing		Q3(B)	Q2(A)	Q3(B)	Q3(B)	Q3(AB)	Q3(C)	Q3(AB)	Q3(B)		Q3(A)	Q3(B)	Q3(C)

General Examination Advice Ordinary Level

Section 1 Short answer questions

1. Short answer questions have only four lines of space for writing answers, so keep your answer short and to the point.

    Write two points of information for each answer (unless told otherwise in the question).
2. Answer all 15 short questions if you have time. The examiner will mark you on your best 10 answers.

Section 2 Long answer questions

1. Answer the required number of questions from part 1 and part 2.
2. Read the questions carefully and ensure you give the required information in your answers.
3. Divide the marks by five to see approximately how many points you are expected to make in your answer.
4. Answer in point form.

Number each point clearly. For each point in your answers:

- State the point
- Explain the point
- Give an example, if possible.

Key verbs in the questions that regularly appear at Ordinary Level

- **Calculate:** Find out or ascertain by using numerical data.
- **Define:** State the precise meaning of.
- **Describe:** Give an account of.
- **Discuss:** Give a detailed explanation.
- **Distinguish:** Show the differences.
- **Draft:** Draw up – Document/letter, sketch, diagram.
- **Explain:** Make clear in a detailed manner.
- **Identify:** Show that you recognise something.
- **Illustrate:** Make clear by means of examples, charts, diagrams, graphs, etc.
- **List:** Write down a number of things that have something in common.
- **Outline:** Give a short summary, omitting detail.

Ordinary Level examination layout – 400 marks – 2½ hours (150 minutes)

Section	Questions	Answer	Marks (%)	Areas covered	Timing
1	15 short answer questions	10 questions	100/400 (25%)	All parts of course.	32 minutes (approx. 3 minutes per question).
2	Eight Questions. Part 1 contains **three** questions. Part 2 contains five questions.	Four Questions. Part 1 answer **one** question. Part 2 answer **two** questions. Answer the fourth question from either Part 1 or Part 2.	300/400 75% Each question is worth 75 marks.	Part 1 questions are taken from units 1, 6, 7. Part 2 questions are taken from units 2, 3, 4, 5.	108 minutes (approx. 27 minutes per question).

Timing above allows five minutes for reading examination paper and selecting questions and five minutes for reading over your answers and checking work at end of exam.

UNIT 1

Introduction to People in Business

Business is primarily concerned with people and their relationships. This section introduces the main parties in business and their roles, and it examines how they work successfully together. It also looks at areas where their interests may not coincide and ways of resolving such situations of conflict.

Objective

To enable pupils to understand the form and the dynamic nature of the relationships between the different parties in business.

- **Chapter 1:** People and Their Relationships in Business
- **Chapter 2:** Conflict Resolution 1: Consumer and Retailer
- **Chapter 3:** Conflict Resolution 2: Employer and Employee

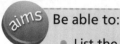

1 People and Their Relationships in Business

aims Be able to:

- List the main parties and people in business.
- Describe the relationships between people as workers, trade union members, managers, entrepreneurs, investors and customers.

HL
- Analyse the relationships between people in business.
- Outline how the elements of contract law help in dealing with conflict.

Main parties and people in business

Business – business is about producing and supplying goods and services.

Stakeholders – groups of people who are involved and play a part in the operation of a business.

People in business – Business is concerned with people and their relationships.

Parties in business include:
- Entrepreneurs
- Service providers
- Investors
- Employers
- Producers/suppliers
- Employees
- Consumers
- Interest groups

Entrepreneurs

- An individual or group who undertake the **risk of establishing and running a business**.
- They follow through on **ideas** and take the chance of failure.
- They **see an opportunity** and set out to exploit that opportunity.
- They take the risk of **organising all the resources** necessary to provide a product or service.

Investors

- Entrepreneurs need **capital** to develop their ideas so they contact one or more investors.
- Investors can be banks, grant agencies, Dragon's Den investors or shareholders.
- **Investors risk money in a project** that may or may not make a profit for them in the future.
- The money is used to **purchase assets and finance the enterprise.**

Producers/suppliers

- These are the **manufacturers and suppliers** of goods and services.
- Producers make goods that satisfy consumers' needs and wants.
- Producers want high prices and profit.

Consumers

- Are the **users** or purchasers of goods and services for personal use.
- They want **quality** and **service** at reasonable **prices**.

Service providers

- These provide a **range of services** for the efficient operation of business (e.g. banking, insurance, transport).

Employers

- These are individuals who **employ people** to work for them for wages/salaries.
- Employers want an **honest and reliable workforce** and good quality work.
- Employer **responsibilities** include paying fair wages and providing a safe working environment and equal opportunities.

Employees

- Employees **work for employers** producing goods or supplying services.
- Their **rights** include reasonable pay, safe working conditions and a contract of employment.
- Their **responsibilities** include honest work, compliance with the contract of employment and compliance with reasonable instructions from the employer.

Interest groups

- An interest group is an organisation which **represents the common viewpoint**, objectives and goals of a particular group.
- Interest groups seek to **influence** decisions and policy affecting their members through negotiation, lobbying, boycotting and possibly legal action.
- Interest groups may or may not succeed in achieving their desired objectives.
- **Business Associations**:
  - The Irish Business and Employers Confederation (IBEC) represents employers.
  - The Irish Congress of Trade Unions (ICTU) represents affiliated trade unions.
  - The Construction Industry Federation (CIF) represents over 3,000 members, covering businesses in all areas of the construction industry.

connections
knowledge
influence

- **Trade Associations**:
  - The Society of the Irish Motor Industry (SIMI) represents members in the motor industry.
  - The Irish Travel Agents Association (ITAA) represents travel agents.

Relationships between parties in business

People in business can either co-operate with each other and help one another or can compete with each other.

- A **co-operative relationship** exists where stakeholders work together towards a common objective to everyone's benefit.
- A **competitive relationship** exists where stakeholders are pursuing different objectives in an effort to achieve particular objectives at the expense of each other.

1. Relationship between entrepreneur and investor

Entrepreneurs are risk takers; they exercise initiative and take a risk in starting up a business with the hope of making a profit.

Investors invest finance in an enterprise; investors can be banks or other financial institutions or private individuals with money who wish to invest. If the investor feels that the venture is a good risk when compared to the possible return in the future, then a decision will be made to invest.

Co-operative relationship

The relationship between the entrepreneur and the investor must be one of co-operation to ensure that both of them gain.

There is a strong relationship when an entrepreneur seeks finance for a new project.

The relationship will remain co-operative as long as the entrepreneur presents a strong business plan with a projected cash flow forecast, profit and loss account and balance sheet.

Investors will also want to see the plans for the repayment of the funds to minimise the risks involved.

Competitive relationship

A competitive relationship will arise if the investor refuses to advance the funds required to establish a new business.

It will also exist if the entrepreneur – having received finance – is not living up to the commitments entered into and is defaulting on repayments.

2. Relationship between producers and interest groups

Producers manufacture goods or supply services that satisfy consumers' needs.

Interest groups are groups that wish to influence the decision-making process but are not part of the accepted political structure.

Interest groups may affect producer interests.

Co-operative relationship

Producers may have their own interest group, which lobbies government on their behalf to change laws relating to taxation or the operation of their industry.

Competitive relationship

Interest groups can affect producer interests.

They can cause bad publicity for a business or cause the image of a business to be damaged (e.g. a fall-off in demand for its products).

This can increase costs as more advertising is needed to counter the bad publicity.

Security may have to be increased because of protest meetings, possible picketing at premises, etc.

3. Relationship between producers and consumers

Producers are the manufacturers and suppliers of goods and services.

Producers are interested in making profit, but they can do so only if they make goods that satisfy consumers' needs and wants.

Consumers are the purchasers or users of goods and services supplied by firms.

Consumers try to satisfy their wants by buying products and services that are of good quality, reasonably priced and come with a good after-sale service.

Co-operative relationship

Producers co-operate with consumers and the relationship is good when:

- Producers provide the products/services demanded by the consumer
- Products are top quality and reasonably priced
- Consumers are satisfied with the product

Competitive relationship

The interests of consumers and producers are sometimes in conflict because the consumer wants low prices and high quality, while producers went high prices and profit.

A competitive relationship between producers is beneficial for the consumer as every business must work hard to satisfy consumer needs.

Producers will compete on prices of goods and services, quality, sales, etc.

Consumers will benefit from:

- Improved quality
- Improved customer services
- Better choice of products
- Better value for money

4. Relationship between producers in the same line of business

Co-operative relationship

A co-operative relationship exists where joint action or effort is required so that producers work together to everyone's benefit toward a common objective.

Example

Producers in the same line of business sometimes co-operate with each other to:

- Protect their industry against an outside threat
- Encourage economic development and to create jobs for the benefit of the community
- Lobby the government in order to solve problems of mutual interest, such as achieving a change in legislation or a reduction in VAT
- Agree on a common scale of discounts for their customers

Competitive relationship

A competitive relationship between producers in the same line of business means each is pursuing different objectives in an effort to achieve a particular objective at the expense of each other. This is beneficial for the consumer as every business must satisfy consumer needs.

Example

Producers in the same line of business may compete on:

- Prices of goods and services
- Quality
- Sales

5. Relationship between employer and employees

Employers aim to:

- Keep production costs low so that the firm will remain competitive
- Increase profits so that retained earnings can be built up to give a good return on the capital invested for the owners

Employees want:

- Reasonable wages, good working conditions and a good standard of living
- Job security and promotion

A good relationship between employers and employees is vital for the success of the business.

Co-operative relationship

When employers and employees have a co-operative relationship the business can be successful.

Employers and employees co-operate when:

- Agreeing pay and working conditions
- Producing goods and services for consumers
- Consulting each other and making decisions together
- Coming to agreement in relation to issues such as profit-sharing, granting share options, maintaining productivity, etc.

Competitive relationship

Employees may want higher pay while the employer wants costs kept to a minimum. Employers want increased profits and cost reductions, which may lead to redundancies, while employees want job security.

A competitive relationship occurs when employees are faced with a wage cut or the threat of losing their jobs.

6. Relationship between an enterprise and its stakeholders

Co-operative relationship

A co-operative relationship exists where an enterprise and its stakeholders work together for their mutual benefit.

This requires joint action or effort and can occur between:

- **People within an organisation** (e.g. employees helping each other in a spirit of teamwork to achieve a certain level of sales or profit), or
- **Organisations** (e.g. one business co-operating with another business in the marketing or distributing of each other's products or services)

Competitive relationship

An enterprise and its stakeholders can pursue different objectives to each other or attempt to achieve particular objectives at the expense of each other.

This can involve people within the enterprise and outside interests which impact on the enterprise.

For example, a competitive relationship **within the organisation** might be where sales people compete with each other for orders or employees compete for promotion. **Outside an organisation** competitive issues can relate to prices, quality, sales, the recruitment of employees, etc.

Make sure that you can explain the co-operative and competitive relationship between people in business and be able to give examples. This is examined almost every year.

Law of contract

A contract is a legally-binding agreement between two or more parties that can be enforced by law.

Elements of a valid contract

1. Agreement

Agreement arises as a result of offer and acceptance. They may be made in these ways:

- In writing (e.g. the purchase of a house or land)
- Oral (e.g. at an auction)
- Implied by conduct (e.g. when a customer goes to a checkout in a supermarket with a basket of groceries)

For a contract to be legally binding there must be:

1. Agreement (offer and acceptance)
2. Consideration
3. Intention to contract
4. Capacity to contract
5. Legality of form
6. Consent to contract
7. Legality of purpose

Offer

An offer is a promise by the person making the offer to be bound by the contract if the offer is accepted.

The offer made has to be clear and it must be communicated to the person receiving the offer so that there is an opportunity to either accept or reject it.

An offer may be made orally, in writing, or it may be implied from the conduct of an individual.

For example, taking goods to a supermarket checkout is an offer to buy them.

Invitation to treat

An invitation to treat is an invitation to someone to make an offer which can be accepted or rejected.

For example, goods on display in a shop window are only inviting customers to enter the shop and make an offer. They can do so by bringing the goods to the checkout and offering to buy them.

Acceptance

When an offer is accepted it is binding on both parties.

Acceptance of an offer must have no conditions attached to it and it must agree fully with the terms of the original offer.

Acceptance can be made orally, in writing, by conduct or by post.

For example, when the checkout assistant accepts the money from the customer, the offer is accepted (by conduct).

2. Consideration

Consideration means that some value (usually money) must move from one party of the contract to the other party in exchange for goods and services.

Consideration refers to what is exchanged between the buyer and seller.

For example, the purchase of a car from a garage. The buyer gives €20,000 to the seller who, in return, receives a car.

3. Intention to contract

There must be the intention by the parties to create a contract.

With business agreements, it is presumed that a legal contract is intended.

With social and personal agreements (e.g. an agreement to go to the cinema), it is presumed that the parties do not intend that a legal contract should exist.

4. Capacity to contract

The parties to a contract must have the capacity to make a contract.

All natural persons and corporate bodies (such as companies) have the legal right to enter into a contract.

The following generally do not have capacity to contract:

- Infants, that is, persons under the age of eighteen (except in certain cases, e.g. necessities)
- Persons under the influence of drink or drugs
- Insane persons
- Bankrupt persons

These people are deemed to be incapable of making valid contracts because it is presumed that they do not fully understand what they are doing. If they enter into a contract, the contract is void.

5. Legality of form

A contract must be drawn up in the correct legal form.

Contracts can be oral, in writing (hire purchase contracts, sale of land contracts, insurance policies) or implied by conduct.

6. Consent to contract

Real consent must exist between the parties to a contract.

The consent must be voluntary. No pressure of any kind can be exerted on the parties to the deal.

A contract may be invalid if pressure is used to get agreement. If there is no real consent, there is no contract.

7. Legality of purpose

The court will not allow action to be taken on illegal contracts such as those which break the law of the land. These include, for example, contracts to:

- Commit a crime
- Evade tax
- Interfere with the court of justice

If an illegal contract exists, no action can be brought for its breach.

Termination of a contract

1. Performance

This is where the contract has been performed exactly as was promised by the parties to it (i.e. whatever was agreed was carried out).

A contract can be terminated by:
- Performance
- Breach
- Agreement
- Frustration

2. Breach

If one of the parties does not perform his/her side of the contract, the other party has the right to take action in the courts against the party who caused the breach.

Breach of a **condition** (a clause that is vital and goes to the heart of the contract) entitles the injured party to treat the contract as terminated and sue for damages for loss suffered.

Breach of a **warranty** (a less important clause) allows the injured party to sue for damages only.

3. Agreement

The parties may mutually agree to the termination. All obligations are released by agreement of the parties.

4. Frustration

Performance of a contract may sometimes be impossible because of something outside the control of the parties (e.g. a fire where goods that were the subject of the contract are destroyed; the contract becomes impossible to perform since the object has been destroyed).

Death or serious illness to one of the parties to the contract may hinder the performance of the contract. In these cases the contract is terminated by frustration.

Remedies for a breach of contract

When there is breach of contract the courts can award the following remedies.

1. Damages

A sum of money is awarded as compensation for any damage or loss caused to the injured party as a result of the breach of contract.

This should put the injured party in the same financial position they would have been in if the contract has not been broken.

2. Specific performance

The party in breach of a contract would be ordered by a court to carry out its agreed obligations, i.e. to do what had been promised in the contract.

This would not be awarded by the courts if an amount of money would have been a remedy. This remedy may be appropriate in a contract for the sale or lease of land.

3. Rescinding the contract

This means that the innocent party (the party that has not breached the contract) has the right to have the contract set aside and to be restored to the position they were in before the contract began.

Describe using examples, one co-operative and one competitive relationship that may exist either between or within organisations. (20 marks)

Source: 2002 Higher Level Section 3

Suggested solution

Co-operative relationship

A co-operative relationship exists where joint action or effort is required so that people can work together to everyone's benefit. (5 marks)

Example

One business co-operating with another business in the marketing or distributing of each other's products or services. (5 marks)

Competitive relationship

This is where parties compete with each other and are pursuing different objectives. These objectives may be achieved by one party at the expense of the other. (5 marks)

Example

Business enterprises competing with each other for market share on areas like price, quality and service. (5 marks)

Marking scheme

Co-operative relationship (10 marks – 5 marks for explanation, 5 marks for example).

Competitive relationship (10 marks – 5 marks for explanation, 5 marks for example).

2 Conflict Resolution 1:
Consumer and Retailer

 aims Be able to:
- Outline non-legislative ways of resolving conflict between retailer and consumer.
- Outline how legislation helps in dealing with conflict between retailer and consumer.
- Describe a possible business conflict and show how the law could be used to solve it.

 HL

Conflict

Conflict occurs where people are in dispute. The pursuit of their goal may result in some damage to the other party with whom they are in conflict.

Methods of resolving conflict

Non-legislative

A non-legislative method of solving a business conflict means that the parties involved don't use a law, or an office or organisation set up under law, to assist in solving their conflict.

 key point

There are two methods of resolving conflict:
- Non-legislative
- Legislative

Legislative

A legislative method of solving a business conflict is to use the law to solve the conflict, or to use an office or organisation set up as a consequence of a law, to help in finding a resolution to the conflict.

Conflict resolution between consumer and retailer

Non-legislative methods of solving conflict between consumer and retailer

1. Contact retailer

The consumer should contact the retailer, giving details of the complaint. Putting things in writing means the problem is taken more seriously.

2. Talk

Discuss the problem to clarify any difficulties

3. Negotiation

This involves parties explaining their position and bargaining to try to reach a mutually acceptable solution.

If negotiations fail, the involvement of a third party may be necessary to resolve the conflict.

4. Third parties

Third parties are independent outside agencies that may be involved in negotiations to help parties resolve their differences.

A. Ombudsman for public services

The office investigates complaints about the activities of government, local authorities, the Health Service Executive and An Post.

The ombudsman only investigates complaints after the person has tried to solve the problem with the public body involved and all other avenues for solving the problem have been exhausted.

Complaints must be made within one year. After reviewing the complaint, the ombudsman decides if it is justified. If it is, the ombudsman makes a recommendation to the public body in order to resolve the problem.

Recommendations of the ombudsman are not legally binding on the parties involved with the complaint.

B. Financial services ombudsman

Investigates claims from consumers about financial service providers including banks, building societies and insurance companies.

C. Consumer Association of Ireland

It is a voluntary association which gives information and advice to consumers about goods, services and consumer law.

It was set up to protect the interest of consumers in Ireland.

It helps consumers to solve complaints.

D. Trade associations

Set standards for their own members which ensure that customers will get the best possible service.

exam focus

Evaluation of the Ombudsman Service

The Ombudsman Service is effective because:

- The ombudsman is impartial and the service is free
- The office of the ombudsman deals with about 3,000 complaints per annum and has over the years advised and guided many others with valid complaints

Consumers can complain to the relevant association (such as the Society of the Irish Motor Industry [SIMI] and the Irish Travel Agents Association [ITAA]) if standards are not being met.

Legislative methods of solving conflict between consumer and retailer

If consumers and retailers cannot reach a satisfactory agreement in a non-legislative manner a legislative approach will have to be pursued.

Sale of goods and supply of services act 1980

1. Rights of buyer in relation to goods sold

Merchantable quality

Product must be of reasonable standard and quality, taking into account what they are meant to do, their durability and their price (e.g. a new car that breaks down is deemed not to be of merchantable quality).

> **key point**
>
> The consumer can insist on their legal rights as set out in the following acts:
> - Sale of Goods and Supply of Services Act 1980
> - Consumer Protection Act 2007

Fit for purpose

Goods must be reasonably fit for the particular purpose indicated by the buyer (e.g. washing machines should wash clothes).

Sale by description

Goods must be as described by the seller as in advertisements and brochures or as stated by a sales person and must match the description given on the packaging.

Sale by sample

If the sale is by sample, then the bulk of the goods must correspond to the sample.

Ownership and quiet possession

The buyer of the goods has a right of ownership and possession of the goods. This means the following:

- The seller has the right to sell the goods.
- The buyer should enjoy quiet possession and be able to use the goods as they wish.

2. Rights of the buyer in relation to services

- That the supplier has the necessary skill to provide the service.
- That the service will be provided with due skill and diligence.
- That any materials used will be sound and fit for their purpose.
- That any goods supplied as part of the service will be of merchantable quality.

3. The retailer/seller is responsible

The seller or the service provider is responsible for putting right defective goods or services. The manufacturer may be at fault, but the contract is with the seller and the duty to put things right lies with the seller.

4. Signs limiting liability are illegal

A seller cannot limit their responsibility by displaying signs to that effect.
It is illegal to display such signs.

5. Guarantees

A guarantee cannot limit the rights of the consumer.
A guarantee is a bonus in addition to a consumer's
normal legal rights.

6. Unsolicited goods

This refers to sending goods to people who have not
ordered them and seeking payment later.

Any person receiving goods in this way may keep
them without payment after giving 30 days written
notice that the goods are not required.

A seller's responsibility is not
limited when they display
signs with messages such as:

- No money refunded
- No liability accepted for
  faulty goods
- Credit notes only

Remedies for breaches of the Act

The remedy will depend on the seriousness of the fault, when the fault happened, and
how soon the consumer complained about it.
Redress can be:

- **A full refund** – If goods are not of merchantable quality or have a major fault from
  the beginning and the consumer acts within a reasonable time of the sale, the goods
  can be rejected by the buyer, and a full refund should provided by the seller.
- **Partial refund, repair or replacements** can be provided by the seller if the consumer
  has used the product or has delayed in acting.

EVALUATION OF THE SALE OF GOODS AND SUPPLY OF SERVICES ACT 1980

The law is effective in protecting consumers because:

- It ensures that consumers receive a refund if they purchase a faulty product or a product that it not up to standard.
- By banning illegal signs (such as 'Credit notes only'), consumers are protected because they do not have to accept a credit note and can insist on a full refund.

Consumer Protection Act 2007

The main elements of the Consumer Protection Act 2007 are:

- It establishes the National Consumer Agency on a statutory basis.
- It updates and modernises consumer law.
- It deals with unfair commercial practices.

1. National Consumer Agency

The main functions of the National Consumer Agency (NCA) are to:

- Promote and protect the interests and welfare of consumers
- Enforce the relevant consumer law
- Encourage compliance with the relevant law
- Investigate suspected offences under any of the relevant laws

national **consumer** agency
gníomhaireacht náisiúnta **tomhaltóirí**

putting **consumers** first

- Refer cases to the Director of Public Prosecutions, where appropriate
- Advise and make recommendations on any legislation or policy which concerns or is likely to impact on consumer protection and welfare and to make proposals for new legislation

2. Consumer protection

This Act deals with unfair business-to-consumer commercial practices. (It does not, however, apply to dealings between businesses.) The Act sets out, among other things, various rules that apply to claims made about goods and services.

In particular, the Act:

- Protects the consumer from **misleading advertisements**
- Requires that the **information in advertisements is fair and accurate**
- Makes it illegal for an advertiser or business to make **false or misleading claims about goods services or prices**

All types of communications that promote goods or services are covered by the Act, including:

- Advertisements
- A notice in a shop
- A claim made by a sales assistant about a product or service

3. Unfair commercial practices

The Act deals with three distinct types of unfair commercial practices:

- Misleading practices
- Aggressive practices
- Prohibited practices

Misleading practices

Misleading advertising, misleading information and withholding material information are considered misleading practices and are prohibited under the Act.

Aggressive practices

The Act prohibits traders from engaging in **aggressive practices,** such as:

- Harassment
- Coercion, which means forcing someone to do something
- Exercising undue influence, which means putting unfair pressure on someone
- Using threatening or abusive language or behaviour
- Taking advantage of a consumer's misfortune or circumstances, when the trader knows the consumer's judgment is impaired

Prohibited practices

Among the **practices that are prohibited** by the Act are:

- Making false claims relating to cures for illnesses
- Offering free prizes when it costs money to claim the prizes
- Running promotions or competitions when the top prize is not available
- Persistently cold calling, having been asked to leave or to stop
- Demanding payment for unsolicited goods
- Pyramid schemes (a scheme where a person pays money, but their primary benefit derives from the introduction of other persons into the scheme, rather than the supply of a product.)

4. Other areas of consumer protection

Price display regulations

The Consumer Protection Act 2007 gives the government minister the power to make regulations requiring that the prices of certain products be displayed in a specific manner. For example, they could provide that prices of certain products must be displayed inclusive of charges, fees and taxes.

Price controls

Price controls can only be introduced in emergency situations and must be by decision of the government and not just the Minister for Enterprise, Trade and Employment.

Codes of practice

The Consumer Protection Act 2007 provides for the recognition of codes of practice drawn up by traders or groups of traders and for the NCA to approve such codes.

5. Enforcement of the Act

The Consumer Protection Act 2007 provides for the following enforcement mechanisms to be available to the NCA:

- The NCA can accept a **written undertaking** from the trader that a prohibited practice will cease. If the trader reneges on the undertaking and resumes the prohibited practice, the NCA may apply for a prohibition order.
- The NCA can apply for a **prohibition order** from the Circuit/High Court prohibiting a trader from engaging in a prohibited practice.
- The NCA can serve a **compliance notice** on a trader whom it considers to have engaged in a prohibited activity. The trader has 14 days in which to appeal the notice. If the trader fails to comply, the NCA may take criminal proceedings.
- The Act provides for the issue of **fixed payment notes**. These are on-the-spot penalties for offences relating to the display of prices.
- **Publication of a Consumer Protection List** – a list of traders convicted of criminal offences, subject to court orders, bound by an undertaking, served with a compliance notice, or subject to a fixed payment notice.

6. Redress for consumers

The Consumer Protection Act allows consumers to apply to the courts for damages if they suffer loss due to misleading practices by a business.

The National Consumer Agency may also apply to the court for an order that requires a business to pay compensation for any loss or damage to the consumer resulting from an offence.

exam focus

EVALUATION OF THE CONSUMER PROTECTION ACT 2007

The law is effective in protecting consumers because:

- Consumers get honest information about the goods and services they wish to purchase and the price they will have to pay; this allows them to make informed choices.
- If consumers are misled, the law ensures that action is taken against the seller.
- Consumers are protected from unfair commercial practices.
- The Act allows consumers to apply to the courts for damages if they suffer loss due to misleading practices by a business.

EVALUATION OF THE NATIONAL CONSUMER AGENCY

This office is very effective in protecting consumers because:

- It has power to investigate and prosecute businesses that break the law.
- Irish consumers have a strong organisation – the National Consumer Agency – to ensure their welfare is protected.
- Irish consumers get honest information about goods and services so that they can make informed decisions and have their rights respected.
- If the agency didn't promote good advertising practices it is likely that consumers would be misled and thus lose out on quality and value.
- The NCA helps businesses realise their responsibility in providing rights to consumers.
- The NCA can apply to the courts for an order requiring a business to pay compensation for loss or damage to the consumer resulting from an offence.

Small claims court

This deals with consumer complaints in relation to goods and services purchased for private use from somebody selling them in the course of business. Claims can be made for faulty goods, bad workmanship and minor damage to privately owned property. Maximum damages that can be claimed are €2000.

A claim is made on a special application form and is lodged with the small claim registrar of the district court with a fee of €15.

Both sides make their case and are encouraged to reach a settlement.

A decision made by the registrar of the court is not legally binding but it is usually accepted.

Appeals can be made through the District Court and heard before a judge.

Since January 2010, the small claims court service is available to businesses pursuing claims against other businesses.

EVALUATION OF THE SMALL CLAIMS COURT

The small claims court is very effective because of the following:

- It is a fast, informal and easy way for consumers to resolve disputes.
- It is an inexpensive method of solving disputes. (A fee of €15 is payable to the District Court when the claim is lodged. No solicitors are required.)
- Consumers receive an unbiased and fair judgment.
- The process can be carried out online; about 50% of claims are now made online.
- It has a very high success rate – approximately 75% of claims are settled through the service.

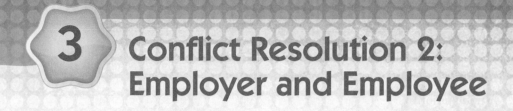

 aims Be able to:

- Outline non-legislative ways of resolving conflict between employer and employee.
- Outline how legislation helps in dealing with conflict between employer and employee.
- Describe a possible business conflict and show how the law could be used to solve it.

Industrial relations

Industrial Relations refers to the relationship that exists between management and employees in an organisation and how they co-operate and communicate with each other.

Good industrial relations will have high staff motivation and morale and high productivity. **Poor** industrial relations will have poor motivation, high labour turnover and low productivity.

Employees may join a trade union to strengthen their bargaining power with management.

Trade unions

An organisation representing employees in negotiations with employers. A shop steward is elected as their official union representative in the workplace.

The functions/benefits of trade union membership to employees

A trade union:

- Protects workers rights
- Seeks better pay and working conditions for members and tries to prevent pay cuts
- Represents members in negotiations with employers/government
- Negotiates with the employer on behalf of its members in a trade dispute
- Provides services for members, such as credit unions and insurance schemes
- Protects the job security of its members in the event of threatened layoffs

Shop steward

A shop steward is an elected representative of union members in a workplace. He/she acts as a communication link between members and their union.

Collective bargaining

Negotiations between employer and employee representatives in a particular firm or industry to determine rates of pay and conditions of employment, etc.

National agreements

Agreements negotiated between government, employers represented by IBEC and employees represented by ICTU (social partners).

This relationship is called 'social partnership' and covers pay and other issues such as tax reform and job creation and other social issues.

Industrial disputes

Factors leading to industrial disputes

1. **Pay** – Employees seeking wage increases/employer seeking wage cuts.
2. **Working conditions** – Employees seeking/improvements in hours of work, safety standards, etc.
3. **Promotion procedures** – Disputes may arise if agreed procedures on promotion are not followed.
4. **Discrimination** – Some employees treated less favourably than others.
5. **Dismissal of employers** – Dismissal without adequate reason.

Types of official industrial action a trade union can undertake as part of a trade dispute

1. Official strike

- It is a complete withdrawal of labour. Workers are entitled to strike pay.
- Union seeks approval of workers in secret ballot.
- Strike confirmed by ICTU.
- Seven days' notice given to employer before industrial action can be taken.

2. Work to rule

- Workers only work as per their contract.
- They follow the rules of their employment contract to the 'letter of the law'.

3. Go slow

- Workers stay on their jobs, but they slow down operations, sometimes making it impossible for the business to operate.
- As the employees are still at work, they are entitled to get paid.

Types of unofficial industrial action a trade union can undertake as part of a trade dispute

Unofficial industrial action/unofficial strike

- Workers go on strike without a secret ballot and without giving employer a weeks' notice and without the approval of the trade union and ICTU.
- Organisers of unofficial strikes do not have legal protection against being sued by their employer.

Conflict resolution – employer and employee

Non-legislative methods

1. Meet and talk

Parties should discuss the situation and clarify any difficulties; negotiation may be required.

2. Negotiation

Negotiation is a process of bargaining to try to come up with a mutually acceptable solution. Employees are represented by their union. Employer is represented by management.

Each party sets out its position, issues are discussed, points of difference are identified and the parties try to reach a solution acceptable to both. This might involve compromise, with parties giving up something in order to reach agreement.

3. Third parties

If negotiations fail, it can be useful to seek the services of third parties to solve the conflict.

Third parties can help solve conflict through conciliation and arbitration.

Conciliation

This is where a third party/conciliator assists the parties in dispute to resolve their differences themselves through continued negotiation.

The conciliation process gets the two sides to listen to each other's point of view, discuss the issues, and negotiate an agreed settlement before the dispute grows into a serious one.

An agreement, if reached, is **not legally binding**, but the aim is to resolve the dispute without strike action.

Arbitration

Arbitration is where the settlement of a dispute is sent before a neutral third party (Arbitrator) for adjudication.

The arbitrator listens to both sides of the dispute and makes a recommendation for settlement. The decision is usually **binding** on both parties. (The parties agree in advance to the arbitration process and that the arbitration decision will be binding on them.)

The main types of disputes dealt with by arbitration are ones that concern employees, trade unions and employers.

Legislative methods

Industrial Relations Act 1990

1. Trade dispute

A trade dispute is defined as 'any dispute between employers and workers that is concerned with employment or non-employment, or the terms or conditions of the employment of any person'.

A **legitimate trade dispute** can arise from any of the following issues:

- Pay and conditions of employment – rates of pay, overtime, holidays
- Physical conditions of work – safety, heating, canteen
- Employee dismissal
- Employment policy of employer – methods of recruitment, etc.
- Trade union recognition in the workplace
- Range of duties required of employees

exam focus

INDUSTRIAL RELATIONS ACT 1990

The main provisions of the Industrial Relations Act 1990 are:

- Definition of a trade dispute
- Trade union immunity from prosecution
- Picketing
- Balloting
- Labour Relations Commission
- Labour Court

2. Trade union immunity from prosecution

Trade unions and workers cannot be sued for damages (or losses) suffered by the employer arising from a trade dispute – provided it is an official trade dispute – if the correct procedures have been followed, that is, if the union held a secret ballot and gave one weeks' notice to the employer.

3. Picketing

It is lawful for workers to assemble at the entrance of a workplace and carry placards giving information about their dispute or strike.

Pickets can only be placed at a workplace and picketing must be peaceful. There must be no obstruction caused.

Placards communicate information to the public and other workers regarding the trade dispute.

Types of picketing

- **Primary Picketing:**
  - Picketing the business premises of the employer involved in the dispute
- **Secondary Picketing:**
  - Picketing another employer not involved in the dispute, e.g. where another employer undertakes the delivery of goods normally delivered by the employer involved in the dispute.
  - This is lawful only if the workers believe that the second employer was acting to frustrate the industrial action by directly assisting their employer.

4. Balloting

A secret ballot must be held before industrial action can take place.

A majority of votes must be cast in favour of industrial action.

One weeks' notice must be given to the employer involved in a dispute.

If the correct procedures are followed, an employer cannot sue unions or workers for damages.

The Labour Relations Commission

Functions/services of the Labour Relations Commission

1. Conciliation service

Conciliation is a voluntary process by which parties in a dispute can meet to resolve their differences with the aid of a neutral and impartial third party called an industrial relations officer.

The industrial relations officer will listen to both sides, get them to understand each others' position and try to arrive at a mutually acceptable solution.

key point

The role of the Labour Relations Commission is to:

- Promote better industrial relations
- Help with resolving industrial disputes

2. Industrial relations advisory service

The Commission offers advice to employers and unions on industrial relations matters and helps them identify underlying problems that cause disputes.

3. Codes of practice

A code of practice is a collection of generally accepted rules, practices and procedures to be followed when dealing with conflict.

The LRC (Labour Relations Commission) prepares, and offers guidance on, codes of practice in consultation with union and employer organisations.

4. Rights commissioner service

A rights commissioner is a person experienced in industrial relations matters whose job is to help settle disputes and grievances which affect only one or a very small number of workers.

The rights commissioner may investigate disputes such as suspension or dismissal of a worker and maternity leave–related issues, but not disputes related to rates of pay, hours of work or annual holidays.

If the recommendations are not acceptable to the parties involved, the decision can be appealed to the Labour Court, whose decision is binding on the parties.

5. Equality officers

The LRC appoints equality officers and staff to investigate cases of discrimination in the workplace.

6. Research

The LRC conducts research into matters relevant into industrial relations and monitors development in the area of industrial relations.

The Labour Court

The Labour Court is a 'court of last resort in industrial disputes'. Cases are referred to the Labour Court when all other efforts to resolve the dispute have failed.

Functions of the Labour Court

1. Investigates disputes

The Labour Court investigates industrial disputes and issues recommendations for their settlement only in the following circumstances:

- If it receives a report from the Labour Relations Commission (LRC) stating that it **cannot resolve** the dispute.

- If the **LRC is unwilling** to investigate the dispute.

- If the Labour Court and LRC agree that **exceptional circumstances** warrant Labour Court intervention.

The Labour Court investigates **trade disputes affecting public interest** at the request of the **Minister for Enterprise, Trade and Employment**.

The Labour Court investigates disputes and issues **recommendations** for their settlement:

- Due to the voluntary nature of industrial relations in Ireland, Labour Court recommendations are not legally binding. However, as the Labour Court is a court

EVALUATION OF THE ROLE OF THE LABOUR RELATIONS COMMISSION IN DEALING WITH INDUSTRIAL RELATIONS CONFLICT

- It is a very effective dispute resolution mechanism; a very high percentage of cases referred to the LRC for conciliation are settled.

- The LRC advisory service helps prevent industrial disputes.

- The use of codes of practice leads to better relationships between employers and employees and results in fewer disputes in the workplace.

- The rights commissioner service provides help for individual workers who may be the subject of unfair dismissal, suspension or disciplinary procedures.

of last resort in the industrial relations process it is expected that the parties will accept the Labour Court recommendation.

- However, if both sides to a dispute request the intervention of the Labour Court (LC) and agree to be bound by its recommendations then the LC recommendation is binding on both sides.

There are certain other categories of cases dealt with by the LC in which the decision of the court is **enforceable**. Such cases include:

- Appeals of decisions of rights commissioners
- Appeals of decisions of equality officers under equality legislation
- Complaints of breaches of registered employment agreements

2. Establishes Joint Labour Committees

The LC establishes a Joint Labour Committee to investigate rates of pay and conditions of employment in industries where workers have no union.

They recommend minimum rates of pay and conditions which, if approved by the LC, become employment regulation orders and are enforceable in law.

3. Registers agreements

Registers agreements made between employers and unions. Once registered with the LC, these agreements become enforceable.

4. Interprets codes of practice

It investigates breaches of codes of practice referred to it by the Labour Relations Commission.

It gives its opinion on the correct interpretation of codes of practice.

EVALUATION OF THE LABOUR COURT

The Labour Court has, since its establishment, played a very important role in Irish industrial relations.

It has enjoyed a high profile, often resolving disputes of great public interest. Overall, it has carried out its dispute-resolution functions with great success. The Labour Court has:

- Intervened and solved very difficult disputes – e.g. public transport disputes
- Resolved disputes that the LRC has failed to resolve

The Labour Court has the respect and confidence of all parties in industrial relations. Its recommendations are not binding on either parties, but in the majority of cases they will be accepted by the parties.

Employment Equality Acts 1998 and 2004

1. Employment discrimination

Discrimination is described as '**the treatment of a person in a less favourable way than another person is, has been or would be treated**'.

2. Discrimination is outlawed

Discrimination is outlawed on a number of grounds, including gender, marital status, etc.

3. Harassment

The Act defines general and sexual harassment and **outlaws** it in the workplace.

4. Equality between men and women

Equal pay for equal work is made a term of every employment contract.

5. Equality Authority

The law set up the Equality Authority, which has the following functions:

- Eliminate discrimination in the workplace
- Promote equality of opportunity in employment on the nine grounds covered by the act
- Provide information to the public on equality legislation

GROUNDS UNDER WHICH DISCRIMINATION IS OUTLAWED:

- Gender
- Marital status
- Family status
- Sexual orientation
- Religion
- Age
- Disability
- Race
- Membership in the Traveller community

6. Equality Tribunal/Director of Equality Investigations

The law set up the Equality Tribunal (previously called the Director of Equality Investigations).

Equality Tribunal

The Equality Tribunal was established to investigate, hear and decide on claims for discrimination and breaches of equality legislation.

Equality mediator

The Director of the Equality Tribunal can, with the consent of both parties, appoint an equality mediator who facilitates both parties to reach a mutually acceptable agreement. If a settlement is reached through mediation, then the terms are legally binding.

Equality officer

If either party does object to mediation or if the process of mediation is unsuccessful, the case will be referred to an equality officer for investigation.

The equality officer will hear evidence from both parties before issuing a legally-binding decision.

Decisions may be appealed by either party to the Labour Court within 42 days.

Remedies

Where an equality officer rules in favour of the complainant the following order can be made:

- In equal pay claims – an order for equal pay and arrears in respect of a period not exceeding three years
- In other cases – equal treatment and compensation up to a maximum of two years' pay

EVALUATION OF EMPLOYMENT EQUALITY ACT 1998

The Act is effective in protecting employees because:

- It sets out nine grounds under which discrimination is outlawed so that all workers must be treated equally.
- The Director of the Equality Tribunal hears cases of discrimination and issues legally-binding decisions.

EVALUATION OF THE ROLE OF THE DIRECTOR OF EQUALITY TRIBUNAL/DIRECTOR OF EQUALITY INVESTIGATIONS

The office is effective as both the equality mediator and equality officer assist in achieving a resolution to complaints of discrimination.

Equality officers can order compensation, which is assured to be paid because the Director's ruling is legally binding.

Decisions assist in the elimination of discrimination, ensuring that all workers are treated equally.

Unfair Dismissals Acts, 1977 to 2007

1. Purpose of the Acts

The purpose of the Acts is to protect employees from being unfairly dismissed from their jobs.

2. Who is covered?

In general, the Acts apply to any person working under a contract of employment. The Acts do not apply to a person who has been in the continuous service of the employer for less than one year. However, the one-year continuous service criterion does not apply where dismissal results from **certain types of leave**, including **maternity, adoptive, parental** or **carer's leave** and/or **trade union membership** or to **rights under the Minimum Wage Act 2000**.

The scope of the legislation has been broadened to include part-time workers who work less than eight hours per week.

3. Burden of proof?

In general, the Acts provide that every dismissal of an employee will be presumed to have been unfair unless the employer can show substantial grounds justifying the dismissal.

4. Grounds for fair dismissal

To justify a dismissal, an employer must show that it either resulted from one or more of the following causes:

- **Incompetence on the part of the employee.** The employee lacks ability to carry out required duties satisfactorily (poor work performance; failure to meet set targets and standard of work expected).
- **Qualifications (misrepresentation by the employee).** Lack of formal technical or professional qualifications as appropriate for the work the employee was employed to do; misleading employer in relation to qualifications.
- **Conduct of the employee.** Improper/unacceptable behaviour by the employee (e.g. theft, substance abuse, violence at work, refusal to obey reasonable orders, breach of employer's rules, causing physical injury).
- **Redundancy.** Due to closure, competition, decline in demand, cutbacks (fair procedures applied).
- **Incapability.** Employee is incapable of carrying out the work he/she was employed to do. (Incapability refers to employee's attendance, i.e. persistent lateness, absenteeism or extended sick leave, illness.)
- **Legal reasons.** If continuation of the job was to break the law in some way (e.g. if an employee's work visa expired, etc.).

5. Unfair dismissals

Dismissals will be unfair under the Acts where it is shown that they resulted from any of the following:

(a) an employee's trade union membership or activities, either outside working hours or at those times during working hours when permitted by the employer

(b) religious or political opinions

(c) race or colour or sexual orientation

(d) the age of an employee; dismissals on the grounds of age, other than being under 16 or reaching the normal retiring age for that particular employment, is deemed to be unfair

(e) an employee's membership of the travelling community

(f) legal proceedings against an employer where an employee is a party or a witness

(g) unfair selection for redundancy

(h) an employee's pregnancy, or any matters connected therewith

(i) the exercise or proposed exercise by the employee of the right to maternity, adoptive, parental or carers leave

Employees claiming dismissal due to (a), (h), (i) may bring an unfair dismissal claim **even though they do not have one year's continuous service with their employer**.

Constructive dismissal

It can also be construed as dismissal if a person's conditions of work are made so difficult that she/he feels obliged to leave. This is called **constructive dismissal**.

6. Claim for unfair dismissals and time limits

If an employee considers that she/he has been unfairly dismissed, she/he may submit a claim for redress under the Acts to a **rights commissioner or a claim may be submitted direct to the Employment Appeals Tribunal**.

Written notice of claim must be made **within six months of the date of dismissal**.

Where a claim is heard by a rights commissioner, the rights commissioner will issue a recommendation and either party may appeal that **recommendation** to the Employment Appeals Tribunal.

Where a claim or appeal is heard by the Employment Appeals Tribunal, the Tribunal will issue a **determination**. There is a right of appeal by either party to the Circuit Court from a determination of the Tribunal.

7. Redress under the Unfair Dismissals Act

Where an employee has been unfairly dismissed, he/she can, under the Acts, be awarded either:

(i) **Re-instatement** – As if the employee had never been dismissed. The employee is entitled to arrears of salary and continuing service will not be considered to have been broken.

(ii) **Re-engagement** – Employee is offered a different, comparable job to the one from which she/he had been dismissed.

(iii) **Compensation** – where financial loss has been sustained by the employee, financial compensation in respect of such loss, subject to a maximum of two years' remuneration.

Employment Appeals Tribunal

The Employment Appeals Tribunal deals with disputes arising out of a number of Acts including those relating to unfair dismissals, redundancy and maternity entitlements. The Tribunal hears evidence from both parties and issues a determination.

(i) Explain the term 'employment discrimination' as set out in the Employment Equality Act 1998.

(ii) List four distinct grounds under which discrimination is outlawed under the Act. (20 marks)

Source: 2009 Higher Level Section 3

Suggested solution

(i) Discrimination is described as the treatment of a person in a less favourable way (8 marks) than another person is, has been or would be treated. (4 marks)

(ii) Grounds under which discrimination is outlawed:

- Gender
- Marital status
- Family status
- Sexual orientation
- Religion
- Age
- Disability
- Race
- Membership of the Traveller community 8 marks (4@2 marks)

UNIT 2
Enterprise

Enterprise is the source of all business. Innovation is central to business development. This section looks at the nature of enterprise, characteristics of enterprising people and associated skills. Unit 2 also examines the application of enterprise in other areas of life.

Objective
To enable pupils to understand the importance of enterprise in business and community life.

- **Chapter 4:** Introduction to Enterprise, Characteristics of Entrepreneurs and Enterprise Skills

4 Introduction to Enterprise, Characteristics of Entrepreneurs and Enterprise Skills

 Be able to:

- Define enterprise.
- Identify the importance of enterprise skills in areas such as the home, school, community, government departments and business start-ups.
- Explain the basic enterprise skills.
- Identify the characteristics of enterprising people.

- Analyse the importance of enterprise in business and in the community.
- Identify enterprise skills, opportunities, risks and rewards from information given.

Enterprise

Enterprise is the activity that provides the initiative and enables individuals to take the risk in setting up a business.

It involves generating an idea or spotting an opportunity in the market and turning it into a reality.

Enterprise is being creative and innovative by showing initiative and taking a risk.

Entrepreneur

An entrepreneur is an individual who undertakes the risk of establishing and running a business (alone or with others).

Entrepreneurs use their initiative in seeking out opportunities and turning them into businesses.

Entrepreneurs typically invest their own money in the business. If the business does not succeed, they lose some or all of their money; if the business is successful, they make a profit.

Examples of **well-known entrepreneurs**:

- Sir Richard Branson – a British billionaire who has built his company (Virgin) into one of the world's biggest brands
- Sean Gallagher – founder of Smart Homes, Ireland's largest home technology company; also a *Dragon's Den* investor

- Brody Sweeney – founder of O'Briens Sandwich Bars
- Eamonn Fallon – Founder of daft.ie, Irelands largest property website

Entrepreneurship

An entrepreneur is an individual who undertakes the risk of establishing a business.

Entrepreneurship is the process of taking the initiatives and carrying the risk of organising all the resources necessary to provide a product or service.

The entrepreneur not only sees an opportunity (e.g. a new product or service) but also sets out to exploit that opportunity.

Profit is the reward entrepreneurs get for their efforts.

Intrapreneur

Intrapreneurs are employees who work within an organisation in an entrepreneurial capacity, creating innovative new products and turning them into profitable activities.

An intrapreneur comes up with new ideas, ways of saving money and new ways of solving problems (e.g. new work methods or new production processes) **within the business** in which he/she is employed. An intrapreneur would therefore work for an organisation such as a transnational company or a government department.

Intrapreneurs need the freedom and resources (human and capital) to pursue their ideas. For example, Intel has a tradition of encouraging intrapreneurship. It gives its employees the freedom to create their own projects and funds their development.

Characteristics of entrepreneurs

1. Control

Entrepreneurs usually need to be in control. They tend to dislike serving under others.

2. Self-confidence

Enterprising people have a lofty self-image and a high degree of self-assurance. They tackle problems with confidence and are persistent in their pursuit of their objectives.

3. Risk taking

Successful entrepreneurs are prepared to take risks to succeed and are not afraid of failing. They take calculated risks which provide a reasonable chance of success.

They take financial risks as well as personal-reputation risks, but try to minimise both.

4. Decisive

Entrepreneurs are prepared to make quick and clear decisions so that they won't miss opportunities. They take responsibility for the decisions they make.

5. Creative/innovative

Entrepreneurs are good at coming up with new ideas or new ways of carrying out existing tasks. They have the ability to see things in new ways, using their imagination and applying their ideas to new situations.

6. Flexible

Entrepreneurs are adaptable and able to respond to change. They are willing to adjust their priorities if necessary.

7. Realistic

Entrepreneurs are very realistic people. They recognise their own limitations and seek advice, if necessary. They are objective when setting goals and will only attempt what is achievable.

8. Energetic

Entrepreneurs are full of energy and eager to work. They are hard-working people who stick with the task until it is completed.

9. Leadership

Entrepreneurs are good leaders. They get on well with people. They can get people to work well together in teams and can motivate people to see and act on opportunities.

10. Opportunistic

Entrepreneurs are always looking for a gap in the market and seeking new challenges. They are proactive, future focused, have vision, anticipate change and always ready to initiate action.

Enterprise skills

1. Planning and goal setting

Entrepreneurs must be able to set short-term and long-term goals. Plans must be drawn up to achieve these goals. When planning, entrepreneurs will carry out a SWOT analysis.

2. Assessing and managing risk

Entrepreneurs must estimate the level of risk involved in a project and compare it with the likely return before a decision is made to proceed with the project.

3. Time management

The ability to use time effectively to ensure that all necessary tasks are completed is an important skill for an entrepreneur to have. This skill also involves taking appropriate action at the appropriate time and prioritising or ranking tasks in order of importance.

4. Decision-making

Entrepreneurs must be good decision-makers. When making a decision, they must choose the best option for the business from many different possible alternatives.

5. Human relations

This is the skill of being able to get on well with people, to develop good working relationships with them and to be able to organise them into teams.

This requires good interpersonal skills and good communication skills.

6. Reality perception

Seeing things as they really are is important for entrepreneurs. They must be able to realise when things are going wrong. They should recognise their own limitations and be able to seek advice when the need arises.

7. Inner control

Entrepreneurs want to control their own situation, and not to be controlled or influenced by others. They want to make things happen themselves.

8. Innovation

This is the skill of coming up with new ideas and better ways of doing things. Entrepreneurs who are innovative try to solve problems by finding new solutions.

Enterprise in different situations

Home	**School**	**At Work** (Intrapreneurship)
• Renovating the home	• Mini enterprises	• Developing new products
• Planning a holiday	• School tours	• Reducing costs
• Household budgeting	• Young scientist	• Better ways of dealing with customer complaints
• Growing organic vegetables	• School disco	• Improved work methods to improve efficiency
• Recycling	• School magazine	
	• New courses	
	• After school study	
	• New teaching methods	

Enterprise in Action

Community	**Public Life**	**In Business**
• Fundraising	• Motor scrappage scheme	• Finding new markets
• Establishing clubs/ associations	• Lotto	• Exporting
• Neighbourhood Watch	• Reform of public service	• Laundry collection service
• Tidy Towns committee	• Training schemes for unemployed	• Expansion
• Local drama Group		• Changing packaging from plastic to paper
• Community centres		
• Allotments to 'grow your own'		

HL Importance of enterprise in business and in the local community

1. Employment creation

Enterprise creates new businesses, which in turn create employment.

2. Increased local business

Workers spend money in the local shops, restaurants, etc. This helps local businesses to survive and expand.

3. Attracts new business

Enterprise attracts entrepreneurs and new business to the area.

4. Government revenue

Increased government revenue results from the success of businesses through PAYE and business taxation.

5. Improved infrastructure

New houses and roads are built and the telecommunications infrastructure in the local area is improved.

Illustrate how entrepreneurial skills might be used to enhance either:

(i) A local community

or

(ii) A government department   (30 marks)

Source: 2003 Higher Level Section 3

Suggested solution

(How entrepreneurial skills might be used to enhance a local community.)

1. Reality perception   (2 marks)

This is the skill of seeing things as they really are. It involves being able to clearly identify the needs of the local community.   (4 marks)

Example: Only by being realistic can enterprising people in the local community see and acknowledge the litter problems existing in the community so that they will be able to act to improve the situation.   (4 marks)

2. Inner control   (2 marks)

This is the skill of taking control of your own situation. They don't want others to influence their life. They want to make things happen themselves. They have the confidence to carry out a project to a successful conclusion.   (4 marks)

Example: Inner control is the skill that allows enterprising people in the community to take the initiative and act themselves rather than wait for others to do things for them. They come up with local community initiatives to address their problems. (4 marks)

3. Decision-making (2 marks)

Entrepreneurs must be good decision-makers. They must decide a course of action and implement it. (2 marks)

Example: A public meeting is called and a decision is made to set up a committee to clean up the area and enter the Tidy Towns Competition. (2 marks)

4. Planning

Planning involves setting short-term and long-term goals and drawing up plans to achieve the goals.

Example: The committee members use their planning skills to plan the work to be done, decide who will do it and determine the number of volunteers required.

5. Time management

This skill involves ensuring that all the tasks are completed within the time available and prioritising or ranking tasks in order of importance.

Example: The committee members use their time management skills to draw up a schedule of time to ensure the area is cleaned before the competition judging.

The most urgent work is prioritised and deadlines are set for the completion of the project.

Marking scheme

- Any 3 Skills @10 marks each
- Naming – 2 marks; development – 4 marks
- Illustration – 4 marks

UNIT 3
Managing I

This unit introduces the concept of management. It examines management as a planning and control process. As management is largely implemented through people, there is an emphasis on the management skills of communication, organisation and motivation.

Objective
To enable pupils to understand the importance of management in business and in the community.

- **Chapter 5:** Introduction and Definition of Management
- **Chapter 6:** Management Skills: Leading, Motivating
- **Chapter 7:** Management Skills: Communication
- **Chapter 8:** Management Activities: Planning, Organising, Controlling

5 Introduction and Definition of Management

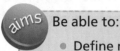 Be able to:

- Define management.
- Identify the importance of management skills in areas such as the home, school, local community, government departments and business start-ups.
- List the characteristics of managers.

- Differentiate between enterprise and management.
- Explain the contribution of both managers and entrepreneurs to business.

Definition of Management

Management is the process of combining personnel and physical resources (money) to create an environment in which the planned objectives/goals of the organisation can be achieved through people (that is, by assigning activities to subordinates).

Managers

Managers are the people responsible for achieving the objectives of the business.

Management skills

Leading – Influencing and directing people.

Motivating – The factors that cause people to behave in certain ways.

Communicating – The process of transferring information from one person to another.

Management activities

Planning – Setting goals and objectives and deciding how to achieve them.

Organising – Arranging the resources in an organisation to achieve the objectives.

Controlling – Monitoring progress by comparing performance with set targets and correcting any differences.

Managers need the **skills** of leading, motivating and communicating to enable them to carry out the **activities** of planning, organising and controlling.

Management in action

Management is used in many situations:

- **Home**: Household manager **plans** household budget, **controls** household expenditure, **motivates** students to study for exams, **communicates** with banks, insurance companies, etc.
- **School**: School principal **plans** curriculum and timetables, **organises** supervision rotas, **controls** school budget, **motivates** pupils and teachers.
- **Business**: Manager **plans** goals to be achieved, **organises** resources (finance and staff), **motivates** employees, **communicates** with customers/suppliers, **controls** stock, quality and credit.
- **Government departments**: Taoiseach **plans** government policies, **controls** departmental budgets, **leads** the Dáil Éireann, **motivates** public service.
- **Local Community**: Committee head **plans** fundraising events, **controls** expeditions, **leads** members, **motivates** volunteers.

Characteristics of managers

1. Leadership

Managers must:

- Lead by example, setting high standards to be achieved by others.
- Be always at hand to impart knowledge to employees.
- Be willing to take responsibility and be accountable for the work of others.

2. Decisive

Managers must:

- Have the ability to make quick and effective decisions and implement them.
- Take responsibly for the outcome of decisions.

3. Hard working

- Managers must be self-disciplined and motivated to work hard to achieve objectives.

4. Communicator

- Managers must be good listeners and be able to communicate effectively within and outside the organisation.

5. Organiser

- Managers must have the ability to organise the resources of the organisation or business in order to run it efficiently.

6. Time management

- Managers must ensure tasks are completed on time. This involves:
  - Making best use of the time available.
  - Prioritising tasks to ensure that the most important ones are completed first.

7. Charismatic

- Managers must have personal appeal and the ability to charm people to get work done.

8. Interpersonal skills

- Managers must understand people, relate to them and be able to deal with them in ways that gets the best results out of them.

Difference between enterprise and management

Enterprise

- Enterprise is the business activity that provides the initiative, generates the idea, identifies the opportunity and underlies the confidence, motivation and determination necessary to take the risk to turn the idea into a reality.
- 'Being enterprising' involves taking risks and, ultimately, being responsible for the success or failure of the business.

Management

- Management is the process of getting objectives achieved effectively and efficiently with and through other people. It is concerned with managing people and resources on a daily basis. Managers must ensure that this is well done so that the aims and objectives of the organisation are achieved.
- Management also involves setting short-term targets and long-term goals, checking to see if they are reached and making changes where necessary.
- The key activities of management are planning, organising and controlling.

In summary

The difference between entrepreneurs and managers is that:

- Entrepreneurs generate ideas **whereas** managers implement ideas.
- Entrepreneurs risk their own money and reputation in setting up a business **whereas** managers do not take the same risk.
- Entrepreneurs are concerned with the future of the business or coming up with new ideas for new businesses **whereas** managers are concerned with the day-to-day operation of the business.

For example, Richard Branson set up Virgin, but Virgin management runs it.

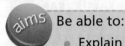

6 Management Skills: Leading, Motivating

aims Be able to:

- Explain the basic management skills of leading and motivating.
- Describe Maslow's hierarchy of needs and McGregor's Theory X and Theory Y.

Management involves getting the best out of people, managers must use the management skills of leading, motivating and communication.

Leading

Setting an example

A leader should be clearly visible in the organisation, a role model, setting an example of what is required of subordinates in terms of behaviour.

Direction

Directing staff by guiding them on the right course so that everyone co-operates and works together to achieve the goals of the organisation.

Leading is the ability to influence and direct people in a particular direction to achieve the goals of the organisation.

It involves **setting an example, directing employees** and **delegating work.**

Delegation

- Delegation involves the passing of authority from a manager to a subordinate, to undertake specific work.
- The manager must ensure that the person to whom the task is delegated has the necessary skills, and is provided with the necessary resources to complete the task.
- The ultimate responsibility for the task remains with the manager.
- Example. In a large firm the managing director must delegate tasks to the sales manager, accountant, human resource manager etc.

Advantages of delegation

- More efficient completion of projects, as manager is not required to do all the work.
- Task may be completed to a higher standard because the subordinate is accountable for performing the work and the results achieved.
- Managers can prioritise tasks, and by delegating the less important work managers can have more time to deal with the important tasks.

Styles of leadership

Authoritarian leadership

- No consultation with subordinates.
- All major decisions are made by the leader, orders are issued and expected to be obeyed without question.
- There is little delegation of tasks to subordinates.
- Objectives are achieved using threats, fear and position of authority to get agreement.

> **key point**
>
> The three **styles of leadership** are:
> - Authoritarian
> - Democratic
> - Laissez-faire

Evaluation of Authoritarian Leadership
An authoritarian style will produce dissatisfied and poorly motivated workers who will not co-operate with the leader.

Evaluation of Democratic Leadership
A democratic style will produce highly motivated and co-operative employees, high morale and greater job satisfaction.

Democratic leadership

- Leader consults subordinates and seeks their opinions, and encourages their participation in decision-making and problem solving.
- Leader delegates authority and responsibility as he/she trusts staff to do the work.
- Persuades employees rather than giving orders.

Laissez-faire leadership

- The leader sets the objectives and subordinate must decide how to achieve them.
- The manager provides little or no direction and gives employees as much freedom as possible.
- All authority or power is given to employees and they must determine goals, make decisions and solve problems on their own.

Evaluation of Laissez-Faire Leadership
This style of leadership is effective when:

- Employees are highly skilled, experienced, and educated.
- Employees have pride in their work and have the drive to do it successfully on their own.

It is not suitable for every business situation.

Importance of effective leadership in an organisation

- An effective leader delegates tasks to employees—staff are trusted and more involved in the business.
- An effective leader sets in example of what is required by subordinates in an organisation.

- An effective leader gives clear directions to employees. They know exactly what is required of them in the organisation.
- A good leader gets everyone to work together to achieve the goals of the organisation.

Motivating

Theories of motivation

Many theories have been developed over the years to help management identify how best to motivate people.

There are two main theories of motivation on how to motivate employees:

Maslow's hierarchy of needs

According to Maslow, most people are motivated by a desire to satisfy a group of five specific needs.

Maslow stated that each individual has a hierarchy of needs and he/she will look to satisfy a higher need only when the lower one has been satisfied.

Motivation can be defined as the factors that cause people to act or behave in certain ways. It is the willingness of people to work hard.

Maslow's hierarchy of needs

Explanation	Needs	How business can satisfy need
The need to reach one's full potential. Being personally fulfilled having developed one's talents to the highest possible level.	Self-actualisation	Challenging job, promotion and the opportunity to reach full potential.
The need for recognition and respect from others.	Esteem	Job titles, recognition for work and effort. Delegation of tasks and responsibility.
The need for interaction with other people. Being part of a group, friendship.	Social	Team work, social outings, staff interaction at work.
Safety and security needs, house, family.	Safety	Secure employment. Health and safety systems.
Most basic survival needs, food, water, shelter.	Physiological	Salaries, good working conditions, canteen facilities.

Evaluation of Maslow's Hierarchy of Needs

- Maslow's hierarchy of needs is very effective because it tells managers that if they want to motivate employees to work harder they must identify the level which each employee is trying to satisfy.
- Managers must then create a suitable work environment to enable employees to satisfy that need.

McGregor's Theory X and Theory Y

McGregor examined behaviour of individuals at work and what managers believe about employees and formulated two theories called Theory X and Theory Y.

Theory X	Theory Y
1. Employees are lazy, dislike work and try to avoid it	1. Employees are interested in work, want challenging jobs.
2. Employees lack ambition, dislike responsibility and prefer to be directed.	2. Employees want to be given responsibility and can be trusted to work on their own.
3. Employees dislike change in the workplace.	3. Employees are motivated to change when they are consulted.
4. Employees are motivated only by money, they need to be controlled to make them function.	4. Employees want to achieve their best and gain respect and recognition.

Characteristics of Theory X manager

- Manager controls employees – possible conflict between management and employees
- Employees are unlikely to use own initiative
- No consultation in decision-making
- Little delegation of work
- Employees become unco-operative and poorly motivated resulting in poor quality goods and services

Evaluation of McGregor's Theory X

McGregor suggested that Theory X managers adopt an autocratic approach to management by:

- Supervising workers closely
- Offering incentives or using sanctions/threats to ensure employee co-operation. This results in poor motivation and unco-operative employees

Characteristics of Theory Y manager

- Manager delegates work
- Employees given extra responsibilities
- Employee participation in decision-making
- Employees more co-operative and motivated
- More innovation, improved quality, increased profitability

Importance of motivation in business

Evaluation of McGregor's Theory Y

McGregor said that Theory Y managers adopt a democratic approach to management which:

- Takes a much more positive view of employees
- Delegates work and gives employees extra responsibilities
- Employees will be motivated and co-operate and will make a better contribution to the business

- Motivated employees will work hard for the success of the business, productivity is improved.
- Motivated employees are more likely to be more innovative and creative, coming up with new ideas to help the business.
- Motivated employees create a positive atmosphere in the workplace. Morale is higher with less industrial relations problems.
- Motivated employees are more likely to stay with the business in the long term, are willing to undergo training to improve their skills to help the business be more successful.

7 Management Skills: Communication

 Be able to:

- Explain the basic management skill of communication.
- Explain the central role of communication in business and management.
- Identify and explain the main barriers to effective communication.
- Demonstrate business information in the form of memos, reports and business letters and draft a visual presentation from given data.
- Identify the duties of a chairperson and secretary and draft an agenda and minutes of a meeting.
- Distinguish between the methods of communication.
- **HL** Discuss the importance of general communication skills.

Importance of good communication in business

1. Industrial relations

Good communication facilitates problem solving without the need for industrial action.

2. Decision-making

Effective communication is important for successful decision-making as managers need good information. Successful communication of information to and from decision-makers is vital.

Communication is the transferring of information from a sender to a receiver and receiving feedback that the message has been understood.

3. Downward communication

Communication is necessary when orders or directions are issued from a superior to a subordinate so that the individual understands the task to be performed and avoids mistakes.

4. Goals/Objectives

Communication allows the activities of all the departments to be co-ordinated in order to achieve the goals of the organisation.

5. Introduction of change

Communication forms the basis for the successful introduction of change.

Communication channels

1. Internal communication

Communication between people inside the organisation.

Downward communication

Instructions, orders, directions are transmitted from a superior to a subordinate (e.g. managing director communicating with marketing manager).

Upward communication

Information, messages, complaints are transmitted from subordinate to superior (e.g. employees complaining to management about working conditions).

Horizontal communication

Communication between people at the same level of authority in an organisation to ensure that all sections of the organisation work together (e.g. marketing manager and finance manager meeting to agree a budget for advertising).

2. External communication

Communication between an organisation and outside businesses (e.g. banks, insurance companies, suppliers, customers, etc.).

3. Communication skills

- **Speaking** – The ability to use language appropriate to listener.
- **Listening** – The ability to listen so that the message is heard and received.
- **Writing** – The ability to write clearly and accurately.
- **Reading** – The ability to read and understand written information.

4. Principles of effective communication

Effective communication can be achieved by considering the following:

- **Accuracy** – All information must be accurate.
- **Brevity** – Communication should be brief and to the point.
- **Clarity** – Language should be clear and easily understood.
- **On time** – Correct timing is essential to allow the recipient time to respond.
- **Feedback** – Communication should allow for feedback from the recipient.

Barriers to effective communication and methods to overcome those barriers

1. Language

If the message is too technical it may be misinterpreted.
How to overcome this barrier: Choose language appropriate to the audience.

2. Not listening

If the recipient is not listening, the information will not be received correctly.
How to overcome this barrier: Repeat the message.

3. Timing

If the message is sent too late the recipient may not be able to act on the information.

How to overcome this barrier: Plan the message to ensure that enough time is given to the recipient to read, understand and respond to the message.

4. Wrong medium

The medium chosen must be appropriate to the message.

How to overcome this barrier: Use the correct medium (e.g. use a letter to deliver a sensitive personal communication such as the termination of employment).

5. No feedback

The sender may require feedback before taking further action (e.g. the marketing manager may require information from the finance manager before deciding on an advertising campaign).

How to overcome this barrier: Build a feedback mechanism into the process (e.g. schedule a specific time slot for feedback).

Methods of communication

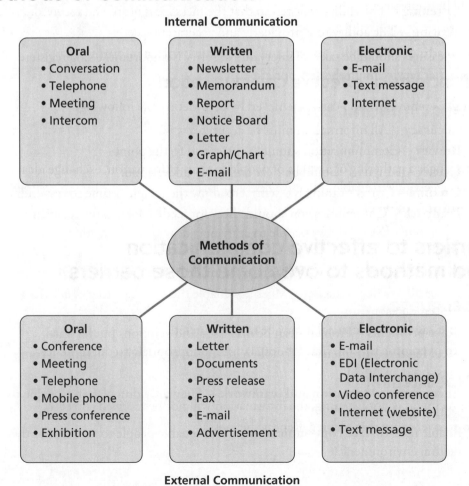

Internal Communication

Oral	**Written**	**Electronic**
• Conversation	• Newsletter	• E-mail
• Telephone	• Memorandum	• Text message
• Meeting	• Report	• Internet
• Intercom	• Notice Board	
	• Letter	
	• Graph/Chart	
	• E-mail	

Methods of Communication

Oral	**Written**	**Electronic**
• Conference	• Letter	• E-mail
• Meeting	• Documents	• EDI (Electronic Data Interchange)
• Telephone	• Press release	• Video conference
• Mobile phone	• Fax	• Internet (website)
• Press conference	• E-mail	• Text message
• Exhibition	• Advertisement	

External Communication

Choosing a method of communication

The following factors must be considered when choosing a method of communication:

1. Cost

Business must choose a method that will minimise costs. E-mail is a cheap method of communication.

2. Speed

If the message is urgent business must choose the quickest method possible. Telephone or electronic communication would be appropriate.

3. Confidentiality

If the information is private, it is important to choose a confidential method of communication. A private meeting would be appropriate.

4. Nature of message

The nature of the message will determine the method to be chosen. If the message is long and detailed and proof of communication is required, written communication would be appropriate.

5. Safety and security

Extra measures should be taken if safety and security is important. Using registered mail or a courier service might be appropriate.

Oral communication

Meetings

A meeting is a gathering of a group of people to share information, exchange ideas and make suggestions to enable collective decision-making.

The **purpose of meetings** is to

- **Exchange ideas** – Allows people to exchange ideas and information and plan ahead.
- **Make decisions** – Allows decisions to be made by voting on proposals.
- **Co-ordinate departments** – Meetings enable the co-ordinating of activities of various departments.
- **Solve problems** – Problems can be discussed and solutions put forward.
- **Meet legal requirements** – To adhere to legal requirements, all limited companies must hold an AGM.
- **Encourage co-operation and teamwork** – They provide a place for people to work together.
- Enable **face-to-face communication** – They enable people to meet each other in a neutral environment.

Types of meeting

There are different types of meetings, including:

- **Annual General Meeting (AGM)** – The meeting of directors and shareholders held once a year.
- **Extraordinary General Meeting (EGM)** – A meeting of shareholders to discuss an important matter that cannot wait until the next AGM.

Terms used in meetings include:

- **Agenda** – A list of matters to be discussed at a meeting and the order in which they will be taken.
- **Minutes of meeting** – A written record of the business transacted at a meeting.
- **Quorum** – The minimum number of people that must be present before a meeting can commence.
- **Standing orders** – The agreed rules for running a meeting.

Chairperson

The chairperson is responsible for running the meeting.

Duties of a chairperson

1. **Planning the meeting** and drawing up an agenda in consultation with the secretary.
2. **Running the meeting**: opening the meeting, ensuring a quorum is present, and that the agenda is followed.
3. **Maintaining order at the meeting**, managing discussion, and ensuring compliance with standing orders.
4. **Putting motions to a vote**, having a casting vote in the event of a tie, and announcing the result.
5. **Summarising decisions made** and concluding the meeting.

Secretary

The secretary is responsible for all administration work in the organisation.

Duties of a secretary:

- **Drawing up agenda** in consultation with the chairperson.
- **Making arrangements for the meeting**, organising the venue, facilities and equipment needed.
- **Sending out notice and agenda** to all entitled to attend in advance of the meeting.
- **Reading minutes** of previous meeting.
- Giving **secretary's report**.
- **Taking notes** on discussion and decisions made and writing up minutes of the meeting.
- Arranging next meeting in consultation with chairperson.

Notice, agenda and minutes of a meeting

Notice

The notice gives the name of the organisation, the type of meeting, the venue, the day, date and time of the meeting and is sent in advance of the meeting.

Agenda

The agenda is the programme for the meeting and contains a list of matters to be discussed and the order in which they will be taken.

Minutes of a meeting

This is a record of the business transacted at a meeting written by the secretary. It includes people present, absences, decisions made, matters discussed, and planning for future meetings.

Agenda and minutes

Draft a typical agenda for, and the minutes of, the AGM of a limited company.

(25 marks)

Source: 2004 Higher Level Section 3

Suggested solution

Agenda and Minutes of the AGM of a Limited Company

Agenda

Notice is hereby given that the 2nd Annual General Meeting of Redcliffe Ltd will be held in the head office of the company at 8 North Main Street, Wexford, on the 10th of April 2011, commencing at 1.30 pm for the following purposes:

1. Minutes of the 2010 AGM
2. Matters arising from the minutes
3. Chairperson's report
4. Auditor's report and accounts
5. Confirm the interim dividend and declare a final dividend for the year
6. Remuneration and appointment of auditors
7. Election/re-appointment of directors
8. Motions
9. Any other business

By order of the Board of Directors.

John Carey
Company Secretary
Date: 2nd April 2011

Minutes of 2nd Annual General Meeting of Redcliffe Ltd

The 2nd Annual General Meeting of Redcliffe Ltd was held in the head office of the company, 8 North Main Street, Wexford, on the 10th April 2011, commencing at 1.30 pm. The chairperson, Mr Kevin O'Halloran, brought the meeting to order.

The attendance included the directors, sixty shareholders and the auditor.

1. The minutes of the 2010 AGM were read and approved.

2. There were no matters arising from the minutes.

3. The chairperson report was given by Mr Kevin O'Halloran, who reviewed the past year and set out plans for the future.

4. The auditors report was presented and the accounts were adopted.

5. The dividend for the year was agreed at 8c per share.

6. The remuneration of the auditors was agreed and Johnson, Mooney and O'Brien chartered accountants were re-appointed as auditors for the following year.

7. Ms J. Creedon and Mr J O'Connor were re-appointed directors for a further year.

8. There were no motions before the meeting.

9. As there was no other business, the meeting concluded at 4.15 pm.

Signed
Kevin O'Halloran
Chairperson
Date: 15th April 2011

Written communication

Memorandum (memo)

Memos are an important form of internal communication providing a written record of a message.

Memorandum

Using today's date, draft a memorandum (memo) from Peter Murphy, marketing manager, to Mary O'Brien, managing director of a retail business, outlining **two** different sales-promotion incentives to encourage sales.

(10 marks)

Source: 2009 Higher Level

Suggested solution

Memorandum	(1 mark)
To: Mary O'Brien, Managing Director	(1 mark)
From: Peter Murphy, Marketing Manager	(1 mark)
Date: 9th June 2009	(1 mark)
Subject: Sales promotion incentives	(1 mark)

Please note that the two methods of sales promotion to be used in the business are:

(1) 'Buy one get one free'	(2 marks)
(2) 'Tokens to be collected for holiday breaks'	(2 marks)
Signature: Peter Murphy	
Marketing Manager	(1 mark)

Business letter

Using fictitious name and address, draft a letter to the Human Resource Manager of a business setting out four characteristics of managers to be looked for when interviewing candidates for management positions.   (20 marks)

Source: 1999 Higher Level Section 3

Suggested solution

P. C. Henderson
Consultant
2 Bank Buildings
Shardon Street
Waterford
Tel: (061) 6899296
Fax: (061) 6899297
www.pchenderson.com

10th September 2011

Mr Liam Mullins
Human Resource Manager
10 Shanakiel Road
Dungarvan
Co. Waterford

RE: Characteristics of Managers

Dear Mr Mullins

Further to your letter of 5th September, I would recommend that when interviewing candidates for managerial positions in your business you appoint candidates who display the following characteristics:

1. Hard working

A hard-working manager sticks with the task until the job is done and does not give up when things get difficult.

2. Good human relations

This means being able to work with and understand other people in the organisation.

3. Well organised

Having a structured and orderly approach to tasks is important.

4. Decisiveness

Good at analysing situations and making choices so that a decision is made and action is taken at the right time.

I hope that this information is to your satisfaction.

Yours sincerely,

P. C. Henderson
Senior Consultant

Report writing

A report is a written document setting out the findings of an investigation into some issue. It also contains conclusions and recommendations.

Reports are used for:

- **Giving information** about the progress of a project, etc.
- **Investigating a problem** – findings are presented and solutions are put forward.
- **Providing a record of an event** and explaining what happened (e.g. an accident).

Structure of a report

1. Title page	Title, writer's name, who report is for, date.
2. Table of contents	Main sections of report, chapters, page numbers.
3. Executive summary	Summary of main findings, conclusions, recommendations.
4. Terms of reference	The purpose of the report; sets out the guidelines to be followed and the problems to be addressed in the report.
5. Findings	Facts discovered are set out in a clear and logical sequence.
6. Conclusions	Evidence is assessed and problems identified.
7. Recommendations	Course of action to be taken.
8. Appendices	Extra information as required.
9. Bibliography	Sources of information used by the writer of the report.

Report writing

Draft a report to the managing director of a limited company explaining the four main barriers to effective communication in business. State relevant assumptions where necessary. (20 marks)

Source: 2002 Higher Level Section 3

Suggested solution

Title: Report to managing director of Kelly Electronics Ltd on effective communication in business.

Report writer: Mr John Hall, management consultant

To: Managing Director, Kelly Electronics.

Date: 10th May 2011.

Table of contents:

Report_____Page 1

Executive summary: The four main barriers to communication are noise, lack of planning, language, and not listening.

Terms of reference: To report on the main barriers to communication in business.

Findings: The following are the four main barriers to communication in business:

1. **Noise** – 'Noise' is any interference from outside which leads to messages being misunderstood or, in some cases, the meaning of the message becoming completely changed.

2. **Lack of planning** – The message may not be properly prepared and planned in advance.

3. **Language** – The language must be suited to the audience. If too much technical language is used, the message may not be understood.

4. **Not Listening** – If the recipient is not listening the information will not be received correctly.

Conclusions: The four main barriers that cause communication to fail that were found in the firm are noise, lack of planning, language used and not listening.

Recommendations: Kelly Electronics must develop a plan to overcome these barriers.

Appendices

Bibliography

Signed: John Hall, Management Consultant

Visual communication

Visual communication allows complex information to be understood more easily. It attracts attention, offers variety and helps reinforce the message.

There are many ways in which information can be presented visually, including:

- Graphs
- Pie charts
- Bar charts

1. Graphs

A graph illustrates a trend over time.

Graph

Draw a line graph to illustrate the following sales information for PDC Ltd 2006–2010.

Year	2006	2007	2008	2009	2010
Sales	€100,000	€130,000	€140,000	€160,000	€150,000

Sales in PDC Ltd, 2006–2010

(10 marks)

Source: 2003 Ordinary Level Section 1

Suggested solution

A line graph illustrating sales information for PDC Ltd from 2006 to 2010.

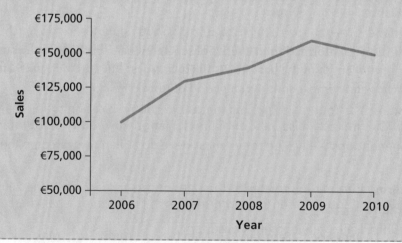

2. Pie chart

A pie chart is a circular diagram divided into segments. Each segment shows a figure as a percentage of the total. Pie charts are useful for showing comparisons.

Pie chart
Create a pie chart using the data on the age of a firm's workforce as shown in the table below.

Age	Under 20	21–40	41–55	56+
% of Workforce	12.5%	37.5%	25%	25%

Suggested solution
Pie chart depicting the age of the firm's workforce.

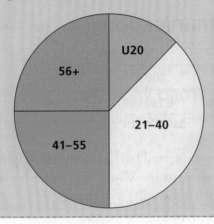

3. Bar chart

A bar chart displays information in a series of separated bars. Each bar is the same width and the height or length of the bars shows the quantities. They are very useful for showing trends and comparisons over a period of time.

Bar chart
The following information relates to the sales of cars for January–June 2009 for Milltown Auto Centre. Present this information in the form of a bar chart.

Month	January	February	March	April	May	June
Sales	50	40	35	30	35	40

(10 marks)

Source: 2009 Ordinary Level Section 1

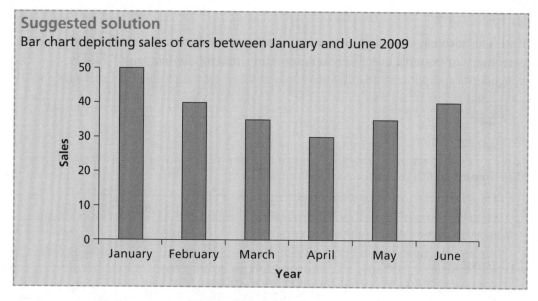

Suggested solution
Bar chart depicting sales of cars between January and June 2009

Electronic communication

Business today operates in a global market and the ability to communicate is greatly increased by using modern information technology.

1. Internet and the World Wide Web

The Internet is a global network of computers facilitating the transmission of data and communication between users.

All computer users who are connected to the Internet through an Internet service provider can access information via the World Wide Web by using a website address or through a search engine, such as Google (www.google.ie).

Broadband is the fastest means of Internet access.

Users may also communicate with each other via e-mail.

The Internet also facilitates e-business, which includes both business-to-business and business-to-consumer activity.

Impact of the Internet and World Wide Web on Business

- Facilitates e-Business – business to business, business to consumer.
- Faster, more cost-effective method of communication – consumers can communicate directly with business.
- A website can be an effective marketing tool – the Internet provides access to global markets.
- Increased scope for flexible working conditions and reduced overhead costs where employees avail of teleworking.
- E-mail provides a record of all communication.

Business can conduct market research through their website.

2. Electronic data interchange (EDI)

EDI is an automated method of processing transactions between suppliers and customers for example ordering stock, invoicing, making payments, etc. EDI is dependent on suppliers and customers having access to compatible EDI software.

The **impact of EDI on business** is as follows:

- It is a fast method of processing transactions.
- It is a cost-effective method of processing transactions. It reduces labour costs and the cost of stationery/office expenses.
- It is an effective stock control system, leading to reduced stock-holding costs (e.g. insurance, storage, etc.). Automated processing ensures speedier stock re-order.
- The scope for human error is reduced as transactions are automated.

3. Videoconferencing

A meeting between two or more people in different locations that is facilitated by the use of videoconferencing technology. Typically, a telephone line, a monitor and a camera are required in each location.

Videoconferencing substitutes for a face-to-face meeting but with the same advantages – parties can see and talk to each other. Visuals in the form of charts and diagrams can be used to support the presentation being made.

Videoconferencing can be a time-saving and cost-effective means of communication. It reduces or eliminates the need to travel to a meeting or conference.

4. E-mail

E-mail is a way of sending a typed message and computer files directly from one computer to another over the Internet.

Each user had an e-mail address and messages are held in a mailbox until read.

The **advantages** of e-mail:

- A fast, efficient, convenient and cheap way of sending messages.
- Copies of a message can be sent to a number of people at the same time.
- Files can be attached to e-mail messages.

However, the use of e-mail in business does present some **problems**:

- **Data security** – Sending information over the Internet is not secure. 'Hackers' may gain access to messages or files sent via e-mail.
- **Incorrect address** – Information could easily be sent to the wrong address.
- **Technological availability** – E-mail can only be used if sender and receiver have computers and e-mail addresses.
- **Computer viruses** – E-mail can be used to spread computer viruses, which, if opened, may damage a computer system.

5. Teleworking/E-working

This is where an employee works on the move or from home (e.g. using home computer or laptop).

It is essential to have access to office systems via e-mail, the Internet, and telephones.

Files can be sent between the home computer and office computer, allowing work to be completed as if the employee were present in the office.

Role of information and communication technology (ICT) and its application in business communications

- **Speed** – Information is transmitted and available worldwide instantly (e.g. e-mail).
- **Location** – Using ICT decision-makers can be far away from their production activities so that face-to-face communication is no longer necessary (e.g. video-conference meeting).
- **Decision-making** – Decision-making needs up-to-date information (e.g. Marketing Department needs up-to-date sales figures). ICT reduces the risk in decision-making.
- **Management structures** – Use of ICT has changed the structure of organisations. Spans of control have been greatly reduced.

Data Protection Act 1988 and 2003

The Data Protection (Amendment) Act 2003 extends the provisions of the Data Protection Act 1988.

What is data protection?

Data protection addresses the safeguarding of the privacy rights of individuals in relation to the processing of personal data. The Data Protection Acts 1988 and 2003 confer rights on individuals as well as responsibilities on those persons processing personal data.

Organisations (such as government bodies, financial institutions, universities, etc.) gather and store data about individuals.

For the purpose of data protection, such organisations or individuals who control the contents and use of personal data are known as 'data controllers'. The Data Protection Acts 1988 and 2003 impose obligations on data controllers and give rights to individuals relating to their personal data.

What types of data are included?

All personal information relating to a living individual is included under the legislation. It covers data that is held on computers as well as data that is held in manual files.

Previously, data protection laws applied only to files in electronic form. The Act of 2003 extends data protection to include manual files.

Data subjects

The **rights of individuals** are:

1. **Right of access** – To **get a copy of the personal information on request**, known as an access request. In order to access data held on you, you must make a written request to the organisation involved.
2. **Correction of errors** – To have your personal data **corrected** or **deleted** if inaccurate.

3. **To have your name removed from a direct marketing list** – To prevent your data from being used for **direct marketing purposes**. This is put into effect by writing to the Data Controller and directing him/her to cease using your information for this purpose. He/she must comply within 40 days.

4. **Right to object** – You may request a Data Controller to stop using your personal data if you consider the use of your data involves substantial damage or distress to you.

5. **Freedom from automated decision-making** – The right of individuals not to be subjected to **automated decision-making,** that is, **to have human input in the making of important decisions relating to you**. Important decisions about you (e.g. work performance, creditworthiness, reliability) may not be made solely by automatic means (e.g. by computer) unless you consent to this. In general, there has to be a human input in such decisions.

6. **To be informed** – To know the identity of the Data Controller and for what purpose they have the information.

7. **To block certain uses of data** – To prevent your personal information from being used **for certain purposes** (e.g. you might want your data blocked for certain purposes where it is held for other purposes). These blocked purposes would include direct marketing activities.

8. **No enforced access/employment rights** – Not to be forced to **disclose information to a prospective employer**. No one can force you to make an access request, or reveal the results of an access request, as a condition of recruitment, employment or provision of a service.

Data controllers

Any organisation involved in the collection, storage or processing of data has responsibilities under the legislation.

The **responsibilities of Data Controllers** are to:

1. **Obtain and process information fairly and openly** – data subject must not be mislead about the purpose of the data. Data subject should be told who the Data Controller is, and for what purpose the data is processed.

2. **Ensure data security** – Data must be protected from unauthorised access (i.e. it must be kept safe and secure and not be disclosed to others).

3. **Keep the data accurate, complete and up to date** – to do this, data should be updated periodically (e.g. an employer should be careful that employment files are current).

4. **Provide a copy of the data** – to an individual, on request, within forty days of receiving a written request from them.

5. **Use data for purpose intended:**
   - It should be kept only for specified and lawful purposes (i.e. information should only be used for the specific purpose provided).
   - It should be adequate, relevant and not excessive for the specified purpose.
   - It should not be retained for longer than is necessary for the specified purpose and deleted when no longer needed.

Data Protection Commissioner

The Data Protection Commissioner is responsible for ensuring that people's rights are respected, and that the persons who keep personal information on computer or in manual format meet their responsibilities.

Functions of Data Protection Commissioner

1. **Investigating Complaints**

   The Data Protection Commissioner investigates complaints received from individuals who feel that personal information about them is not being treated in accordance with the Acts.

2. **Enforcing Compliance with the Acts**

   The Data Protection Commissioner may require a Data Controller to correct data, block data from use for certain purposes, erase data by providing a written notice called an **'Enforcement Notice'** to the Data Controller.

3. **Power to Obtain Information**

   The Data Protection Commissioner may require any person to provide him with whatever information is needed to carry out his functions, such as to pursue an investigation by providing a written notice, called **'information notice'**, to the person.

4. **Prosecution of offences**

   Prosecuting data controllers found guilty of offences under the Acts.

5. **Keeping a register of data controllers**

   All Data Controllers e.g. financial institutions, public bodies, universities and anyone keeping personal data on individuals must register with the Data Protection Commissioner.

exam focus

Evaluation of Role of Data Protection Commissioner

- The data protection commissioner is very effective in protecting data subjects by ensuring that individuals have access to their personal data, and getting it corrected or deleted.
- The Data Protection Commissioner also investigates complaints and prosecutes offenders.

Notice and agenda

Assume you are the secretary of a local youth club. Draft the notice **and** agenda to be posted to all members of the youth club notifying them of the annual general meeting. (The agenda must contain five items.)   (10 marks)

Source: 2005 Higher Level Section 3

Suggested solution

Notice and Agenda AGM of Youth Club

Notice is hereby given that the 5th **Annual General Meeting** (1 Mark) of the **Wexford Youth Club** (1 Mark) will be held in the **Clubhouse, Mary Street, Wexford (1 Mark) on the 10th February 2011 (1 Mark)** at 8.00 p.m.   (1 Mark)

Agenda for Meeting

1. Minutes of the 2010 AGM   1 mark (compulsory)
2. Matters arising from minutes
3. Chairperson's report   1 mark (compulsory)
4. Secretary's report
5. Treasurer's report   1 mark (compulsory)
6. Subscriptions for 2011
7. Election of officers   plus 2 other items
8. Election of club committee   @ 1 mark each
9. AOB

Marking scheme

- Notice 5 @ 1 mark each
- Agenda 5 @ 1 mark each

 **Management Activities: Planning, Organising, Controlling**

 Be able to:

- Explain the basic management activities of planning, organising and controlling.
- Discuss the nature of management activities and their linkages.

Planning

Planning is the process of setting goals or objectives and deciding how to achieve them.

Steps involved in planning

- Carry out SWOT analysis
- Draft mission statement and objectives
- Identify types of planning to be used

SWOT analysis

When planning, an organisation must carry out a SWOT analysis by analysing its internal **Strengths** and **Weaknesses** and identify external **Opportunities** and **Threats**.

This is an analysis of the present position of a business and is usually done before drawing up plans.

The aim is to maximise the potential strengths and opportunities while minimising the impact of weaknesses and threats.

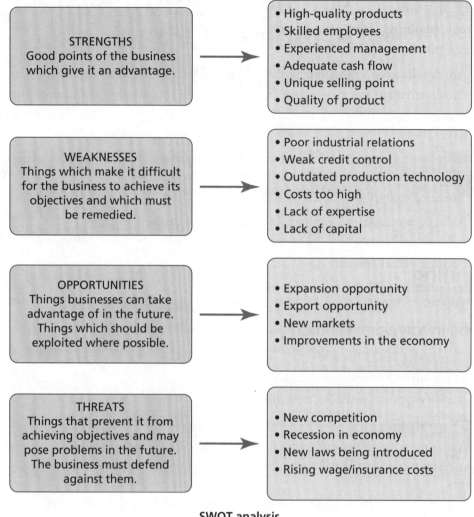

SWOT analysis

Mission statement and objectives

Mission statement – A mission statement sets out the general purpose and objectives of the organisation, the reason for its existence and what it sees for itself in the future.

Objectives – Objectives of an organisation are aims that it is trying to achieve (e.g. 'to cut costs and become more competitive').

These are the targets to be aimed at – they motivate people to achieve results. Objectives must be **SMART**:

- **Specific** – They must be clear and precisely expressed (quantifiable).
- **Measurable** – The success of the plan should be easily measured.
- **Agreed** – The plan must be agreed by all the management team.
- **Realistic** – They must be capable of being achieved with the resources available.
- **Timed** – There must be a timescale for achieving the objectives.

Types of planning

Strategic planning (long-term planning)

Strategic plans:

- Are developed over the long term and normally cover five years or more.
- Are drawn up by top management and focus on the organisation's mission or purpose.
- provide a guide for where the business is going in the long term, and how it's going to get there.

Strategic planning requires an examination of the organisation's strengths, weaknesses, opportunities and threats so that the objectives can be achieved.

Here are some examples of objectives:

- Achieve entrance into a foreign market or a new market
- Achieve an increase in market share
- Become a market leader

Tactical planning (short-term planning)

The long-term plan is broken down into more manageable short-term plans.

Some short-term plans relate to a particular function of the organisation, (e.g. advertising).

They cover a period of about one to two years and are developed by a management team which deals with getting the work done to carry out the strategic plan.

Short-term plans have their own objectives. Some examples of short-term objectives are:

- Launch a new advertising campaign aiming to increase sales by 25%
- Improve customer service
- Open a new branch of the business
- Launch a new product
- Reduce employee turnover

Short-term plans are tactical plans. If they are achieved they help the business to meet its long-term goals.

exam focus

THE IMPORTANCE OF PLANNING FOR THE SUCCESS OF A BUSINESS

It identifies a business's strengths (and builds on them) and weaknesses (which must be overcome).

It identifies a business's opportunities (and exploits them) and threats (which must be eliminated).

It tries to anticipate problems facing the business in the future and identify steps that can be taken to deal with these problems.

It sets targets against which the success of the business can be measured.

Planning helps an organisation cope with change.

Co-ordination

Co-ordination means ensuring that all departments work together with a common purpose of achieving the goals of the organisation.

Example: The Production department must contact the Purchasing department about types and quantities of raw materials needed.

Organising

Organising involves arranging all the resources, people, equipment and finances into the most suitable form to achieve the objectives of the business.

Organising means setting up a formal structure in an organisation so that the activities are co-ordinated and objectives achieved.

An organisation chart shows how an organisation expects to get things done. It will start with the heads of departments and move down to subordinates at lower levels of responsibility.

Good organisation is important for the success of a business because:

- It identifies different levels of authority and sets out who is responsible to whom so that each person can understand his/her role in the achievement of the objectives.
- Work that is shared among the various departments gets completed faster and quality is improved.
- A good organisation structure will improve communication between the various departments. (Good communication is essential for a business that wants to achieve its objectives in the most efficient way possible.)

Types of organisation structure

Functional structure

This is an organisation structure that shows the organisation divided into departments according to their function (such as finance, production, sales and marketing, purchasing, and human resources).

All sales people are grouped together, all production people are grouped together and tasks are carried out more effectively as they are consistent with the training of each individual in his/her department.

A person is in charge of each department who is responsible for achieving its objectives.

The structure is also called 'line organisation' because each person in the line is answerable to the person above. Responsibilities are well-defined and so this type of structure is easy to understand.

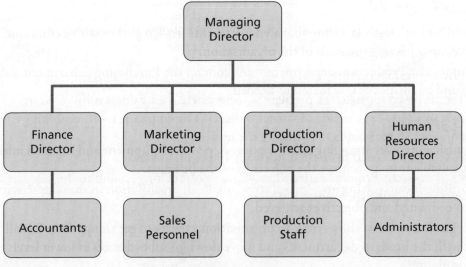

Functional structure

Chain of command

The chain of command is the path on which orders/instructions/decisions are passed down from the top to the bottom of the hierarchy and feedback is passed back up. There is a clear structure to the organisation and clear lines of authority exist. Instructions flow downwards along the chain of command and accountability flows upwards.

Span of control

A span of control is the number of subordinates who are delegated authority and report to the supervisor or manager. In the illustration below the span of control of the managing director is three.

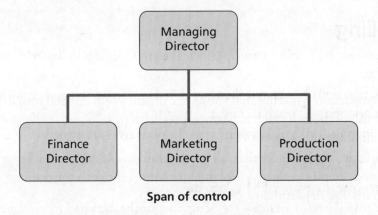

Span of control

A manager's span of control can be wide (many employees) or narrow (few employees). Its size depends on the type/difficulty of work, the quality of the manager and staff, the service being provided and the type of products being made. Products which are easy to make will need less supervision and can have a wider span of control.

Matrix structure

This type of structure is a combination of two types of organisation structure:

- Functional structure
- Project team structure

It is a team-based approach to problem solving where the business is involved in complex projects (e.g. a major construct project). The emphasis is on combining the skills of many departments to complete the project.

Employees are removed from their normal job to work on the project.

They report to the Project Leader when working on the project and to their department manager when doing their normal work.

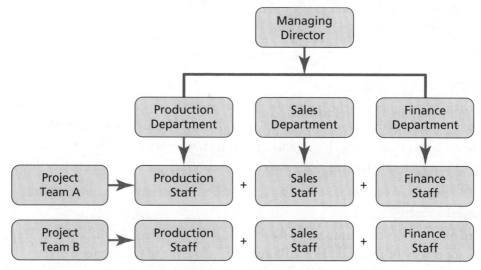

Matrix structure for a manufacturing organisation

Controlling

Controlling means measuring actual performance to see if it is in line with the target set out in the plan.

Corrective action must be taken if there are deviations from planned performance so that the organisation will reach its target.

Control is concerned with making sure that the objectives are achieved.

Principles of control

1. **Set target** – e.g., increase sales by 25% this year
2. **Measure actual performance** – e.g. after six months sales had increased by 8%
3. **Compare performance with target** – e.g. result off target
4. **Take corrective action** (to ensure that the business stays on target to achieve its objectives) – e.g. increase advertising

Types of control

The main areas of control in business are:

- Stock control
- Quality control
- Credit control
- Financial control

Stock control

This is the monitoring of stock levels to ensure that there is enough stock to meet demand while keeping costs to a minimum.

The aim of stock control is to ensure that the business has the correct amount of stock at all times – never too much, never too little.

The following are **benefits of stock control**:
- Cash will not be tied up in too much stock.
- There will be no shortages of raw materials for production.
- Insurance costs will be lower.
- The business will always have the correct amount of stock, ensuring no lost sales and improving sales and profits in the future.
- The firm will be able to identify goods that are on demand as well as slow-moving goods, which may be subject to deterioration or obsolescence.

Just in Time – This is a method of stock control where materials and products are delivered at the exact time they are needed (e.g. materials delivered just in time for manufacture). The aim is to minimise the cost of holding stock while at the same time never running out of stock.

Quality control

This is checking the efficiency of production to ensure that the product meets the standards expected by customers.

Inspections are carried out during the production process to ensure that high-quality standards are achieved.

A good-quality control system can lead to significant cost savings, fewer customer complaints and an improved reputation for the business.

Quality control can be achieved by:

- Obtaining **recognised quality standards** such as the Q mark and ISO award. The Q mark is a quality standard recognised in Ireland. The ISO (International Standards Organisation) is an internationally-recognised quality standard.

- Having a **quality assurance system** to guarantee customers that the firm's products are of the highest quality.
- Establishing a **Quality Circle** – a group of employees who meet to discuss and solve quality problems.
- **Training** employees in quality control.

Effective quality control is important because it ensures that:
- The goods produced are of the highest standard.
- Costs are reduced as no faulty goods should be sold to customers, which means no repairs and no cash refunds.
- There will be fewer customer complaints and improved reputation for the business.

Credit control

This means controlling the amount of goods sold on credit, monitoring the credit period given to customers and ensuring that payments are made on time.
Credit control involves:

- Confirming the creditworthiness of customers
- Setting credit limits and credit periods
- Establishing penalties for late payments
- Minimising the risk of bad debts

The importance/benefits of a good credit control system:
- Firm controls the amount of goods sold on credit.
- Debtors pay for goods on time.
- Bad debts are kept to a minimum.
- The creditworthiness of customers is checked in advance.
- Firm will not have to rely on bank overdrafts to deal with cash shortages.

Financial control

Financial control is used to monitor the financial position of the business.
A budget is a financial plan that sets out the expected income and expenditure for a future period of time.

A comparison is made between the actual financial performance and the budget figures. The difference (known as a 'variance') should be investigated.

Example: A cash flow forecast shows planned cash inflows and cash outflows for a future period and ensures that the business does not run out of cash.

The importance of controlling to management

Controlling ensures that:

- Plans are being implemented as agreed in order to enable the business will achieve its objectives.
- Action will be taken if things are not going according to plan.
- Plans will not fail and that the business will grow.

Here are some **examples** of how controlling serves important purposes in a business:

- Effective quality control – Ensures goods meet the standard expected by customers.
- Effective stock control – Ensures that the business will always have the correct amount of stock.
- Effective credit control – Ensures that debtors pay for goods on time, which reduces the risk of bad debts.
- Effective financial control – Monitors the finances of the business and ensures that debts can be paid as they arise.

Applied Business Question (ABQ) (Higher Level)

Based on Units 1, 2 and 3
This is a compulsory question for Leaving Certificate 2014/2019

Renewable Energy Solutions (RES) Ltd

Liam Best, an electrical engineer, established Renewable Energy Solutions (RES) Ltd ten years ago. The business imports, supplies and installs energy-efficient solar panels that are used to heat homes and businesses. While attending a trade fair in Germany on behalf of his previous employer, Liam identified a niche in the market for an Irish supplier of solar panels. With twenty years' experience in the heating and plumbing supplies business and with no opportunity for promotion, he decided to start his own business. Impressed with Liam's knowledge and belief in his product, Liam's bank manager and a number of private investors were happy to provide the necessary finance. The business grew rapidly and by the end of 2007 had a turnover of €30 million and a workforce of thirty.

The past year, however, has been difficult for the business. As the construction of new houses has fallen, there has been a steady decline in the sales of solar panels. Costs are rising and the business is finding it more difficult to pass on price increases to customers. Cash flow is tight and Liam is particularly concerned by the fact that two of his largest customers have not paid their bills on time. In addition, the company is finding it difficult to raise short-term finance due to the current credit squeeze. Rising stock levels in the warehouse are also causing problems. A number of customers have recently returned solar panels, as a result of damage caused while in storage in the warehouse or in transit.

Liam is confident that the demand for green energy sources in Ireland will increase again. He believes that the government's new Building Energy Rating (BER) regulations, combined with the increasing demand for more cost-effective and environmentally friendly heating systems, will provide opportunities for his business.

However, Liam has e-mailed all staff informing them that action will need to be taken swiftly if the business is to survive the current downturn in the economy. To avoid the introduction of compulsory redundancies, Liam explains in his e-mail that it will be necessary to implement a 10% pay cut, with immediate effect for all workers. The staff contacted their trade union to express their concerns about the proposed pay cuts. A trade union meeting has been organised to discuss staff concerns and agree a response to the pay cut proposed by Liam.

(A) Illustrate, using examples from the previous text, **four** enterprising characteristics/skills shown by Liam. (20 marks)

(B) Discuss **three** types of management control that you would recommend Liam put in place to secure the future of RES Ltd. (30 marks)

(C) **(i)** Describe, using the previous text, **one** possible **non-legislative** and **one** **legislative** solution for the industrial relations problem facing RES Ltd.

(ii) In your view how should Liam have dealt with the issue to lessen the likelihood of an industrial relations conflict? (30 marks)

(80 marks)

Suggested solution

(A) Illustrate, using examples from the previous text, *four* enterprising characteristics/skills shown by Liam.

(i) Liam is a **risk taker** (1 mark). Successful entrepreneurs are not afraid of failing or taking risks. Liam has seen an opportunity in the market for a new product/service, and is prepared to take the chance to set up his own business. He is taking both a personal and a financial risk in setting up RES Ltd. (2 marks)

Link to text
With twenty years' experience in the heating and plumbing supplies business and with no opportunity for promotion he decided to start his own business. (2 marks)

(ii) Liam is **innovative/creative** (1 mark). Entrepreneurs are good at coming up with new ideas and recognising opportunities as they present themselves. They are constantly looking for new ideas and ways of improving what they do. Liam identified an opportunity to introduce solar panels to the Irish market and set up his own business, RES Ltd (2 marks).

Link to text
Liam identified a niche in the market for an Irish supplier of solar panels.
(2 marks)

(iii) Liam is **confident/positive** (1 mark). Entrepreneurs have a strong sense of self-belief and conviction about their own business ideas. Liam recognised a business opportunity and believed that his twenty years' experience in the heating and plumbing business provided him with the necessary skills and expertise to develop the idea into RES Ltd. His confidence in his business idea convinced others to invest in the business. (2 marks)

Link to text
Impressed with Liam's knowledge and belief in his product, Liam's bank manager and a number of private investors were happy to provide the necessary finance.
(2 marks)

(iv) **Liam is resilient/determined** (1 mark). Despite the downturn in the economy Liam has no intention of giving up. Liam is now looking for other opportunities to sustain RES Ltd. He views the introduction of the BER positively and believes the BER will present more opportunities for RES Ltd. **(2 marks)**

Link to text

Liam is confident that the demand for green energy sources in Ireland will increase again. **(2 marks)**

Marking scheme

(A)	Four enterprising Characteristics/Skills Must be linked to text of ABQ.	Four characteristics/skills 5 marks each (1 + 2 + 2) **(State, explain, relevant link)** **Separate relevant link for each characteristic/skill**	**20 marks**

(B) Discuss *three* types of management control that you would recommend Liam put in place to secure the future of (RES) Ltd.

(i) **Stock Control** **(2 marks)**

This is the monitoring of stock levels to ensure that there is enough stock to meet demand while keeping stock holding costs to a minimum. Establishing the optimum stock level reduces the costs associated with being overstocked or understocked.

Benefits of effective stock control

- Ensures adequate stock levels to satisfy customer demand thus avoiding potential loss of sales
- Minimises storage costs, while making effective use of storage space available
- Identifies slow moving stock
- Reduces risk of stock going out of date/becoming obsolete/goods being damaged/stolen
- Aids working capital management – less money tied up in stock
- Reduces insurance costs   2 points @ 3 marks each.

Link to text

Rising stock levels in the warehouse are also causing problems. **(2 marks)**

(ii) **Quality Control** **(2 marks)**

This is the process of checking the quality standard of the goods or services provided by a business to ensure they are up to required standards/meet expectations of the market. The quality of the goods and services provided is fundamental to the business reputation. Poor quality goods and services will result in loss of customers and sales.

Benefits of Quality Control

- Consistent quality – enhances the reputation of the business, helps maintain customers and wins new customers
- Reduces costs associated with faulty goods (e.g. returns, refunds, court cases, damage to reputation of business, loss of customers, etc.)   2 points @ 3 marks each.

Link to text

A number of customers have recently returned solar panels, as a result of damage caused while in storage in the warehouse or in transit.   (2 marks)

(iii) Credit Control   (2 marks)

It involves checking creditworthiness of customers, setting credit limits and periods, deciding penalties for late payments in an effort to avoid or minimise bad debts.

Benefits of Credit Control

- Firm controls amount of goods sold on credit
- Firm controls to whom goods are sold on credit – creditworthiness of potential customers is checked.
- Debtors pay debts on time
- Reduces risk of bad debts   2 points @ 3 marks each.

Link to text

Cash flow is tight and Liam is particularly concerned by the fact that two of his largest customers have not paid their bills on time.   (2 marks)

Marking scheme

(B) Three types of Management Control	Three types of Management Control	30 marks
	10 marks each	
	(2 + 3 + 3 + 2)	
Must be linked to text of ABQ.	(State, explain two points, relevant link)	
	Separate relevant link for each type	

(C) (i) Describe, using the previous text, one possible *non-legislative* and one *legislative* solution for the industrial relations problem facing (RES) Ltd.

(a) Non-legislative

1. Negotiation/discussion/third parties

Liam could meet with the Shop Steward/workers to discuss his concerns and try to reach an agreement in relation to the proposed pay cut.   (2 marks)

Link to text

The staff contacted their trade union to express their concerns about the proposed pay cuts. (3 marks)

2. **Grievance procedure**

lternatively, shop steward may invoke the grievance procedure whereby:

- Shop steward makes an official complaint in writing in relation to the proposed 10% pay cut
- Liam must respond and meet with the shop steward (2 Marks)

Link to text

The past year has been difficult for the business. As the construction of new houses has fallen there has been a steady decline in the sales of solar panels. (3 marks)

- If the shop steward is dissatisfied with the outcome of the meeting with Liam she/he may either:
- Request the intervention of Head Office in negotiations

or

- Opt to pursue a legislative route to try and solve the conflict

(b) Legislative

The Labour Relations Commission

1. The Labour Relations Commission offers a conciliation service to solve disputes. This is where the parties to the dispute can meet with the help of a third party to sort out their differences. (2 marks)

Link to Text

Liam wants a 10% pay cut with immediate effect for all workers (3 marks) *while the workers. Want to 'Express their concerns about the proposed pay cuts'.* (3 marks)

2. The LRC can appoint an industrial relations officer to try and resolve the dispute between Liam and his employees at RES Ltd.

   The officer tries to get the two parties to come to an agreement using conciliation. The process involves a series of meetings with all parties involved in the dispute. A settlement occurs when both parties come to agreement or where they accept a proposal for settlement that the Industrial Relations Officer puts to them. The recommendation is not legally binding and can be rejected by either side. It can be appealed to the Labour Court. (2 marks)

(ii) In your view how should Liam have dealt with the issue to lessen the likelihood of an industrial relations conflict?

Liam has chosen the wrong medium to communicate a significant change in terms and conditions of employment to his employees.

Link to text

He has sent an e-mail to staff to inform them that it will be necessary to implement a 10% pay cut, with immediate effect for all workers.

Effective communication reduces conflict, and enhances working relationships.

A face-to-face meeting with the employees would have:

(i) Allowed Liam to present to employees the current financial position and challenges faced by RES Ltd.

Link to text

The past year has been difficult for the business, costs are rising and the business is finding it more difficult to pass on price increases to customers.

(ii) Facilitated a recognition by employees of the impact of the downturn on RES Ltd.

Link to text

The company is finding it difficult to raise short-term finance due to the current credit squeeze.

(iii) Afforded staff with a sense of dignity, respect and inclusion in decisions affecting their future.

(iv) Provided an opportunity to discuss and explore possible alternative courses of action rather than an immediate 10% pay cut.

Marking scheme

(C)	(i) **One** non-legislative/**one** legislative solution.	**One non-legislative solution**	30 marks
		10 Marks	
		5 marks (2 + 3) + 5 marks (2 + 3)	
		One legislative solution	
		10 Marks	
		5 marks (2 + 3) + 5 marks (2 + 3)	
	(ii) What should Liam have done to lessen likelihood of conflict?	**10 Marks**	
		5 marks (2 + 3) + 5 marks (2 + 3)	

UNIT 4

Managing II

The theme of this unit is the applications of management. It looks at those functions that are common to managing a household and a business. It examines organisational applications, including human resource management and the changing role of management.

9 Household and Business Manager 1: Finance

aims Be able to:
- Outline the difference between managing a household and managing a business in relation to finance.
- Explain the importance of finance for a business.

Cash flow forecast – household and business

The purpose of a cash flow forecast for a business

- It identifies when a business might find itself facing a **cash flow problem**.
- It identifies times of high expenditure and **shortages** so that finance can be arranged to deal with the deficit.
- It identifies future cash **surpluses** so that the business can make plans to invest this extra money.

> **key point**
>
> A **cash flow forecast** shows the planned flow of money in and out of a business or household over a period of time.

- Comparing figures in the cash flow forecast with the actual receipts and payments figures allows the business to see if it is on target with its cash flow projections, aiding **financial control**.
- It shows future cash inflows and outflows their sources and timing, which assists in the **decision-making process**.
- A cash flow forecast is vital for a **business starting up** and is essential if making an **application for a loan** to show that repayments can be made.

Household Cash Inflows and Outflows

Inflows	Outflows
Wages/salaries	Fixed expenditure (mortgage/rent)
Interest	Irregular expenditure (telephone/electricity)
Child benefit	Discretionary expenditure (holidays/entertainment)
Social welfare payments	
Tax rebate	
Loans	

Business Cash Inflows and Outflows

Inflows	Outflows
Cash sales	Purchase of assets
Receipts from debtors	Purchases of goods
Interest	Payments to creditors
Grants	Payment of taxes
Share capital	Payment of expenses
Sale of assets	Paying dividends to shareholders
Tax refund	

Cash flow

'Cash Flow is the lifeblood of any business and its management is critical to business survival.'

In September 2008, Buttercup Garden Centre prepared the following Cash Flow Forecast.

Cash Flow Forecast of Buttercup Garden Centre – October to December 2008

Cash Flow Forecast of Buttercup Garden Centre, October to December 2008				
	October	November	December	Total
	€	€	€	
Receipts				
Cash Sales	12,500	9,500	10,000	32,000
Credit Sales	2,000	1,500	3,500	7,000
Total Receipts	**14,500**	**11,000**	**13,500**	**39,000**
Payments				
Cash Purchases	1,000	2,500	4,000	7,500
Credit Purchases	5,000	2,000	1,000	8,000
Wages	6,000	6,000	7,500	19,500
Equipment	12,000	—	—	12,000
Total Payments	**24,000**	**10,500**	**12,500**	**47,000**
Net Cash	(9,500)	500	1,000	(8,000)
Opening Cash	3,000	(6,500)	(6,000)	3,000
Closing Cash	(6,500)	(6,000)	(5,000)	(5,000)

(i) Explain the benefits to Buttercup Garden Centre of preparing a Cash Flow Forecast.

(ii) Based on the information provided above, outline how Buttercup Garden Centre could improve the Cash Flow position of its business. (20 marks)

Source: 2009 Higher Level Section 3

Suggested solution

(i) The **benefits** to Buttercup Garden Centre of preparing a Cash Flow Forecast are:

- Identifies the timing and sources of cash inflows
- Identifies the timing and sources of cash outflows
- Establishes net inflows/outflows – business can then plan effectively to meet cash shortages (or, alternatively, consider their options in relation to a large cash surplus)
- Provides a benchmark against which actual performance can be compared, aiding financial control
- Aids access to finance from financial institutions

(ii) Buttercup Garden Centre could **improve** the cash flow position of its business through the following:

A. Purchase of equipment – capital expenditure

Buttercup Garden Centre plans to purchase and pay for equipment out of cash flow in October 2008. Equipment is an item of capital expenditure and will most probably be used in the business over a period lasting a number of years. Buttercup should consider taking out a medium-term loan to pay for the equipment. This would ease their cash flow position considerably, and provide access to badly needed cash.

B. Access to credit/bank overdraft

Buttercup Garden Centre will need to negotiate a bank overdraft with its local bank. If trade continues as per the month of December, and there are no changes in overheads or other unforeseen expenses, it will take at least another five months to clear the forecasted deficit of €5,000.

C. Credit control

Information provided in the cash flow forecast for Buttercup Garden Centre shows that:

- Cash sales are expected to decrease, while the level of credit sales is expected to increase over the three-month budgeted period.
- Cash purchases are expected to increase, while credit purchases are expected to decrease over the three-month period.

Both sales and purchases forecasts are putting pressure on cash flow, and the availability of cash. Buttercup needs to review its credit policy – to decrease cash purchases if possible and increase cash sales.

D. Control of overheads

Wages increased from €6,000 to €7,500 (a 25% increase) from October to December, yet sales fell in the same period. Buttercup Garden Centre needs to review and control the amount of money spent on wages.

Marking scheme

(i) Benefits **2 @ 5 Marks (2 + 3)**

(ii) Suggestions for improvement (reference to purchase of equipment a compulsory point) **2 @ 5 Marks (2 + 3)**

Sources of finance

Most household and businesses need finance to pay bills or purchase assets.

Sources of finance can be **short term, medium term,** or **long term.** Businesses must match the source of finance with its use.

Short-term sources of finance (less than one year)

exam focus

Sources and Uses of Short-term Finance	
Household	**Business**
Sources:	**Sources:**
Bank overdraft	Bank overdraft
Creditors	Creditors – trade credit
Accrued Expenses	Accrued expenses
Credit card	Taxation
Uses:	**Uses:**
Pay day-to-day expenses	Purchase stock
Purchase clothes	Pay wages/expenses
Purchase services	Pay creditors

Short-term finance

This is finance for less than one year and is used to finance short-term assets, such as stock and pay expenses.

The main sources of short-term finance include:

- Bank overdraft
- Creditors
- Accrued expenses
- Taxation
- Credit cards

Bank overdraft

A bank overdraft is a short-term loan given to current account holders designed to meet short-term expenditure needs.

The current account holder is given permission by the bank to withdraw more than the amount in the account, up to a specified limit.

Security is not usually required.

Interest is calculated on a daily basis on the overdrawn balance.

Creditors

Suppliers give an agreed period of credit to their customers, who then sell the goods and have the use of the money until the invoice has to be paid.

No interest is charged and no security is required. However, if the invoice is not paid by the due date discounts may be lost.

Accrued expenses

These are expenses that do not have to be paid until after the service has been provided (e.g. telephone, electricity).

By delaying the payment of these bills, the business can use the money as a short-term source of finance for other purposes.

Taxation

The business collects taxes on behalf on the Revenue Commissioners (e.g. PAYE, PRSI and VAT).

These taxes are held by the business for a period of time before being forwarded to Revenue.

Credit card

A credit card allows a card holder to purchase goods and services up to a specified limit.

At the end of the month the credit card company sends a statement.

No interest is charged if the balance is paid by the due date.

Medium-term sources of finance (one to five years)

exam focus

Sources and Uses of Medium-term Finance	
Household	**Business**
Sources:	**Sources:**
Hire purchase	Hire purchase
Leasing	Leasing
Personal loan	Medium-term loan
Uses:	**Uses:**
Cars	Computers
Televisions	Office equipment
Electrical appliances	Vehicles
Furniture	Machinery

Medium-term finance

This is finance for one to five years and is used to finance office equipment, vehicles and machinery. The main sources of medium-term finance include:

- Hire purchase
- Leasing
- Term loan

Hire purchase

Purchasing assets and paying by instalments over an agreed period of time.

Buyer obtains immediate possession and use of the asset but does not become the legal owner until the last instalment is paid.

The rate of interest is high and interest is charged on the initial sum borrowed.

No security is required to obtain the finance.

Leasing

Leasing is a medium-term source of finance for households and businesses and involves the renting of an asset from a finance company.

The lessee has the possession and use of the asset during the period of the lease but does not own it.

The lessee does not have to use cash lump sum to buy the asset.

No security is required.

Lease repayments can be set against profits to reduce tax.

Medium-term loan

A term loan from the bank is repaid in fixed instalments over an agreed period.

It is negotiated with the bank after completing a loan application form and is granted for a stated reason.

Banks may demand security (collateral) in the event of non-repayment.

Interest on a business term loan can be offset against tax in the profit and loss account.

Long-term sources of finance (over five years)

exam focus

Sources and Uses of Long-term Finance	
Household	**Business**
Sources:	**Sources:**
Long-term loan	Long-term loan/debenture loan
Mortgage	Owner's capital/share capital
Savings	Retained earnings
Uses:	**Uses:**
Buy a house	Purchase of land and buildings
Pay for house improvements	Pay for business expansion
	Buy another business

Long-term finance

Finance for more than five years and used to purchase property, build an extension or expand the business.

The main sources of long-term finance include:

- Long-term loans
- Share capital
- Retained earnings

Long-term loans

Long-term loans for a household are available from banks and building societies to purchase a residence. These are called mortgages and are secured on the asset purchased.

A debenture loan is a long-term loan to a company usually for expansion.

Security will usually be the title deeds of the property.

Interest payments on loans are an allowable expense against tax in the profit and loss account.

They are used for large capital expenditure.

Share capital (equity)

Share capital is provided by the shareholders (owners) who buy shares in a company.

Shareholders receive a share of the profit in the form of a dividend if the company makes profit.

Ordinary shareholders have votes at the AGM giving them a say in the running of the business – one share = one vote.

There are no interest payments and no security has to be provided to raise this finance.

Equity capital is used to purchase expensive assets that will last more than five years.

Retained earnings

This is profit not paid out in dividends but re-invested back into the business as extra capital for expansion or for purchasing assets.

It is a free source of finance and no security is required.

If this source of finance is continuously used, shareholders may become dissatisfied with the lack of dividends.

Read the information supplied and answer the question that follows.

Capdata is a small software writing business located in the south of Ireland and employing four employees. It has the opportunity to grow but has little experience of the day-to-day running of a business. It needs premises, equipment and employees not only with computer technology skills but also with business management and sales skills.

In choosing either a short-, medium- or long-term source of finance, Capdata has been advised that it should always match the source of finance with the purpose for which the finance is to be used.

Explain, using examples from each type of finance why this is so.   (20 marks)

Source: 2001 Higher Level Section 3

Suggested solution

When raising finance a business should always match the sources and uses of finance. This will reduce the cost of finance (i.e. a short-term source for a short-term use, a long-term source for a long-term use).

Sources of finance

1. Short-term finance

This is finance available for less than one year. The main sources include trade credit, bank overdraft, accrued expenses and taxation.

Example: Capdata needs employees. **Employing staff** leads to wage costs (4 marks), so a suitable source of finance here is a **bank overdraft,** which is a short-term source of finance due for repayment within one year (3 marks).

2. Medium-term finance

This is finance between one and five years. The main sources include hire purchase, leasing and term loan.

Example: Capdata needs equipment. **Purchase of equipment** can be financed using a medium-term source of finance (4 marks). **Hire purchase** or **leasing** would be suitable as they are good for a firm's working capital and cash flow because only the regular instalments/leasing payments have to be made (3 marks).

3. Long-term finance

This is finance for more than five years and includes long-term loans (debentures), equity capital and retained earnings.

Example: Capdata needs premises. This is **capital expenditure,** which requires a long-term source of finance (i.e. a source available for more than five years (4 marks). **Long-term loan** would be suitable to buy premises which are very expensive and would require large borrowings to be repaid over a long period of time (2 marks).

A firm that mismatches the source with the use is not using the most cost-effective source of finance. (So, for example, a firm using a bank overdraft to purchase premises would put huge pressure on its ability to repay the loan.)

Marking scheme

- Sources of finance: 7   +   7   +   6
  (4 + 3)   (4 + 3)   (4 + 2)

aims Be able to:

- Outline the difference between managing a household and managing a business in relation to insurance.
- Explain the importance of insurance to a business.

Insurance

Insurance is a contract whereby a person (the insured) pays a fee (premium) to an insurance company (the insurer), which in return promises to compensate the person for any financial loss suffered.

Risk management

Risk management is having a planned approach to the handling of the risk to which an individual or business is exposed. It involves:

- Identifying all possible risks facing a business (e.g. risk of fire)
- Identifying the cause of the loss (e.g. personal injury)
- Measuring the likelihood of the event occurring
- Calculating the costs of the methods of protecting the business from loss (e.g. reduce risks by insurance, training of staff in health and safety)

Methods of risk reduction

1. Take out insurance in order to transfer the risk to an insurance company for a premium where the company will compensate for any loss suffered.
2. Train personnel in health and safety and provision of safety equipment and/or protective clothing.
3. Appoint a health-and-safety representative in the workplace who would report safety issues, provide a health-and-safety statement, identify hazards and carry out regular safety inspections.
4. Install security systems, alarms, security guards, CCTV.
5. Introduce safer production processes to improve employee health and safety.

Principles of insurance

1. Insurable interest

- The insured person must have a personal financial interest in the item being insured.
- The policyholder must benefit by the continued existence of the item and suffer by its loss.
- The owner of property has an insurable interest in the property.

The **principles of insurance** are:
1. Insurable interest
2. Utmost good faith
3. Indemnity
4. Subrogation
5. Contribution

Example: Everyone has an insurable interest in their personal possessions, such as their house, but your next door neighbour would not have an insurable interest in your house.

2. Utmost good faith

- All material facts must be disclosed to the insurer.
- A material fact is one that would influence the insurer into accepting or rejecting the risk or in setting the premium.
- This means that all the information that might have a bearing on the decision to enter the contract must be supplied on the proposal form, even if the information is not requested.
- The insurer can declare the contract void and claims made by the insurer can be refused if all the facts are not disclosed.

Example: A person with a heart problem looking for life assurance would have to disclose this to the insurance company as this is a relevant fact related to life assurance.

3. Indemnity

- There must be no profit from insurance – only recovery of actual loss.
- The contract is for the reinstatement of the actual property insured. That is, putting the claimant in the same position as was the case prior to the accident or loss.

Example: A two-year-old car insured for €20,000 but with a market value of €15,000 is written off in an accident. The maximum compensation for the loss suffered is therefore €15,000.

4. Subrogation

- Having paid compensation to the insured, the insurer takes over the rights of the insured to sue a third party who was responsible for causing the loss.

Example: If A injures B, and B is paid compensation by the insurance company, then the insurance company can sue A to recover the money.

- The insured also has the right to take over what is left of the property after compensation is paid.

5. Contribution

- If the loss suffered is insured by more than one insurer, then the amount claimed is divided proportionally between them.
- The loss is shared by the insurers. Contribution usually occurs where two or more companies insure the same risk (e.g. insuring the same property with two different insurance companies).

Underinsurance

Average clause

- The average clause states that if a partial loss is suffered and the property is underinsured, then only a proportion of the amount insured will be paid.
- The full value of the loss is not paid – all claims are reduced to a proportion of the insured value.

John O'Neill owned a house worth €350,000 and had insured it for €300,000 when a fire caused a partial loss of €63,000.

(i) Calculate the amount the insurance company will pay. (Show your workings.)

(ii) Explain your answer. (10 marks)

Source: Higher Level Section A 2008

Solution

(i) Answer €54,000

(ii) The average clause applies for partial loss. As the house is underinsured, only a proportion of the amount insured will be paid.

Workings

$$\frac{\text{Value Insured} \times \text{Loss}}{\text{Value of House}} = \text{Compensation}$$

$$\frac{€300,000 \times €63,000}{€350,000} = €54,000 \text{ Compensation}$$

Relationship between risk and cost

The relationship between risk and cost is:

- The higher the risk, the higher the cost.

  Example: Car Insurance – a male, aged 20 and holding a first provisional licence will be a higher risk and thus pay a higher premium than a female aged 40 who has been insured for a number of years and holds a full licence.

Insurance and assurance

Insurance is a protection against a risk that **may** happen – for example, a fire or accident. **Assurance** provides for a risk that **will** happen – such as death.

1. Motor insurance

- **Third-party fire and theft insurance**

  Compensation is provided to third parties for damage to them and their property by the insured while driving a car.

  It does not cover the insured person or his/her car for damage caused by the insured. Compensation is paid to the insured only when damage results from a fire or theft of the car.

- **Comprehensive insurance**

  Comprehensive insurance provides compensation to third parties for damage to them or their property by the insured while driving a car. It also covers the insured person's car against all risks.

2. House and contents

Covers buildings and contents against fire, flooding, burglary or accidental damage. It would provide compensation to the owner in the event of loss or damage to the specified items covered by the policy.

3. Health insurance

Covers the cost of hospital care in the event of accident or illness. Private healthcare insurance is provided by VHI Healthcare, Quinn Healthcare and Aviva Health.

4. Life assurance

Life assurance provides compensation on the death of the insured. Types of life assurance include:

- **Whole life assurance** – The insured pays a premium for the rest of his/her life and compensation is paid to dependents on the death of the insured.

- **Endowment life assurance** – The insurance pays the premium, and compensation is paid either on the insured reaching a certain age or on their death, whichever comes first.

5. Mortgage protection

If the borrower dies before the mortgage is fully paid, the policy will cover the balance due on the mortgage.

6. Permanent health insurance

This covers a person's income if they are unable to work because of an accident, serious accident or disability.

Business insurance

1. Motor vehicle insurance

All cars, vehicles and delivery trucks owned by a business must be insured. The same types of policies and rules apply as for households.

2. Property insurance – buildings and contents

This policy covers buildings, equipment and stock against loss or damage as a result of fire or accident.

3. Public liability insurance

This protects the business against claims by members of the public from injury or loss resulting from an accident on the business premises.

Types of Insurance a **business** should have:

1. Motor vehicle insurance
2. Property insurance – buildings and contents
3. Public liability insurance
4. Employer's liability insurance
5. Fidelity guarantee insurance
6. Product liability insurance
7. Burglary insurance

4. Employer's liability insurance

This policy protects employers against claims made by employees as a result of an accident at work.

5. Fidelity guarantee insurance

This protects the business against financial losses as a result of theft or fraud by an employee.

6. Product liability insurance

This protects the business against claims by members of the public for loss or damage suffered as a result of a defective product.

7. Burglary insurance

This protects the business against loss/damage caused by theft/break-ins.

Taking out insurance/insurance documents

Private Car Insurance
Proposal Form

ZURICH®

Agent's Name

Agent's Number	Policy Number

A. Proposer
1st Proposer

Title (Mr, Mrs, Ms, Miss etc.)	First Name

Surname

Date of Birth

Type of Licence (e.g. Irish, EU, Full, Provisional)

Daytime Tel. No.	Email

Evening Tel. No.

Postal Address

Address at which vehicle is kept (if different from Postal Address)

Occupation	○ Full time ○ Part time
Employer's Business	○ Full time ○ Part time

Cover to commence from: □□□□□□   to: □□□□□□

B. The Vehicle

Make and exact Model (e.g. DL, GL)

Type of Body (e.g. Saloon, Soft Top)

CC	Fuel (e.g. petrol/diesel)	Transmission (e.g. Manual/Automatic)

Registration No.	Year of Make
Date Purchased	Present Value
Left Hand Drive?	No. of fixed seats

1. Insurance proposal form

An application form that must be filled out if a person or firm is taking out insurance. All material facts must be disclosed and the proposal form is governed by the principal of utmost good faith.

2. Premium

Fee paid annually to the insurance company by the person seeking insurance. In return, the insurance company will compensate the insured for the loss or damage covered by the agreement.

3. Policy

Contains details and terms of the insurance agreement. Policy excess means the insured has agreed to forgo, say, the first €250 of any compensation.

4. Claim form

This form is used by the insured when seeking compensation for a loss that has occurred. It describes what happened and the amount being claimed.

The importance of insurance for business

1. Protection against risks

The business will be protected against risks. A large claim against the business or loss of property could put the business in severe financial difficulty.

2. Business survival

The business can continue and survive despite unforeseen events (e.g. fire or flood).

3. Improved safety standards

Insurance companies will insist on improved safety and security standards before granting insurance cover. This should reduce the number of accidents in the workplace.

'Watertight Ltd' is a family-run plumbing and central-heating business. It has a parts outlet that sells to the public and to the trade. It employs three qualified plumbers who work throughout the area using the enterprise's vans.

Describe the various types of insurance which you would expect Watertight to be familiar with. Give reasons for your choice.

(10 marks)

Source: 1999 Higher Level Section 3

Suggested solution

1. Public liability insurance (1 mark)

This protects the business against claims by members of the public for accidents while on the firm's premises.

'Watertight has a parts outlet dealing with members of the public so it will need this policy to cover claims by the public as a result of accidents on its premises.'

(3 marks)

2. Employer's liability (1 mark)

This covers the business against claims by employed injured at work.

'Watertight employs three people and therefore requires cover against claims made by employees for accidents or injury suffered at work.' (2 marks)

3. Motor insurance (1 mark)

All businesses with vehicles are obliged by law to have third-party cover, but it would be advisable to take out comprehensive insurance to cover all people and vehicles in the event of an accident.

'Watertight has a number of vans driven by staff so it needs motor insurance.'

(3 marks)

Marking scheme

Three types of Insurance [4m + 3m + 3m]:

- 4 marks (name – 1 mark; information – 3 marks)
- 3 marks (name – 1 mark; information – 2 marks)
- 3 marks (name – 1 mark; information – 2 marks)

11 Household and Business Manager 3: Taxation

aims Be able to:
- Outline the difference between managing a household and managing a business in relation to taxation.
- Explain the implications of taxation to a business.
- Identify activities common to managing a business and a household in relation to finance, insurance and taxation, including the completion of relevant forms.
- Identify activities that are different in managing a business and a household in relation to finance, insurance and taxation.

Taxes paid by households and individuals

Tax is charged by the government on the income of individuals and businesses and on goods and services. This money is used by the government to finance its spending and to provide services.

1. Income tax (PAYE)

This is charged on peoples wages/salaries. Income tax is deducted by the employee from wages/salaries and sent to the Revenue Commissioners. This is called the PAYE system (Pay As You Earn). PRSI (Pay Related Social Insurance) is also collected through the PAYE system as well as the Universal Social Charge.*

The PAYE system

The PAYE system applies to anyone who earns income from employment.

Form P12A

Form P12A must be completed by all employees before commencing employment.

It is used to apply for a certificate of tax credits and a standard cut-off point.

'Tax credit'

A tax credit reduces the amount of tax payable by the taxpayer and is determined by personal circumstances.

exam focus

Taxes paid by **households and individuals**:
1. Income tax (PAYE)
2. Value added tax (VAT)
3. Capital Gains Tax
4. Capital Acquisitions Tax
5. Deposit Interest Retention Tax (DIRT)
6. Motor Tax
7. Employee PRSI
8. Universal Social Charge

exam focus

The PAYE system requires the completion of a number of tax forms, including:
- P12A
- P60
- P45
- P21

*The Universal Social Charge is a tax payable on income from all sources

Tax credits that a person may be entitled to include:

- Personal Tax Credit (single, married)
- PAYE Tax Credit
- Gross tax less tax credits = tax payable

'Standard cut-off point'

This is the amount of a taxpayer's income on which they pay tax at the standard rate. Any income earned over the standard cut-off point will be subject to the higher rate of tax.

In the absence of a certificate of tax credits, emergency tax must be deducted by the employer.

Form P60

Issued by an employer to an employee after the end of the tax year.

It shows gross pay, income tax and PRSI paid by the employee for the tax year.

Form P60 will be required by the employee when claiming a refund on overpaid tax or overpaid PRSI contributions.

Form P60 can also be used as proof of income for various purposes (e.g. education grants, medical services, etc.).

Form P45

Issued by an employer to an employee on leaving employment.

Form P45 provides details of the amount of gross pay, tax and PRSI paid by the employee up to the date of leaving employment.

Form P45 will be required by an employee when:

- Entering new employment – the new employer will require the P45 to calculate the correct amount of tax payable
- Claiming social welfare benefits
- Claiming a tax refund

Form P21

This is known as a balancing statement and all PAYE taxpayers are entitled to receive a P21 annually. It compares tax paid with the amount of tax that should have been paid.

If tax was overpaid by a taxpayer, they are entitled to a refund.

If tax was under paid by a taxpayer, a demand for further tax will be made.

Income tax calculation

From the following information, calculate the net annual take home pay of Ms Joan McCormack.

Joan McCormack is an employee of Lynch Printers and earns a gross salary of €84,000. She is allowed the following tax credits:

Single person tax credit of €1,650 and PAYE tax credit of €1,650. The income tax rates are 20% on the first €32,800 (standard cut-off point) and 41% on the balance. Employee PRSI is €3,360. The universal social charge (USC) is €5,880.

Suggested solution

Joan McCormack – Net Annual Take Home Pay

Gross Salary +(BIK)					€84,000
Tax					
€32,800 @ 20% Take away from 84,000 to get	€6,560				
€51,200 @ 41%	€20,992				
Gross Tax		€27,552			
Less Tax Credits					
Single person	€1,650				
PAYE	€1,650	(€3,300)			
Tax to be paid			€24,252		
PRSI			€3,360		
USC			€5,880		
Tax, PRSI and USC				€33,492	
Net annual take home pay				€50,508	

2. Value added tax (VAT)

Value added tax is paid by households when they buy goods and services.
VAT is added to the price of the goods or services. Here's an example:

Price of computer (excluding VAT)	€800
Add value added tax 21%	€168
Price of computer (including VAT)	€968

Householder will pay €968, and of this amount €168 is VAT.

3. Capital gains tax

This is tax paid by the households on profit from the sale of assets such property or shares.
Capital gains tax does not apply to the profit on the sale of a principal private residence.

4. Capital acquisitions tax

This tax is paid by the recipient of:

- A gift taken other than on death
- An inheritance taken on death

The amount of tax payable depends on the amount of the gift or inheritance and the relationship between the giver and receiver.
A certain amount of the gift or inheritance is tax free.

5. Deposit interest retention tax (DIRT)

The interest a person receives on a savings account in a bank, building society or post office is subject to a tax called Deposit Interest Retention Tax (DIRT) at a rate of 25%. The tax is deducted by the bank before the interest is paid to the person and is sent to the Revenue.

6. Motor tax

Motor tax is paid to the local authority on all motor vehicles owned by the household. The amount payable depends on the car's emissions levels.

7. Employee pay related social insurance (PRSI)

Every person in employment must pay PRSI. It is a compulsory payment and is calculated as a percentage of the employee's gross wages. There is a wide range of benefits available to people who have paid PRSI, including jobseeker's benefit, illness benefit, maternity benefit, and dental and optical benefits.

Taxes paid by business

1. Income tax – self-assessment

Self-assessment income tax applies to all self-employed people.

Self-employed people calculate their own tax liability for the year and pay it by 31 October of that year. They must also send in a full tax return for the year by 31 October of the following year.

Self-assessment tax returns are subject to random audits by Revenue inspectors to ensure that the returns made are accurate.

exam focus

Taxes paid by **businesses** include:

1. Income tax – self-assessment
2. Value added tax (VAT)
3. Corporation tax
4. Commercial rates
5. Employer's PRSI

2. Value added tax (VAT)

VAT is a tax on consumer spending. It is chargeable when a business sells goods or services to a consumer.

Business charges VAT on sales and is entitled to deduct from this amount VAT paid on purchases.

VAT owed by a business must be sent to the Revenue Commissioners every two months. There are various rates of VAT depending on the product or service sold.

3. Corporation tax

Corporation tax is charged on profits of companies resident in the state.

The rate of corporation tax is 12.5% on trading income.

4. Commercial rates

Rates are a charge payable by all commercial businesses to fund services provided by local authorities, including housing, water supply and sewerage, roads, etc. Rates amounts are based on property valuations.

5. Employer's pay related social insurance

Employers must also pay PRSI. It is calculated as a percentage of an employee's gross wages. This is the employer's contribution to the national social insurance fund, which pays for social insurance benefits and pensions.

Effects of taxation on business

1. Collecting and recording tax is a huge cost for business. They do not get paid anything for collecting tax for the state.
2. Tax reduces profit, which reduces the dividends paid to shareholders and the amount of retained profit in the business.
3. Customs duties increase the price of raw materials imported, thus increasing the cost of production.
4. High rates of personal taxation reduce the incentive to work and seek promotion.

Similarities and differences in managing a household and managing a business

Similarities

1. Taxation

Both households and businesses must pay taxes, so income tax/PRSI is common to both. Business must also pay VAT on purchases and corporation tax on profits.

2. Insurance

Both must assess risk and insure people and property.

3. Finance

Both must raise suitable sources of finance. Households need finance for the purchase of a house, car and other expenses (such as the education of children and family holidays).

Businesses need working capital to finance operating expenses and long-term finance to the purchase of fixed assets.

4. Official Forms

Both household and business must complete forms such as tax forms, loan applications and insurance proposal and claim forms.

5. Records

Both must keep financial records and keep documents such as tax forms and insurance polices safe.

6. Management Activities

Both must plan, organise and control to achieve goals and objectives.

Differences

1. Taxation

Different taxes apply to households (PAYE, capital acquisitions tax) and to businesses (VAT, corporation tax).

2. Insurance

Businesses need to cover a wider range of risks than households (e.g. public liability, employee's liability and fidelity guarantee).

3. Finance

Businesses have a wider range of sources of finance (e.g. share capital).

4. Scale of Operation

Business is on a much bigger scale then a household (e.g. finance and personnel).

5. Motivation

Motivation in business is mainly profit, whereas in a household the main motivating factor is family love.

6. Legislation

A business is subject to much more legislation than a household. Areas such as company law and competition law do not directly affect households.

7. Management Expertise

Specific kinds of management expertise are regularly used in running a business. Bookkeeping and budgeting skills are relevant to the running of a household, but not to the extent required in business.

Taxes paid by a business

Read the information supplied and answer the question that follows.

Capdata is a small software business located in the south of Ireland that employs four people. It has the opportunity to grow, but has little experience of the day-to-day reality of running a business. It needs premises, equipment and employees not only with computer technology skills but also with business management and sales skills.

Describe the taxes that Capdata would be liable for, give reasons for your choice.

(20 marks)

Source: 2001 Higher Level Section 3

Suggested solution

Capdata would be liable for the following taxes. (It is assumed Capdata is a limited company.)

1. PAYE (Pay as you earn) (2 marks)

This is income tax. It is deducted from employees' pay by the employer each time wages/salaries are paid.

The tax is sent to the Revenue Commissioners by the employer. (2 marks)

As Capdata employs four employees, it must operate the PAYE system. It must deduct tax from employees' wages /salaries and send it to the tax office. (3 marks)

2. Corporation Tax (2 marks)

This is tax on company profits. (2 marks)

Capdata must be familiar with the corporation tax system as they will be liable to pay corporation tax on their profit. (3 marks)

3. Value Added Tax (VAT)   (2 marks)

This tax is charged when a business sells goods and services to a consumer. The amount of tax is calculated as a percentage of the price charged. VAT is paid every two months to the Revenue Commissioners.   (2 marks)

Capdata is a service provider and must charge VAT on services provided.   (2 marks)

Marking scheme

| **7 marks** | + | **7 marks** | + | **6 marks.** |

2 m + 2 m + 3 m   2 m + 2 m + 3 m   2 m + 2 m + 2 m

(Name Explain Link)   (Name Explain Link)   (Name Explain Link)

Income tax calculation

Peter Collins is single. He is a manager earning €50,000 annually. He is allowed the following tax credits:

- Single person tax credit €1,650
- PAYE tax credit €1,650

The income tax rates are 20% on the first €32,800 (standard cut-off point) and 41% on the balance.

Employee PRSI is €1,736 and the Universal Social Charge (USC) is €2,819. Calculate the net annual take home pay of Peter Collins.

Suggested solution

Peter Collins – Net Annual Take Home Pay

Gross Salary				€50,000
Tax				
€32,800 @ 20%		€6,560		
€17,200 @ 41%		€7,052		
Total Tax		€13,612		
Less Tax Credits				
Single person	€1,650			
PAYE	€1,650	€3,300		
Tax payable			€10,312	
PRSI			€1,736	
Universal Social Charge			€2,819	
Total Tax, PRSI and USC				€14,867
Net Annual Take Home pay				€35,133

12 # Human Resource Management

Human resource management

Human resource management is the function of management that recruits, trains and rewards the workforce so that the objectives of the firm are achieved.

1. Manpower planning

Manpower planning involves:

- Identifying the human resource needs of the organisation and ensuring that they are met
- Conducting an audit of existing staff skills and expertise
- Identifying additional staff needed
- Preparing a plan to recruit or reduce human resources

2. Recruitment and selection

Recruitment – The process of attracting suitable candidates to apply for vacancies in a firm.

Selection – Selecting the most suitable candidates for the job.

Stages in recruitment and selection

Prepare a job description

This describes the duties and responsibilities of the job. It includes details of the job, conditions of employment place of work, etc.

 exam focus

The **functions of human resource management** are:

1. Manpower planning
2. Recruitment and selection
3. Training and development
4. Employer–employee relationships
5. Performance appraisal
6. Rewarding employees
7. Teamwork

Prepare a person specification

This describes the ideal person to do the job. It includes the skills, qualities, experience and qualifications that the person should possess to do the job effectively.

Advertising the job – The human resource manager uses the information from the job description and person specification to draw up an advertisement for the job. Candidates may be asked to submit a CV or complete an application form.

Attract a group of suitable candidates

The next job of the human resource manager is to encourage suitable candidates to apply for the job.

A. Methods of recruiting employees:

- Advertising in newspapers or local radio is a popular way of recruiting staff. Newspapers carry recruitment supplements and reach a wide audience.
- Posting an advertisement online (such as on Irishjobs.ie)
- Using the Local Job Centre
- Using FÁS, which keeps a register of jobseekers
- Head hunting (targeting a good employee in another firm and encouraging him/her to change jobs)
- Using recruitment/employment agencies
- Recruiting at colleges and training centres

B. Internal and external recruitment

Internal – Finding someone from those already employed in the business.

External – Finding someone from outside the business.

The advantages of **internal recruitment** are:

- **Motivation** – Employees will see that hard work and commitment can be rewarded through promotion.
- Less expensive to promote internally.
- Knowledge – Existing employees know the business better than external recruits.
- The business knows the employee's achievements, strengths, weaknesses, etc.

The advantages of **external recruitment** are:

- An external candidate may have new ideas or new ways of doing things.
- The person with the most suitable skills can be employed.
- An outsider will bring a range of experiences gained in other organisations.

C. Decide on the application process

The most common methods are:

- Application form
- Curriculum vitae (CV)

Application form

Many firms develop their own application forms, asking a series of questions regarding education, work experience, interests and hobbies, etc. The application form is completed by the applicant and returned to the firm.

Curriculum vitae (CV)

The CV sets out:

- Personal details
- Skills and qualities
- Education and qualifications
- Achievements
- Employment history
- Referees

The applicant applies for the job by sending his/her curriculum vitae along with a covering letter to the company.

Screening of applicants

Once the application forms or CVs are received, the selection process begins. Screening is carried out to compile a short list of candidates for the job.

Selection tests

A number of selection tests may be carried out to assist in the selection process:

- Intelligence tests – measures general intelligence
- Aptitude tests – tests a candidate's skills
- Personality tests – measures personality type

Interview

The interview allows the employer to acquire information about the candidate and assess their suitability for the job. It also enables the candidate to obtain information about the job and the organisation. Interviews can be one on one, in a panel interview, or in a group interview.

Checking references

The checking of references is undertaken to confirm the information already obtained and to establish past performance.

Offer job to successful candidate

A written offer of the job is made to the most suitable candidate. A contract of employment is drawn up and is signed by both parties and given to the employee.

3. Training and development

Training involves supplying the skills, knowledge and attitudes needed by employees to do their jobs better.

Types of training

Induction training

The training received by new employees to help them in the workplace. It includes:

- Health and safety training
- Presentation of the organisation's rules and codes of ethics
- An introduction to co-workers and management

On-the-job training

Involves experienced staff teaching the employee the skills and knowledge required for the job in the workplace.

Off-the-job training

Involves doing courses outside the workplace (e.g. in a training centre or college).

Staff development

Development involves preparing the employee to take on more responsibility and new challenges in the workplace. This includes certificate/diploma/degree/post-grad courses, management courses, etc.

Importance/benefits of training and development:

- Better quality service to customers, resulting in fewer complaints.
- Improved quality of production.
- Flexible and adaptable workforce allowing for changes to take place/new work methods and technologies are facilitated.
- Less industrial relations problems/staff are better cared for and more motivated.
- Lower labour turnover due to high staff morale
- Adds to the reputation of the firm, and thereby attracting quality staff.

4. Employer–employee relationships

The human resource manager is responsible for ensuring good industrial relations in business. The term 'industrial relations' refers to the quality of the relationship that exists between employer and employees in business.

If relations between employer and employees are good, workers will be motivated to work hard and morale will be high.

A **good industrial relations climate and high morale in the organisation** can be achieved by:

- **Open communication** – Regular meetings between management and staff
- Providing for the **health, safety** and **welfare** of staff
- **Valuing employees** – Recognising the contribution of employees to the organisation
- **Grievance procedures** – Ensuring that employees have a formal means of making a complaint
- **Teamwork** – Developing teams within the organisation
- **Reward** – Rewarding employees fairly for effect

The **importance/benefits of a good employer–employee relationship in business** include:

- **Motivation** – Employees are motivated to work to the best of their ability
- **Co-operation** – Employers and employees are working towards the same goal/objectives
- **Less risk of industrial action** – If good relations exist
- **High productivity** – Employees have a positive attitude towards work
- **Problem solving** – Problems are resolved quickly as there are agreed procedures for solving disputes

5. Performance appraisal

This is the process of reviewing the performance of an employee in business.

Performance appraisals involve a meeting/interview between the human resource manager and employee to:

- Examine their performance and discuss their progress
- Set targets/objectives/expectations
- Discuss any problems employee may be having
- Identify training and development needs/resources needed by the employee to achieve targets
- Discuss the employee's pay and rewards

Many organisations now relate reward (i.e. salary scales) to how the employee performs in the organisation.

The importance/benefits of conducting performance appraisals in business:

- **Review rewards** (benefits structures) – It may be used in determining pay increases or promotion.

- **Decide about selection and training** – It helps a business decide if too much or too little training is being delivered in various departments of the business. (For example, they may need to reduce training in some departments that have a high staff turnover and thereby reduce business costs.)

- **Retain the right staff/identify poorly performing staff** – It helps a business identify top talent and ensure that these employees are retained and guided towards reaching the business plans and objectives. A business can also identify employees who are not reaching their potential and take steps to address the issue.

- **Improve industrial relations** – Conflicts in the workplace may be highlighted through performance appraisals. This enables the business to help solve problems between management and employees and helps improve industrial relations in the workplace.

- **Increase productivity** – Performance appraisals are important for staff motivation, communicating and fostering a positive relationship between management and staff. This leads to greater productivity from employees.

- **Identify hidden strengths** – Performance appraisals help to identify hidden strengths in staff members, which can then be brought out for the good of the business. This can be achieved by developing individual skills and thus improving the overall performance of the business. It can be used to assess employees' potential for promotion.

- **Delegate tasks** – Managers can decide to delegate tasks to certain employees who are performing well in business. This will relieve pressure on managers.

- **Form judgements** – It requires the human resource manager to form a judgement on a person's work by reviewing the quality of the work and the progress that the person has made or the capability of the person.

6. Rewarding employees

It is the function of the human resource manager to negotiate the remuneration package employees are to receive. This package can include both financial and non-financial rewards.

Financial rewards

- **Wages and salaries** – Pay may be calculated by flat rate, time rate, piece rate, bonus or commission.

- **Flat rate** – Employees receive an agreed rate of pay per week or month based on a standard number of hours worked.

- **Time rate** – Employees are paid a fixed rate per hour. Overtime is paid at a higher rate.

- **Piece rate** – Payment is based on number of units produced. The more units produced, the more earned.
- **Bonus** – Payment to employees for reaching a target.
- **Commission** – Payment is made according to the value of the amount sold (e.g. a 10% commission to a sales person based on the level of sales achieved).

Non-financial rewards

- **Fringe benefits** – Fringe benefits include benefits in kind given to employees in the form of goods or services rather than money (e.g. meal/lunch vouchers, company cars, subsidised health insurance, etc.).
- **Profit sharing** – A profit-sharing scheme is where the firm share part of their profit with employees. It is paid to them in addition to their wages. It motivates employees to increase the profit by increasing output and reducing costs. The more successful the company is in making profits, the more the employees earn.
- **Employee share ownership scheme** – Shares in the business may be given to employees instead of cash bonuses.
- **Share options** – A share option scheme gives employees the option to buy shares in a company at a specified price.

7. Teamwork

A team is a group of people working together towards a common objective.

Stages in team formation

Objectives are set for the team and then people with the right skills are selected.
The process of team development takes place as follows:

- **Forming** – The team is formed and begins to meet and discuss the project.
- **Storming** – Team members argue with each other until their various roles are clarified. (This is called 'storming'.)
- **Norming** – The team then begins to work as an effective unit. They set 'norms' or rules and standards for working together.
- **Performing** – The team begins to perform and achieve its goals.

IMPORTANCE/BENEFITS OF TEAMS IN ORGANISATIONS

- **Motivation** – Teamwork encourages greater effort and recognition is given for everyone's achievements.
- **Better decisions** – People working in teams are likely to reach better decisions.
- **More ideas** – Members of a team are more forthcoming with ideas and solutions.
- **Support** – Team members share responsibility and help each other out.
- **Same objectives** – All team members are working towards the same objectives.

Be able to:

- Explain the changing role of management, from controller to facilitator.
- Explain the importance of employee participation.
- Understand how technology changes the role of management.
- HL Identify the strategies for managing change.
- Discuss the importance of Total Quality Management (TQM).

The changing role of management

People working in management today have to cope with rapid change.

The following are among the factors that force managers to change.

1. Changing consumers

Management must respond to changes in consumer tastes and focus on high-quality goods and services to achieve customer satisfaction.

2. Changing technology

There have been rapid developments in ICT in recent years. The advent of video-conferencing, e-business and the Internet has led to significant changes in the conduct of business. As a result, most organisations are in a state of change.

3. Changing employees

Employees are better educated and want a say in decision-making. Companies must respond to this change and provide opportunities for employees.

4. Competition

Organisations face competition on a global scale, so in order to compete smaller firms have to change their structures and operations.

5. Changing legislation

Management must respond to new Irish and EU laws that affect business (e.g. employment laws, consumer rights, etc.).

Change from controller to facilitator

In a changing business world, businesses must change their management style from 'controller' to 'facilitator'.

Controller manager

The manager is:

- **The Boss** – Gave orders to employees which are to be carried out without question.
- **The Controller** – Constant supervision and direction from manager – employees had no say in decision-making.
- **The Critic** – Told employees where they went wrong.
- **The Expert** – Knew all the answers – employees did it his way.

Facilitator manager

The manager is:

- **The Leader** – Gives direction.
- **The Coach/Trainer** – Trains employees to develop their skills and fully utilises their talents.
- **The Resource Provider** – Provides all the necessary resources necessary to carry out the job (finance, training, technology).
- **The Facilitator** – Does the following:
  - Provides advice and support
  - Delegates responsibility to employees
  - Encourages new ideas
  - Consults staff on issues concerning their job
  - Promotes new relationships through involvement and empowerment of employees

Employee participation

Achieving employee participation

Employee participation can be achieved by:

- Involving employees in the affairs of the firm
- Offering share ownership
- Job enlargement, rotation, enrichment

Involving employees in the affairs of the firm

This can be achieved through:

- **Works councils** – Allows representatives of the workers to have a say in the plans and strategies of the firm.
- **Worker directors** – Employees are elected to the board of directors. This gives employees a say in decision-making.

Offering share ownership

Employees are given an opportunity to purchase shares in the company. They become owners and have a vote at the AGM.

Job enlargement, rotation, enrichment

Employees can also participate in the organisation through:

- Job Enlargement
- Job Rotation
- Job Enrichment

Job Enlargement

- Increasing the number of tasks in the job.
- Provides more varied work and reduces boredom.

Job Rotation

- Switching workers between a number of jobs.
- Greater variety will lead to greater job satisfaction.

Job Enrichment

- Employees are given a variety of more difficult tasks with more authority and more responsibility.

Empowerment

Empowerment is placing real power, responsibility and decision-making in the hands of the workers who work close to the customer.

Empowerment is more than delegation in that real power is given to employees, including the freedom to decide what to do and how to do it. Employees are then responsible for the achievement of the goals set.

Workers who deal with customers every day are given great influence over the operation of the enterprise. Decision-making and control is in the hands of the workers, who use their skill and knowledge in the interests of the organisation.

exam focus

BENEFITS OF EMPOWERMENT IN ORGANISATIONS

- Improved service to customers.
- Improved morale – Workers have control over how they work.
- Improved skills – Gives the workers the opportunity to improve existing skills and develop new skills.
- Improved motivation – Empowerment allows staff to influence business decisions.
- Improved productivity – Empowerment makes the working of the organisation more effective and because employees are using their own initiative, productivity is improved.

Total quality management (TQM)

Total quality management is a process which tries to
ensure quality in all aspects of a firm's operation so
that it can produce the best products or services for
its customers.

Total quality management puts the focus of the firm
into meeting and satisfying the needs of its customers.
Employees are given responsibility to ensure that the
products meet the requirements of customers.

There are basically **five
principles** to a TQM approach:
1. Focus on customers
2. Continuous improvement
3. Empowerment
4. Teamwork
5. Quality assurance

1. Focus on customers

Business must find out what customers want and
then make that product to meet their requirements.

2. Continuous improvement

To achieve continuous improvement, management must concentrate on improving
processes and products, improving quality and reducing costs.

Continuous improvement is a step-by-step bettering of business processes.

3. Empowerment

TQM will not happen without the empowerment of workers. They must be given real
power, including the responsibly and authority to decide what to do. They must be
allowed make decisions and changes where necessary to improve the quality of the
product.

4. Teamwork

For TQM to succeed, there must be teamwork – people working in groups to achieve improvement in specific areas. The sharing of ideas and solving problems together in groups makes work more rewarding and satisfying.

5. Quality assurance

Quality assurance means management ensuring that the product or service is of the highest quality and that quality standards are agreed and met throughout the organisation to insure customer satisfaction. Quality must be the responsibly of all employees.

BENEFITS OF TOTAL QUALITY MANAGEMENT IN ORGANISATIONS

- Improved quality – There should be an improvement in the quality of products produced.
- Reduction in cost – There will be less waste.
- Workers are better motivated – Because they see management are committed to quality.
- Increased sales – The firm will develop a reputation for providing quality goods, which will increase sales.
- Increased customer satisfaction – Products and services are of the highest standard.

Strategies for managing change

1. Management Commitment

There must be total senior management commitment for the proposed changes. If this is not present, the change process will not progress.

2. Consultation

Consultation must take place with trade unions and employee representatives regarding the proposed changes and the effects of the change on them. Employees must understand fully the implications of change on them.

3. Communication

Effective communication between all parties throughout the change process is essential. This will reduce uncertainty and insecurity.

4. Negotiation

Negotiations between management and employees on options for implementing change, remuneration packages, productivity agreements, changes in work practices and a general improvement in working conditions may all be part of the change process.

5. Funding

Finance is required for training and retraining of employees in the new skills needed to do the work as a result of the change.

6. Reward

Employees must be rewarded for implementing the change process. This means remuneration packages for staff.

Managing technology

How technology has changed the way management operates

Technology has changed the way management operates in the following ways:

1. Information and Communication Technology (ICT)

Management use technology to communicate developments. The use of the Internet, e-mail, EDI, fax and videoconferencing have greatly facilitated information exchange.

Electronic Data Interchange (EDI) – used to exchange business documents in a highly **efficient way**.

Videoconferencing – This enables people in businesses worldwide to communicate person to person.

2. Decision-making

Management use computers for financial forecasting and planning. Data can be downloaded, enabling them to make critical decisions more quickly.

3. Production

Advances in production technologies have resulted in higher levels of automation. For example,

- **Computer Aided Design (CAD)** allows a business to design new products or **redesign existing products**.
- **Computer Aided Manufacture (CAM)** is computer software that controls the manufacturing process.

4. Motivation

Many organisations are using computers, the Internet and fax to enable employees and managers to work from home – Teleworking. Productivity and motivation may increase because employees are free to work at home at their own pace.

5. Marketing

Most companies use a website to advertise and sell their goods and services. Market research can also be carried out on the Internet.

Impact of technology on personnel

- **Teleworking**

ICT enables managers and employees to work on a computer from home or from other remote locations and be linked to the office computer. The time and cost of travelling to and from work is reduced.

- **Reduced workforce**

Technology has replaced many jobs leading to redundancies. Fewer workers are required in offices and on production lines.

- **Training**

In many occupations, the training of workers can be done by or with the help of computers and the many different software packages available.

- **Job satisfaction**

Technology makes routine or boring tasks easy to carry out, increasing job satisfaction.

Impact of technology on business costs

The introduction of technology may **increase business costs** in the following ways:

- **Investment in technology**

There is a high capital cost associated with new communication and production technology, including installation and maintenance costs.

- **Training costs**

Training costs can be high and must be ongoing to keep up to date with technological developments.

New technology can also reduce business costs

The introduction of technology may **reduce business costs** in the following ways:

- **Better quality goods** – Better quality products, less waste and fewer complaints can lead to significant cost savings.
- **Reduced administration costs** – Teleworking reduces the amount of office space required and reduces administration costs.
- **Less Travel** – Videoconferencing reduces the amount of travel to meetings.

Impact of technology on business opportunities

- **New products** – Some new products owe their existence and success to technology (e.g. reserving airline seats and hotel reservations from any part of the world at any time).
- **Marketing** – Many businesses now use the Internet to market their goods and services. By creating a website, a large number of potential customers can be reached at minimal cost.
- **New methods of conducting business for individuals** – Using a home computer or laptop allows people to engage in many business-related activities from home (using online banking, seeking insurance quotes, working from a home office, etc.).
- **E-business** – Many business functions can be carried out using the Internet (e.g. EDI [Electronic Data Interchange], where goods can be ordered automatically from a supplier when stocks fall below a certain level).

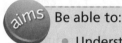 **Monitoring the Business**

Accounts and business information

Financial information tells the owners or shareholders and the management how the business is performing and allows them to make decisions. It also provides useful information to other interested parties.

Trading account

This shows the gross profit or gross loss made by a business in the trading period.

Gross profit is the profit made by buying and selling goods before deducting expenses.

key point

Final Accounts

The financial statements used by a business are:

- Trading account
- Profit and loss account
- Balance sheet

Sales − Cost of Sales = Gross Profit/Loss

Cost of Sales = Opening Stock + Purchases − Closing Stock

Profit and loss account

This shows the net profit or net loss made by a business in the trading period that is profit after deducting expenses.

Gross Profit − Expenses = Net Profit

Balance sheet

A balance sheet is a statement of assets, liabilities and share capital of a business on a particular day.

A balance sheet shows:

- **Assets:** Profit a business owns.
- **Fixed assets:** Permanent assets in the business.
- **Current assets:** Assets that can be easily turned into cash (e.g. stock, debtors, bank, cash).
- **Liabilities:** Debts that a business owes.
- **Current liabilities:** Debts that have to be repaid within one year (e.g. creditors, bank overdraft, expenses due).
- **Long-term liabilities:** Debts that will be repaid in the long term (e.g. mortgage, long-term loans).
- **Share capital:** Money invested in the company by its owners or shareholders.
- **Reserves:** Retained earnings built up over a number of years and used to finance expansion.
- **Working capital:** Money available to pay short-term debts as they arise. It is calculated by deducting current liabilities from current assets.

> Current Assets – Current Liabilities = Working Capital

If current assets are greater than current liabilities, working capital is positive and the firm is said to be liquid.

If current liabilities are greater than current assets, working capital is negative and the firm is said to have a liquidity problem and to be overtrading, i.e. cannot pay its debts as they arise.

Interpretation of accounts using ratios

A company can be assessed in the following areas:
- **Profitability**: Profitability ratios measure the efficiency of a firm in generating profit.
- **Liquidity**: Liquidity ratios measure the ability of a business to pay its short-term debts.
- **Debt–Equity**: Ratio that identifies how the business is structured financially.

1. Profitability ratios

Profitability ratios shows how successful the management was in making profit in the business.

The profitability ratios are:

- Return on Capital Employed/Return on Investment
- Gross Profit Percentage/Margin
- Net Profit Percentage/Margin

	Ratio	Formula	Information Given by Ratio
1.	Return on Capital Employed/Return on Investment	$\dfrac{\text{Net Profit} \times 100}{\text{Capital Employed}}$ Ans = %	Shows the return on the total amount of money invested in the business. Should be compared with the return from risk-free investments in financial institutions.
2.	Gross Profit Percentage/Margin	$\dfrac{\text{Gross Profit} \times 100}{\text{Sales}}$ Ans = %	This is gross profit as a percentage of sales. This is profit made from buying and selling before paying expenses.
3.	Net Profit Percentage/Margin	$\dfrac{\text{Net Profit} \times 100}{\text{Sales}}$ Ans = %	This is net profit as a percentage of sales. This is profit made after payment of expenses.

Financial information published in financial statements such as profit and loss accounts and balance sheets are useful for decision-making. Consider the following figures and answer the questions that follow:

	2005	2004
	€	€
Sales	500,000	400,000
Expenses	50,000	40,000
Net Profit	70,000	60,000
Capital Employed	650,000	600,000

(i) For 2004 and 2005 calculate the gross profit margin, the net profit margin and the return on investment.

(ii) Analyse these profitability trends and discuss how shareholders might use them in making decisions.

(40 marks)

Source: 2006 Higher Level 2006 Section 3

Suggested solution

(i)

Profitability Ratios	Formula	2004	2005
1. Gross Profit Margin	$\dfrac{\text{Gross Profit} \times 100}{\text{Sales}}$ ②	③ * $\dfrac{100,000 \times 100}{400,000}$ ① 25% ①	③ * $\dfrac{120,000 \times 100}{500,000}$ ① 24% ①
2. Net Profit Margin	$\dfrac{\text{Net Profit} \times 100}{\text{Sales}}$ ②	① $\dfrac{60,000 \times 100}{400,000}$ ① 15% ①	① $\dfrac{70,000 \times 100}{500,000}$ ① 14% ①
3. Return on Investment	$\dfrac{\text{Net Profit} \times 100}{\text{Capital Employed}}$ ②	① $\dfrac{60,000 \times 100}{600,000}$ ① 10% ①	① $\dfrac{70,000 \times 100}{650,000}$ ① 10.76% ①

Net Profit + Expenses
* 2004 Gross Profit = 40,000 + 60,000 = 100,000
Net Profit + Expenses
* 2005 Gross Profit = 70,000 + 50,000 = 120,000

(ii)

The gross profit margin has decreased from 25% in 2004 to 24% in 2005. This indicates that the firm's profitability has decreased and it is less efficient in buying and selling, even though sales and gross profit both increased.   (2 marks)

The net profit margin has decreased from 15% in 2004 to 14% in 2005. The firm's profitability has disimproved over the year, even though the net profit has increased from €60,000 to €70,000. The expenses increased from €40,000 to €50,000, and as the net profit is calculated after deducting expenses, this indicates that the firm is less efficient at controlling expenses in 2005.

Expenses must be examined closely for possible savings and unusual unnecessary increases and controlled.   (2 marks)

Return on investment has improved from 10% in 2004 to 10.76% in 2005. A return of 10.76% is very good when compared with the return from risk-free investment of 3.5% to 5% at present.   (2 marks)

How Shareholders Might Use Profitability Ratios When Making Decisions

Profitability ratios are very useful to shareholders when making decisions about their investment in a business:

- The return on investment shows the return on the total funds invested in the business. It indicates how successful management was in making profit in the business. (2 marks)

- If shareholders are to invest in business the return on investment should be higher than the return to be earned elsewhere in banks, building societies or other risk-free investments because of the element of risk involved. (2 marks)

- In this business, the return in 2005 of 10.76% would be attractive to shareholders as it is much better than alternative investments. (2 marks)

2. Liquidity ratios

Liquidity is the ability of a business to pay its short-term debts as they arise. It is measured by subtracting current liabilities from current assets.

Current Assets − Current Liabilities = Working Capital

Working capital is the day-to-day finance available for running a business. If working capital is positive, the firm said to be **liquid**. If working capital is negative, the firm is said to be **overtrading**, that is, it cannot pay its debts as they arise.

The liquidity ratios are:

1. Current Ratio/Working Capital Ratio
2. Acid Test Ratio/Quick Acid Ratio

	Ratio	Formula	Information Given by Ratio
1.	Current Ratio	$\dfrac{\text{Current Assets}}{\text{Current Liabilities}}$	Tells us whether the company has enough current assets to pay its current liabilities. The recommended ratio is 2:1 – that is, current assets should be double current liabilities.
2.	Acid Test Ratio	$\dfrac{\text{Current Assets} - \text{Closing Stock}}{\text{Current Liabilities}}$	This ratio measures a firm's ability to meet its short-term debts out of liquid assets. Stock is omitted from current assets as it may not be quickly turned into cash. Thus it is a better measure of liquidity. The recommended ratio is 1:1, so that a healthy firm should have €1 in liquid assets for every €1 owed in short-term debts.

Examine the following figures from Savin Ltd.

	2007	2006
Current Assets	€91,500	€80,450
Current Liabilities	€62,400	€43,200
Closing Stock	€49,000	€40,100

(i) Calculate for 2007 and 2006:
  - Current Ratio
  - Acid Test Ratio

(ii) Applying your knowledge, comment on two trends that you notice developing in the business. Suggest what you would do about them.

(30 marks)

Source: Sample Paper Higher Level Section 3

Suggested solution

(i)

Ratio	Formula	2007	2006
Current Ratio	$\dfrac{\text{Current Assets}}{\text{Current Liabilities}}$ ❷	❶ $\dfrac{91,500}{62,400}$ ❶ 1.46:1 ❶	❶ $\dfrac{80,450}{43,200}$ ❶ 1.86:1 ❶
Acid Test Ratio	$\dfrac{\text{Current Assets} - \text{Closing Stock}}{\text{Current Liabilities}}$ ❷	❶ $\dfrac{91,500 - 49,000}{62,400}$ ❶ $\dfrac{42,500}{62,400}$ ❶ 0.68:1 ❶	❶ $\dfrac{80,450 - 40,100}{43,200}$ ❶ $\dfrac{40,340}{43,200}$ ❶ 0.93:1 ❶

(18 marks)

(ii) Trends and Suggestions

Current Ratio

Trends Developing

The ratio has decreased from 1.86:1 in 2006 to 1.46:1 in 2007. This is well below the ideal ratio of 2:1. The trend shows a worsening of the liquidity in the business. This has been **caused** by a large increase in current liabilities. (3 marks)

Suggestions for Action
Some action is necessary to improve the situation. Current liabilities have to be reduced by raising cash from some source, perhaps selling stock at reduced prices to increase cash flow and so pay creditors and a bank overdraft. Reducing the length of credit to debtors would also improve the liquidity position.   (3 marks)

Acid Test Ratio

Trends Developing
The acid test ratio has disimproved from 0.93:1 to 0.68:1. Both of these ratios are well below the ideal ratio of 1:1 and indicate that the firm will take difficulty in paying its debts as they fall due. The business has only got 68c available to pay each €1 of short-term debts.   (3 marks)

Suggestions for Action
Cash must be obtained from some source. Maybe giving discounts to debtors to pay quickly would allow the firm to reduce its current liabilities.   (3 marks)

3. Debt–equity ratio

This shows the finance structure of the company the Debt–Equity. Show the relationship between debt capital and equity capital in a company.

Debt Capital = Long-term debt
Equity Capital = Ordinary Share Capital + Reserves

Debt Capital : Equity Capital

The ratio shows how much the business has borrowed relative to amount invested by owners:

- **Low Gearing**: Debt capital is less than equity capital. This means business has borrowed less money than the amount invested by shareholders.
- **High Gearing**: Debt capital is greater than equity capital. This means business has borrowed more money than the amount invested by shareholders.
- **Neutral Gearing**: Debt capital = equity capital. The business has borrowed the same amount of money as that invested by shareholders.

Advantages of low debt–equity ratio (low gearing)

1. **Owners Capital**

   A greater amount of the capital of the company is provided by the owners.

2. **More Profit Available for Dividends**

   As there are no major interest commitments, a large proportion of the profits is available to pay dividends or to re-invest in the company.

3. **Easier to Borrow in the Future**

The business can borrow more easily in the future.

4. **Easy to Sell Shares in the Future**

It should be easier to sell additional shares in the future because of good dividends to shareholders.

Consequences of high debt–equity ratio (high gearing)

1. **High Interest**

High interest payments on borrowings must be met before the company can pay dividends to shareholders.

2. **Difficult to Sell Shares in the Future**

It may be difficult to sell shares in the future because of the poor outlook on dividends.

3. **Difficult to Borrow in Future**

Additional borrowings may be almost impossible to get since assets will have been used as security for loans already issued.

4. **Low Dividends–Low Share Price**

If profits fall, interest on loans must still be paid. There may be little profit left to pay dividends to shareholders. Shareholders may become dissatisfied with their investment and may sell their shares, resulting in a fall in the share price.

(i) Using the figures given below calculate the debt–equity ratio of SES Ltd for the years 2006 and 2007. (Show your workings.)

	2006	2007
Long-term Loans	300,000	364,000
Ordinary Share Capital	450,000	450,000
Retained Earnings	50,000	70,000

(ii) Comment on the significance of the trend in the debt/equity ratio over the two years for the existing shareholders.

(20 marks)

Source: 2009 Higher Level Section 3

Suggested solution

(i) The debt–equity ratio provides an indication of the financial structure/gearing of the business.

> The debt–equity ratio is calculated as follows:
>
> Debt Capital : Equity Capital

	2006	2007
Debt–Equity Ratio	**①**　　　**②** 300,000:500,000 0.6:1　**②**	**①**　　　**②** 364,000:520,000 0.7:1　**①**

(2 Calculations @ 5 marks (1+2+2))

(ii) Significance of the trend in the debt/equity ratio over the two years for the existing shareholders.

The debt–equity ratio in 2006 was 0.6:1, while the debt–equity ratio for 2007 has **increased** to 0.7:1. This is a worrying trend for the existing shareholders.

Significance

- Higher interest payments may reduce profits.
- If profits fall, the payment of dividends to ordinary shareholders will be affected.
- Reduction in dividends may lead ordinary shareholders to sell their shares. The increased supply of shares on the market will reduce the market price of the shares.

(2 Comments @ 4 marks (2+2))

The importance of the profit and loss account and balance sheet for the good financial management of a business

Profit and loss account

The profit and loss account has two sections:

- Trading account
- Profit and loss account

Trading Account

The trading account shows:

- Sales – cash sales and credit sales
- Cost of sales – all costs incurred producing the goods

> Cost of sales = opening stock + purchases − closing stock

- **Gross profit** – profits after the all costs have been taken away

Sales − Cost of Sales = Gross Profit

Profit and Loss Account

All expenses of the business are deducted from gross profit to arrive at net profit.

Gross Profit − Expenses = Net Profit

THE IMPORTANCE OF THE PROFIT AND LOSS ACCOUNT

The profit and loss account shows:

- The figure for **net profit** for the year. By comparing the figure with the previous year the performance of the business can be assessed.
- The level of **expenses**. If expenses have increased from the previous year they must be investigated and controlled to increase profits.
- How much of the net profit **is retained** in the business and how much is distributed to the shareholders in **dividends**. Prudent financial management ensures that the level of profit retained is adequate for future expansion or investment.

Balance sheet

A balance sheet is a statement of assets, liabilities and capital of a business on a particular day.

Assets

- **Fixed assets**: Permanent assets in the business (e.g. lawn and buildings machinery).
- **Current assets**: Assets held in the business for less than one year (e.g. stock, debtor's cash and bank.

Liabilities

- **Current liabilities**: Amounts the business owes and are due to be paid within one year (e.g. creditors, bank overdraft, accrued expenses).
- **Long-term liabilities**: Debts that will be repaid in the long term, that is, over 5 to 25 years (e.g. long-term loans).
- **Share capital**: Money invested by the owners and that is made up of issued share capital and profit and loss account.

THE IMPORTANCE OF THE BALANCE SHEET

The balance sheet shows:

- The **value** of the fixed assets in a business and whether there is adequate **security** available for future borrowings.
- The company's **liquidity position** – the ability of the firm to pay its debts as they arise. Working capital is calculated by deducting current liabilities from current assets. The current ratio should be 2:1, otherwise the firm may be in danger of overtrading.
- How the business is **financed**. The debt–equity ratio compares the amount of equity in the business with the amount of debt capital. The lower the ratio, the less is being paid out in interest payments.

Users of accounts and business information

The following parties are interested in the performance of a business.

1. **Owners/shareholders**

   Owners/shareholders will be interested in:

   - How much profit the business made.
   - How much they can expect in dividends.
   - The value and security of their investment.

2. **Management**

   Accounting information is important to management in assessing the performance of a business. It is also useful in decision-making.

3. **Financial institutions**

   Financial Institutions will be interested in:

   - The liquidity position of the firm and its ability to pay interest and repay loans and overdrafts when due.
   - Whether to give finance to the firm in the future.

4. **Creditors and suppliers**

   Creditors and suppliers will be interested in the liquidity position of the business and in particular:

   - Whether it can pay for goods supplied on credit.
   - Whether it is advisable to give credit in the future.

5. **Potential investors**

   Investors will be interested in:

   - The return on their investment in dividends.
   - The long-term share values and security of investment.

6. **Employees**

   Employees will want to assess:

   - Security of employment and prospects of promotion.
   - The future prospects of the company
   - The company's ability to meet wage demands in the future.

7. **Revenue Commissioners**

   The Revenue Commissioners require accounts and information to accurately calculate the tax liability of the organisation.

(i) Using two ratios in each case, analyse the profitability and liquidity trends in Calty Construction Co. Ltd, from the following figures for 2002 and 2003.

(ii) Suggest how the trends might be improved.

	2002	2003
Current Assets	15,900	16,800
Net Profit	15,100	12,285
Equity Share Capital	100,000	105,000
Current Liabilities	8,100	7,400
Closing Stock	9,100	12,400
Gross Profit	45,150	40,950
Retained Earnings	20,000	21,000
Sales	169,500	157,500

(40 marks)

Source: 2004 Higher Level Section 3

Suggested solution

(i)

(a) Gross Profit Margin

	2002	2003
$\dfrac{\text{Gross Profit} \times 100}{\text{Sales}}$ ❶	❶ $\dfrac{45,150 \times 100}{1,69,500}$ ❶	❶ $\dfrac{40,950 \times 100}{1,57,500}$ ❶
	= 26.64% ❶	= 26% ❶

The gross profit margins decreased from 26.64% in 2002 to 26% in 2003. The margin is steady, even though sales and gross profit have both decreased. ❷

(b) Net profit margin

	2002	2003
$\dfrac{\text{Net Profit} \times 100}{\text{Sales}}$ ❶	❶ $\dfrac{15,100 \times 100}{1,69,500}$ ❶	❶ $\dfrac{12,285 \times 100}{1,57,500}$ ❶
	= 8.9% ❶	= 7.8% ❶

The net profit margin decreased from 8.9% in 2002 to 7.8% in 2003. This reflects the reducing sales and gross profit figures. ❷

(c) Return on Investment

	2002	2003
$\dfrac{\text{Net Profit} \times 100}{\text{Capital Employed}}$ ❶	❶ $\dfrac{15,100 \times 100}{120,000}$ ❶	❶ $\dfrac{12,285 \times 100}{126,000}$ ❶
	= 12.58% ❶	= 9.75% ❶

The return on investment decreased from 12.58% in 2002 to 9.75 % in 2003.
It is still better than the return on risk free investments of 3.5% to 5% at present. ❷

(d) Liquidity

Current Ratio	2002	2003
$\dfrac{\text{Current Assets}}{\text{Current Liabilities}}$ ❶	❶ $\dfrac{15,900}{8,100}$ ❶	❶ $\dfrac{16,800}{7,400}$ ❶
	= 1.96 : 1 ❶	= 2.27 : 1 ❶

The current ratio has increased from 1.96:1 in 2002 to 2.27:1 in 2003. It is slightly above the recommended ratio of 2:1. While current assets have increased and current liabilities decreased, the level of stock held has increased. There is a danger of obsolescence and increased costs for storage and insurance. ❷

(e) Acid Test Ratio

	2002	2003
$\dfrac{\text{Current Assets} - \text{Closing Stock}}{\text{Current Liabilities}}$ ❶	❶ $\dfrac{15,900 - 9,100}{8,100}$ ❶	❶ $\dfrac{16,800 - 12,400}{7,400}$ ❶
	$\dfrac{6,800}{8,100}$	$\dfrac{4,400}{7,400}$
	= 0.83 : 1 ❶	= 0.59 : 1 ❶

The acid test ratio has deteriorated from 0.83:1 in 2002 to 0.59:1 in 2003. The ratio in both years as well below the ideal ratio of 1:1 and indicates that the business will have difficulty in paying its debts as they fall due. The business has only 59c available to pay each €1 of short-term debts in 2003.   (2 marks)

(ii)

1. A decline in the gross profit margin can be improved by:

   - Increasing selling price if there has been an increase in cost of sales.
   - Changing the sales mix towards more products with a higher profit margin.
                                                                 (2 marks)

2. A decline in the net profit margin can be improved by:

   - Controlling expenses – all expenses areas should be examined and tightened for possible savings and investigate unusual and unnecessary increases.   (1 mark)

3. **Acid Test Ratio**

   The firm's liquidity position is deteriorating cash must be obtained from some source by:

   - Giving discount to debtors to pay, thereby quickly improving the cash position which would allow the firm to pay its current liabilities.
   - Selling stock at reduced prices to increase cash flow and pay current liabilities.   (2 marks)

Marking scheme

- Any two trends @ 2 marks each.

Applied Business Question (ABQ) (Higher Level)

Based on Units 2, 3 and 4
This is a compulsory question for Leaving Certificate 2015/2020

(HL) Stone products Ltd

Paddy Murphy was very proud of himself for having set up a successful business. Ever since he left school and trained with his father as a stone mason, he had wanted to own a quarry and building business of his own. He worked hard at everything he did, at school, as an apprentice and now in his own business. He always concentrated on the future and because of this he tried to make the best decisions in the interest of the business.

Over the past twenty years the stone and concrete business had changed a lot, especially in the areas of quality, customer service and in stock and financial management. The changes caused some difficulties in the business, but Paddy's approach was to collaborate with the staff to tackle the challenges. He liked to train his own employees in general but also, when necessary, to recruit people from outside.

Stone Products' customers were mainly in the construction industry and they returned to trade with the company on a regular basis. Customers were happy with the way Paddy did business. Success resulted from finding out as much as possible before making a decision and having as many of the employees as possible organised into teams and involved in making the decisions. He liked people with initiative to work for him, especially those who would stick with jobs, spot challenges early and find solutions quickly. He allowed his staff to deal with customers directly, paid them well but expected targets to be met.

(A) Illustrate, from the above information, the enterprising characteristics shown by Paddy. (20 marks)

(B) Analyse the management activities used by Paddy in the running of his successful business. Refer to the above text in your answer. (20 marks)

(C) Paddy often said that good Human Resource Management was the key to his success. Would you agree with his view? Using the information available about Stone Products Ltd, explain your answer fully. (40 marks)

(**80 marks**)

Suggested solution

(A) Characteristics of entrepreneurs

1. Control

They usually need to be in control of situations. They are independent and have a need for achievement. *'Paddy had always wanted to own a business of his own.'*

2. Risk taking

Successful entrepreneurs are not afraid of failing. They can take both financial risk and personal reputation risks. *'Paddy set up a successful business.'*

3. Flexibility (feedback and review)

Entrepreneurs accept change as natural. They learn from mistakes and failures and are always checking feedback to see if the job can be improved. Their self-imposed standards are high. *'Paddy adapted and was flexible with the changes that occurred in the business.'*

4. Confidence

Entrepreneurs have high self-image and self-confidence. They look for solutions rather than problems. They like to get things done by the most efficient ways.
'He did good research before making a decision and involved teams of all employees.'

5. Realism

Entrepreneurs are very realistic people. They are honest with themselves. They choose things that are achievable rather than desirable all the time. Entrepreneurs accept what can happen and do not go for the impossible. *'Paddy expected targets to be met.'*

6. Decisiveness

Entrepreneurs have the ability to make quick and clear decisions and take responsibility for the actions and decisions they make. If a decision is a bad one then they accept the result without blaming other people. *'He concentrated on the future and made good decisions.'*

7. Determination

They do not give up easily due to obstacles and failures. They are determined at tackling problems and succeeding at the task on hand. They cope with disappointments on the way to success and can take setbacks regularly. *'Paddy worked hard at everything he did.'*

8. Leadership

Entrepreneurs are good leaders. They can get people to work together in teams and motivate people to see opportunities and use the opportunity to everyone's benefit. *'Paddy liked people with initiative and he allowed his staff to deal with customers directly.'*

9. Energetic

Entrepreneurs are not lazy people. They are 'get up and go' and hard working people who stick at a task until it is completed. *'Paddy worked hard at everything he did.'*

Marking scheme

(A)	Five enterprising characteristics. Requires reference to the ABQ text.	Five characteristics at 4 marks each (2 + 2, characteristic plus reference).	20 marks

(B) Management activities

1. Planning

Selecting the goals of the organisation and finding out ways to achieve them. The targets to be aimed at.

The main objective is to survive and be profitable while meeting the needs of customers. Plans reduce risk and uncertainty and give an organisation purpose and direction.

Planning is a method of looking ahead to the future that helps us to make decisions.

Long-term planning – One to five years into the future. Planning is vital. Forecasting the future.

The mission statement – The purpose of the organisation is what it was set up to achieve. *'Paddy always concentrated on the future'*

Short-term planning – One to two years.

SWOT analysis – Examine the organisation's strengths. Weaknesses opportunities and threats both:

- Internal (e.g. good people, lots of work, good suppliers, etc.)
- External analysis (e.g. trends affecting building business, what the competition are up to, government proposals that affect the industry, etc.)

  'Paddy found out as much as possible before making a decision.'

2. Organising

Organising involves getting things done through some form of organised structure. Building a structure in an organisation so that its activities are co-ordinated and its objectives are achieved. Possible structures are line organisation and matrix structure. Build project teams to start and finish the building jobs.

Collaborate with the staff. Employees organised into teams.

3. Controlling

The activities that measure the deviations from planned performance and takes action to correct them. Elements in a business requiring control include: Quality control, Stock control, credit control, budgetary control. *Changes in quality, customer service and stock and financial management.*

Expected targets to be met.

Marking scheme

(B)	Management Activities Planning, Organising, Controlling	Two points at 7 marks (2 + 5) and one at 6 marks (2 + 4). Reference must be made to the text.	20 marks

(C) The key functions of HRM and relate them to text.

1. Manpower planning

Manpower planning involves examining the human resource needs of the organisation and ensuring that they are met. An audit of existing employee skills and expertise may be conducted. Plans for the future are laid and employee-development programmes designed.

Link to text

Paddy always concentrated on the future

2. Recruitment and selection

Personnel in an organisation change for many reasons (e.g. retirements, transfers, illness, resignations, promotions, maternity leave, etc.). For this reason, the HR specialist must maintain a supply of personnel to meet all requirements.

Link to text

Paddy Murphy was prepared to recruit people from outside the firm when necessary.

3. Training and development

As organisations and people change over time, all personnel must be ready to meet the challenges of changes in the market place. Personnel are helped in this area with programmes of training and development.

Link to text

Paddy liked to train his own employees in general

4. Performance appraisal

Most organisations now relate reward (i.e. salary scales and bonuses) to how the employee performs in the organisation. The design and development of appraisal systems is now a central function of HRM (i.e. putting a value on employee performance).

Link to text

Paddy allowed his staff to deal with customers directly paid them well but expected targets to be met.

5. Industrial relations

Industrial relations are the relations existing between employers and employees on such matters as pay and conditions of employment. Negotiations must take place between the parties, not only on pay, but also on complaints, grievance and disciplinary procedures and on issues like redundancy, early retirement and dismissal.

Link to text

Paddy's approach was to collaborate with the staff to tackle the challenge.

6. Rewarding employees

Since the main asset of all organisations is its workforce, particular care will be paid to maintaining the attractiveness of working for the organisation. Care will be taken to reduce the risk of key personnel leaving.

If the market rate of pay is not offered then new, talented employees will not work for the organisation, they will leave and work for other organisations.

Link to text

Paddy paid his staff well.

Marking scheme

(C)	Human Resource Management	Four points at 10 marks each (3 + 7 [3 + 4]). Reference must be made to the text.	40 marks

UNIT 5

Business in Action

This unit views business as a living, dynamic activity. It examines a business start-up from the generation of the original idea to the development of the business plan. There is an emphasis on the relationship between the business and its customers and on how the business must develop in response to changes in the market.

Objective

To enable pupils to understand the stages involved in setting up a business enterprise.

- **Chapter 15:** Identifying Opportunities
- **Chapter 16:** Marketing
- **Chapter 17:** Getting Started
- **Chapter 18:** Business Expansion

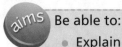

Be able to:

- Explain the importance of researching business ideas.
- Identify techniques for developing business ideas and researching them.
- Contrast the main sources of new product ideas.

Sources of new product or service ideas

Business ideas and opportunities come from a wide variety of sources. These include:

- **Internal sources** – by examining their own strengths and weaknesses
- **External sources** – by looking at the opportunities and threats in the market place

Internal sources

1. The research and development department

The R&D department in a business is typically staffed with technical experts such as scientists and engineers seeking to devise new applications and products.

Example: Pfizer – The world's largest research-based pharmaceutical company, invests more than $7 billion annually in research and development to create new products to treat diseases.

2. Employees

Idea generation and development techniques (such as brainstorming) can be encouraged by rewarding employees who come up with ideas with cash bonuses and fringe benefits or any incentive that encourages the idea-generation process (entrepreneurship).

Example: At 3M, company employees may spend 15% of their time working on any projects they like for the betterment of the company. (After the initial success of the project, 3M funded it for further development.)

3. Existing products of business

Employees may improve or develop new products or services based on existing products of the business.

4. Community needs

Recognising community needs and wants that are not being met at present may provide an opportunity to fill a gap in the market.

Example: A late-night takeaway or a shop in a housing estate.

5. Hobbies or occupations

These can be a source of new product ideas.

Example: Oscar De La Hoya, a retired American boxer, founded Golden Boy Promotions, a national boxing promotional company in Los Angeles, California.

External sources

1. Changes in society

Changes in society (such as new legislation) can give rise to a need for new products and services.

Example: Legislation banning the use of mobile phones while driving led to the development of hands-free mobile phones.

2. Customers

Customers can often suggest ideas for improvements in a product and innovative ideas may come from customer feedback, customer complaints or the changing needs of customers.

3. Competitors

Ideas can be found by monitoring competitors to see what products they are developing and what customers they are neglecting.

4. Market research

A business may carry out market research or surveys to find out what product or service is not provided. The firm can identify customer needs and wants by using a variety of research approaches, including customer surveys and interviews.

5. Organisations/state agencies

Organisations such as An Bord Tráchtála/The Irish Trade Board, the Central Statistics Office, and country and city enterprise boards can provide statistical information which may be used to produce a successful product or service idea.

6. Products in other countries

Products or services that are available in other countries but not yet in Ireland could be adapted for the Irish market. If a product has not been patented it may be freely copied.

Market research

- Market research is the systematic gathering of important and relevant information about markets and trends.
- Market research provides a business with a method of collecting important information on customers and their likes and dislikes in an organised and systematic way so that the information is accurate and reliable.

Reasons why businesses carry out market research

- **Market:** It provides information about the size of the market and whether it is growing. It also provides information about the characteristics of the market (age of people in it, their income, their location).
- **Competitors:** It reveals information about competition in the market, their products, the market share and their strengths and weaknesses.

- **Marketing mix**: It helps a business decide on the marketing mix it will use to sell its products in terms of the Four P's – product, price, promotion and place (the product, its price, the method of promotion and the place where it will be sold).
- **Consumer reaction**: Businesses can find out the reasons why consumers buy a particular product and what influences their buying behaviour.
- **Reduces risk**: Market research makes it more likely that a product will succeed. It reduces the risk of the business using resources to produce products that the consumer does not want.
- **Sales**: It assists a business in working out the likely sales for its products.

Market research techniques

There are many different types of market research, including:

- Desk research
- Field research

Desk research

Desk research is based on secondary sources of information (that is, on research that has already been conducted by others). Internal and external sources of information may be used in desk research.

Example: The total number of cars sold in 2010 can be found through research conducted by the CSO or the Society of the Irish Motor Industry (SIMI).

Internal sources of information are available in the firm's files and will include:

- Company reports
- Customer feedback
- Sales figures, marketing records, and salesperson reports, on file

External sources of information include:

- Reports from state agencies (CSO, Enterprise Ireland, FÁS)
- Trade Associations (such as SIMI)
- Websites
- Trade statistics for the country (imports and exports)
- Household budget surveys

Field research

This is research based on primary sources of information. Field research seeks to discover new information about a target market.

Field research methods include:

- Surveys
- Questionnaires
- Observation

Example: A car dealership that wishes to check the satisfaction ratings of customers who purchase new cars may gather this information by using a questionnaire.

Surveys

The main purpose of a survey is to determine from the responses how consumers will react to new products or services.

Survey methods include:

- Personal interviews
- Telephone interviews
- Postal surveys
- Online surveys

Potential customers are interviewed by researchers and responses recorded.

A representative sample of people from the entire market is selected for the survey.

Questionnaires

The data-collection method is usually the questionnaires. Questionnaires must be prepared in such a way that the information is useful and relevant. A questionnaire contains a series of structured questions designed to generate information required to meet the objectives of the research.

Observation

This is a technique that requires a researcher to observe and watch the reactions and behaviour of individuals.

Example: A researcher in a bank observing the average queue length for each hour of the day.

New product and service development process

The development of a new product or service goes through a number of stages:

1. Idea generation
2. Product screening
3. Concept development
4. Feasibility study
5. Prototype development
6. Test marketing
7. Production and launch

HL

The stages involved in the development process of a new product.

Olympion Ltd is a company that produces a range of high-quality sportswear. Following a lengthy market research process, the firm is now expanding its business to include a new range of Hoodie Tracksuits aimed at the teenage market.

Outline the stages involved in the development process of the new range of Hoodie Tracksuits.   (20 marks)

Source: 2009 Higher Level Section 3

Suggested solution

The following stages would be involved in the development process of the Hoodie Tracksuits:

1. Idea generation

Initial ideas for the new product are identified. This can take the form of brainstorming, where many ideas are discussed, or from market research.

Example: 'Hoodie Tracksuits'

The idea for a new range of Hoodie Tracksuits came from market research carried out by Olympion.

2. Product screening

The ideas are analysed and the impractical and unworkable ideas are eliminated, leaving the one which has the best potential to succeed in the market place.

A SWOT analysis may help identify ideas with potential.

Example: 'Hoodie Tracksuits'
The new range of Hoodie Tracksuits under consideration may be of much better quality than existing ones from competitors.

3. Concept development
This involves turning an idea into an actual product or service that will appeal to customers. A **unique selling point** (USP) is identified, which will distinguish it from other products.

Example: 'Hoodie Tracksuits'
The USP of the Hoodie Tracksuit could be 'Climacool', a feature designed to keep the user cool at all times.

4. Feasibility study
This is carried out to assess whether the product is viable and can be successfully developed and brought to the market. Break-even analysis is done to check if the product can be profitable.

Example: 'Hoodie Tracksuits'
If the break-even quantity is 40,000 tracksuits and market research shows that potential sales is 60,000, that would suggest that the product would be profitable.

5. Prototype development
An original working model of the product is developed and tested. It is produced to see if the product can be made and what materials are required to make it. The prototype is used to test the product to see what improvements can be made.

Example: 'Hoodie Tracksuits'
Samples of the Hoodie Tracksuit can be produced.

6. Test marketing
The product is tested on a sample of consumers. Consumer feedback is gathered at this stage.

Example: 'Hoodie Tracksuits'
The final version of the product can be tested packaged and shown to a small number of customers for reaction to its quality, price, etc.

7. Production and launch
The product is put into production and introduced to the market. The firm will select a suitable marketing strategy to persuade consumers to buy the product.

Example: 'Hoodie Tracksuits'
Olympion should advertise the launch and use other promotion methods. It should also contact shops and get them to support the launch.

Marking scheme
6 Stages – @3 marks (1+2)
Link to Olympion – 2 marks   (20 marks)

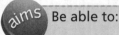 **Marketing**

Marketing

Marketing is defined by the Institute of Marketing as 'The process responsible for identifying, anticipating and satisfying customer requirements profitably.'

It is the process of:

- **Identifying customer requirements** through market research. It is only by finding out the needs of customers that the business can respond to those needs.
- **Anticipating customers' future needs**.
- **Satisfying the identified need** by producing products and services in the quality and quantity required by customers.

Marketing concept

The marketing concept has been defined as:

- Understanding the needs and wants of customers
- Developing products to satisfy consumers' needs
- Supplying the desired product more efficiently than competitors
- Making every effort to satisfy customer wants profitably

Advantage to a business of adopting the marketing concept

Business will be able to compete in the most competitive of markets, because they will produce what its customers need rather than attempt to get customers to purchase what the firm has produced.

Marketing strategy

The marketing strategy (or marketing plan) will be made up of a plan on how the policies relating to the 4 P's (product, price, place and promotion) will be used to achieve the marketing objectives.

Particular emphasis is placed on 'market segmentation policy' and the needs of customers in different markets.

A SWOT analysis should be carried out in advance of drawing up a marketing plan.

Advantages of marketing plan

It sets out the steps needed by a firm to achieve its objectives. Management must choose the best way forward to achieve the objectives.

The business can measure its performance against the goals set in the marketing plan, thus helping to control the business. Changes can be made if required.

The marketing plan helps to present the case for finance to financial institutions. It can be used to show where the enterprise is going.

Market segmentation

Market segmentation involves dividing up the market into clearly identifiable sections which have common characteristics.

It allows a firm to identify its target market.

The main ways to segment a market include:

- **Demographic** – This involves dividing a market according to factors such as age, income, gender.
- **Physiological** – This involves dividing the market according to attitudes and tastes.

Advantages to a business enterprise of segmenting the market

The Marketing strategy will focus on customers who are most likely to buy the product.

It will help the business to avoid markets which will not be profitable.

It gives the business a competitive advantage in the market.

Target market

A target market is a particular segment that has been identified as containing likely customers of a product or service.

The target segment will be the one in which the firm has a competitive advantage and in which it believes that it can satisfy customers better than competitors.

Having selected a target market, a business can develop the correct marketing mix (product, price, promotion, place) to reach the target market.

For example, the target market for the *Less Stress More Success* book series is Junior and Leaving Certificate exam students.

Niche market

A niche market is a specialist market for a particular type of product or service (e.g. *Less Stress More Success* for students).

A niche market is identified through market segmentation.

A business that focuses on a niche market is addressing a need for a product or service that is not being addressed by mainstream providers.

A niche market can be thought of as a narrowly defined group of potential customers.

For example: Instead of offering a general cleaning service, a cleaning business might establish a niche market by specialising in a cleaning window blinds.

Marketing mix

The marketing mix consists of the 4 P's (product, price, promotion and place) used by a firm to implement its marketing strategy.

Marketing Mix

The Four P's of the Marketing Mix:

- Product – product or service
- Price – price to charge
- Promotion – how to promote a product or service to potential customers
- Place – where to sell the product or service

Product

This is the physical product or service offered to the consumer and includes its distinctive features (form, shape and colour) as well as guarantees and after-sales service.

The key elements involved in a product are:
- Product design
- Packaging
- Branding
- Product life cycle

Product design

The product must be designed reliably to satisfy the needs of the target market.

It must comply with safety standards and perform well.

Its distinguishing feature is its **Unique Selling Point (USP)**.

Packaging

Good packaging make product attractive and appealing to consumers.

Packaging makes a product recognisable to the consumer.

Attractive packaging demonstrates an image of quality and reliability.

Packaging provides information regarding the product.

Branding

A brand is a distinctive name symbol or design that identifies the goods or services of a firm, and distinguishes them from those of competitors.

Branding allows immediate recognition by consumers.

The unique mark or name used to brand goods is a form of trade mark. By registering the trade mark the enterprise has exclusive rights to use the mark. Well-known brands include L'Oréal Paris, Lacoste, Pepsi-Cola, Kellogg's, Microsoft, Sony, Kodak.

Benefits of branding to the business:

- **Marketing**: Having a brand name makes it easier to distinguish the product from competitor's products and instantly recognisable. Can be used as a marketing tool for advertising purposes. (For example, Kellogg's is a well-known brand and they have use a range of promotion strategies to keep the brand to the fore of consumer's minds.)
- **New products are easier to introduce** if the brand name is already well known. (Kellogg's releases different products under the Kellogg's brand.)
- **Pricing**: A well-known brand name can command a premium price. (Kellogg's brands command higher prices than, for instance, own-brand labels and so Kellogg's can charge premium prices.)
- **Sales increase**: Repeat purchases increase sales.
- **Market segmentation**: Individual market segments can be identified and targeted with different products under the brand name (e.g. Kellogg's Rice Krispies).
- **Customer Loyalty**: Over time consumers become loyal to a particular brand and will not change.

Benefits of branding for the consumer:

- Branding helps the buyer to **identify** a particular supplier's goods and creates and **maintains their confidence** in the performance of the brand.
- Brands help consumers/buyers to judge the quality of a product. Country of origin can influence consumers in making judgments as to whether a product is of value or not (e.g. French perfume, Italian leather, Swiss watches).
- The purchase and use of brands allows a consumer/buyer to fulfil their need for self-expression and also communicate his or her self-image. A consumer/buyer who defines himself or herself as successful and powerful may drive a Mercedes!

Own brands

Large retailers sell goods under their own brand name – e.g. Marks and Spencer (St Micheal), Dunnes Stores (St Bernard).

The goods are produced by manufacturers to the retailer's specifications and are usually sold at lower prices than other brands.

Product life cycle

1. Product Development

During the development phase there is no cash inflow (sales). There is substantial cash outflow because of the costs associated with the development process.

2. Introduction

This is a period of slow sales growth and high expenditure on advertising and promotion as the

exam focus

Products follow a life cycle of six distinct stages:
1. Development
2. Introduction
3. Growth
4. Maturity
5. Saturation
6. Decline

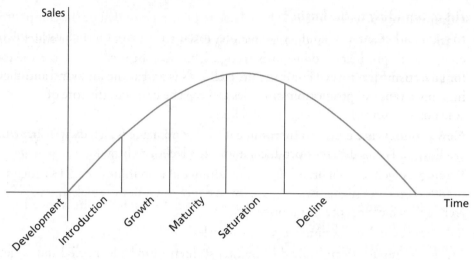

Product Life Cycle

product is introduced to the market. There is very little cash inflow from sales at this stage and no profit.

3. Growth

The product is known and is demanded by consumers. There is rapid sales growth, positive cash flow and increasing profit.

4. Maturity

Sales and profit reach a peak and start to level off. Profits stabilise as the product is accepted by most consumers.

5. Saturation

Sales slow down as most consumers have bought the product. The business must cut its price to maintain its market share and/or bring out new and improved versions of the product.

6. Decline

Sales decline and profits fall as more technically advanced products take over the market. The product is eventually withdrawn from the market.

Price

Price is the amount of money charged for the product or service.

Price is an important element in a purchasing decision because the demand for a product or service is influenced by price.

Factors to be considered when deciding on the selling price of a product

The factors which should be taken into account when deciding on the selling price include:

- **Costs** – The price should cover the firm's costs (production, marketing, distribution, etc.) and include a profit margin.

- **Competitor's prices** – The price will have to be similar to that of the competitors to gain market share. If competition is very intense the price to be charged will be affected.
- **Stage of product life cycle** – If the product is new and at the introduction stage, a high price may be charged to recover costs. Products at end of the life cycle may be sold at a low price to keep sales from falling.
- **Consumers** – The type of buyers will determine the price which can be charged.
- **Demand** – If demand for the product is high, the firm can charge a high price.

Pricing policies

- **Cost plus pricing** – All costs are calculated and a margin for profit is added to determine the selling price.
- **Competitive pricing** – To compete in the market prices must be set at the same level as those of competitors.
- **Penetration pricing** – This involves setting prices lower than competitors in order to gain market share.
- **Premium pricing** – This is charging a high price to reflect the high-quality image of a product or service.
- **Tactical pricing** – This involves the use of discounts, promotional prices and special offers. Cash discounts are often granted to customers who pay immediately by cash. Businesses often offer trade discount to buyer who buys in bulk.

Break-even analysis

Breaking even is when a firm is just covering its costs, making neither a profit nor a loss. The purpose of break-even analysis is to ascertain the sales level, in units and value, that a company must achieve to break even.

1. Costs

$$\text{Total Costs} = \text{Fixed Costs} + \text{Variable Costs}$$

Fixed costs are costs that remain unchanged, irrespective of the level of production (e.g. rent and rates, insurance, management salaries). These costs have to be paid whether or not anything is produced.

Variable costs are costs that change directly with the level of production (e.g. the raw materials used and direct labour). These will tend to double if output doubles.

$$\text{Total Variable Costs} = \text{Variable Cost per Unit} \times \text{Number of Units Produced}$$

2. Revenue

Total revenue is the money received by a firm from the sale of its goods or services.

$$\text{Total Revenue} = \text{Selling Price} \times \text{Quantity Sold}$$

3. Contribution

This is a measure of the amount of money that each unit sold contributes towards covering the fixed costs of a business. Once fixed costs are covered, all further contribution is profit.

> Contribution = Total Revenue − Variable Costs
> Contribution per Unit = Selling Price per Unit − Variable Costs per Unit

4. Break even

This is the level of output and sales at which a firm generates just enough income to cover fixed and variable costs, earning neither a profit nor a loss.

If the selling price of a product exceeds its variable cost, each unit sold will earn a contribution towards fixed costs. If total contributions cover fixed costs, the firm breaks even.

5. Break-even point

The break-even point (BEP) is the level of sales at which the firm breaks even, making neither a profit nor a loss.

$$\text{Break-even point} = \frac{\text{Fixed Costs}}{\text{Contribution Per Unit}}$$

6. Margin of Safety

This is the difference between sales volume and the break-even point, and is the amount by which sales can fall before a firm incurs a loss.

> Margin of Safety = Sales Volume − Break-even Point

Break-even chart

All costs (fixed and variable), together with the sales income expected from the product, can be represented on a **break-even chart**, which will show the break-even point.

Uses of a break-even chart:

- It is used to determine how many products a business must sell in order to break even.
- It shows the margin of safety at different levels of output.
- It shows the profit the firm can make if it operates at full capacity.
- It shows the impact of changes in selling price on profitability.
- It shows the impact of changes in costs on profitability.

Break-even chart

Illustrate by means of a break-even chart the following figures, showing (a) break-even point, (b) profit at full capacity, and (c) margin of safety:

Fixed costs:	€20,000
Variable costs:	€3 per unit
Forecasted output (sales):	12,000 units
Selling price:	€5 per unit
Full capacity:	15,000 units

Suggested solution

Calculate break-even point

Calculate the break-even point. This allows you to position the diagram properly on the page.

Break-Even Point

$$\text{Break-even point} = \frac{\text{fixed costs}}{\text{contribution per Unit}}$$

Contributions per Unit = Selling Price per Unit − Variable Cost per Unit

$$= €5 - €3$$

Contribution per Unit = €2

$$\text{Break-even point} = \frac{€20,000}{2} = 10,000 \text{ units}$$

This means that 10,000 units must be sold in order to break even.

Break even in Euro (€) = 10,000 × €5 = €50,000

Drawing the break-even chart

Step 1. Draw the axis

Label the horizontal axis as **Output (units)** and the vertical axis as **Costs and revenue**.

Decide the scale, making sure the break-even point (BEP) is positioned in the middle of the chart.

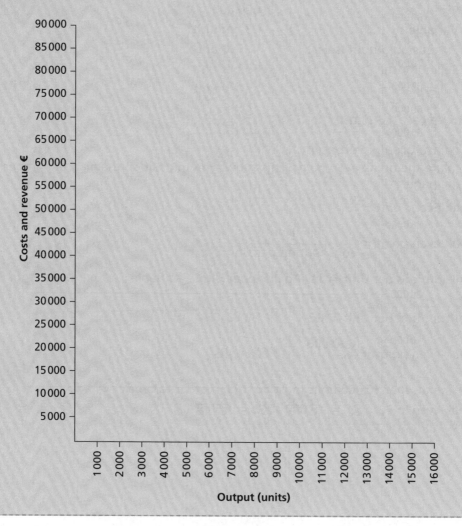

Step 2. Draw the fixed cost (FC) line

Draw the fixed cost line. This will be a straight line parallel to the horizontal axis at the appropriate level (€20,000).

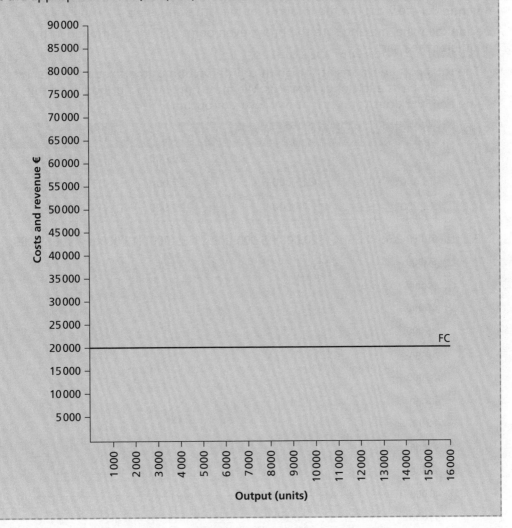

Step 3. Draw the total cost (TC) line

Draw the total cost line (TC = FC + VC). This line starts at the point of intersection of the fixed cost line and the vertical axis and slopes upwards. To draw this line it is necessary to work out the total cost at two different levels of output.

Workings for drawing the total cost line

The total cost line starts at the point of intersection of the fixed cost line and the vertical axis and slopes upwards. We must find two other points on this line and work out total cost at two levels of output.

Units	Variable Costs	Fixed Cost	Total Cost
0	0	€20,000	€20,000
5,000	€15,000	€20,000	€35,000
15,000	€45,000	€20,000	€65,000

Points on line are (0 units, €20,000) (5,000 units, €35,000) (15,000 units, €65,000)

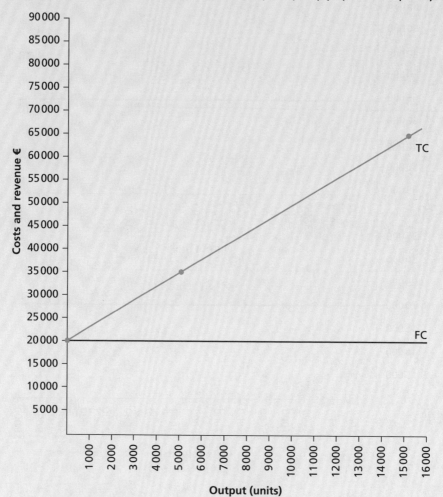

Step 4. Draw total revenue (TR) line

Draw the total revenue line. This line starts at 0 and slopes upwards. To draw this line it is necessary to work out total revenue at two different levels of output.

Workings for drawing the total revenue line

The total revenue line starts at 0 and slopes upwards. Find two other points on this line and work out total revenue at two different levels of output.

Units	Selling Price	Revenue
0	€5	0
5,000	€5	€25,000
15,000	€5	€75,000

Points on line are (0 units, 0 revenue) (5,000 units, €25,000) (15,000 units, €75,000)

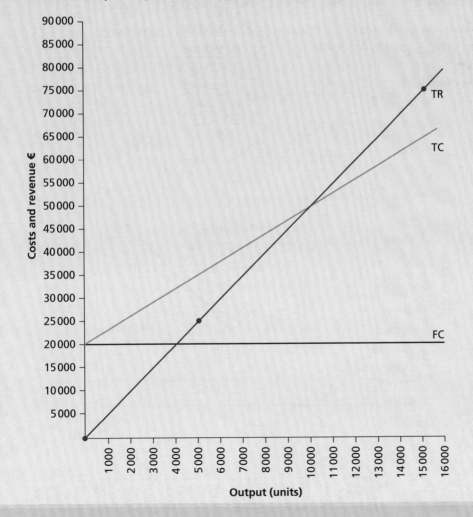

Step 5. Show the break-even point, the margin of safety and the profit at full capacity

Break-even point

Establish the break-even point (BEP), which is where the total cost line and total revenue line intersect. Before this point the business is making a loss; after this point the business is making a profit.

Margin of safety

Show the margin of safety using this formula:

Sales − Break-even Point = Margin of Safety.

12,000 units − 10,000 units = 2,000 units

This means that sales can fall by 2,000 units before a loss is incurred.

Profit at full capacity

Show profit at full capacity by using this formula:

Total Revenue − Total Costs = Profit at Full Capacity.

Sales (15,000 units × €5):	€75,000
Less variable cost (15,000 × €3):	€45,000
Contribution	€30,000
Less fixed costs	€20,000
Profit	€10,000

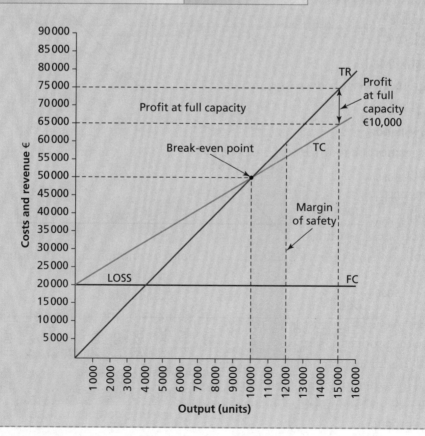

Promotion

Promotion consists of all communication used by a business to let customers know about the products on offer and to get them interested in buying them.

The methods of promotion are:
- Advertising
- Sales promotion
- Public relations
- Personal selling

Advertising

Advertising is the communication of information to persuade customers to buy a particular product or service.

Function of advertising

The function of advertising is to:

- Provide information about the product or service
- Persuade consumers to buy the product or service
- Remind consumers that the product is still available
- Increase sales and profits

Advertising media

The medium used will depend on the:

- Market segment
- Type of product or service
- Message
- Cost

Advertising Media

The main locations for advertising include:

- Television
- Newspapers
- Magazines and journals
- Radio
- Cinemas
- Online
- Poster sites/hoardings
- Public transport

Sales Promotion

Sales promotion consists of short-term incentives to encourage customers to purchase the product or service.

It is used in addition to normal advertising.

It is ideal for promoting a new product.

The aim is to give an immediate boost to the sales of a product.

Sales promotion methods include:
- Special offers
- Free samples
- Extra quantities for same price
- Competitions – holidays, cars, etc.
- Tokens for holiday breaks
- Two-for-the-price-of-one offers
- Money-off packs
- In-store demonstrations

It is popular in large multiples (such as Dunnes, Tesco) in an effort to increase market share.

Public relations

Public relations is concerned with creating and maintaining a good public image in relation to a company and its products and services.

It aims to generate favourable publicity and a good corporate image of the business amongst its customers and the general public.

Public relations is about building a relationship with the public. It is not directly concerned with increasing sales of products.

The person in business who manages public relations is called the public relations officer (PRO).

Public Relations Officers (PRO)

The role of the public relations officer is to deal with:

- Media relations – through press releases and press conferences
- Customer relations
- Local community relations
- The generation of favourable publicity for firm

Developing public relations

Methods of developing public relations include:

- Press conferences, press releases conveying information to the media
- Sponsorship – A payment made for the right to be associated with an activity or event (the product name will be displayed – e.g. Heineken Cup rugby)
- Donations – to communities, sports clubs, schools
- Open days – to allow the general public to visit the company site

Personal selling

This is the use of personal contact to persuade customers to purchase the product or service.

Face-to-face meetings are useful for the sale of expensive products or products that require a high degree of expertise or technical knowledge and need to be demonstrated to the customer.

Place

This is the process of getting the product to the consumer.

A distribution system is essential to move goods from manufacturer to consumer.

Channels of distribution

The term 'channels of distribution' refers to the movement of goods from manufacturer to wholesaler to retailer to consumer.

The main channels of distribution are:

- **Direct** – Manufacturer sells directly to consumers. For example, furniture manufacturers selling directly from the factory.
- **Modern** – Large retailers (e.g. Dunnes, Tesco) bypass wholesalers and purchase large quantities of goods directly from manufacturer at a discount and sell to consumers.
- **Traditional** – The path through which goods normally pass on their way to the final user. The goods are manufactured by the manufacturer, which sells them to the wholesaler, who distributes them to the retailer, who sells them directly to the consumer.

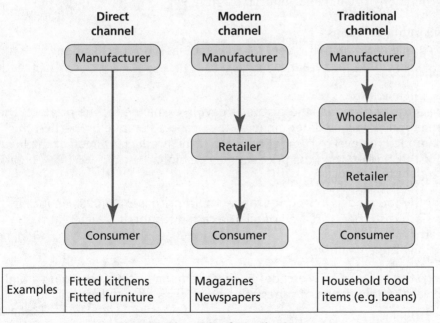

Main Channels of Distribution

Wholesaler and retailer

Wholesaler – A firm that buys products in bulk from the manufacturer/producer and then resells in smaller quantities to the retailer (e.g. Musgraves Cash and Carry).

Retailer – A firm that sells products directly to the consumers. They normally buy in large quantities from wholesalers. (A newsagent is a retailer.)

Marketing mix

Evaluate the elements of the marketing mix using a product or service of your choice.

(35 marks)

Source: 2003 Higher Level Section 3

Suggested solution

Product: Mercedes-Benz SL-Class Roadster

Product

A product is a good or service offered for sale to the consumer. The product is made up the detailed characteristics of the item on offer (e.g. its distinctive features; its form, shape and colour as well as its quality; after-sales service; guarantees; brand name and image). (3 marks)

Mercedes-Benz – Roadster

This is one of a range of German-made Mercedes cars. It offers excellent safety features, highly advanced engines, air conditioning and many other features.

(3 marks)

Evaluation

This is an excellent product. It is very reliable and has high specifications. It is a prestige vehicle with good resale value. (3 marks)

Price

Price is the amount of money the customer pays in exchange for the product. The price of the product will be determined by the product's unique properties, the cost of manufacture, level of competition, etc. If the product is aimed at the luxury segment of the market, then the price set may be high. (3 marks)

Mercedes-Benz – Roadster

It is one of the top models in its price range. Its list price is €110,000. Finance is available. Cash customers can avail of a large cash discount. It is aimed at high income earners. (3 marks)

Evaluation

The pricing strategy used by Mercedes-Benz is premium pricing – charging a high price to create on impression of superior quality. This is an excellent pricing strategy. (3 marks)

Promotion

Promotion is made up of all forms of communication used to inform customers about the product on offer and to get them interested in buying it. The promotional methods are advertising, sales promotion, public relations and personal selling. (3 marks)

Mercedes-Benz – Roadster

The product is advertised on television and in business magazines and on the Mercedes-Benz website. Mercedes are sponsors of many prestige events. Emphasis is placed on brand loyalty. A free test drive is available at any Mercedes garage nationwide. Brand emphasis is on safety, reliability and high quality.　　(3 marks)

Evaluation

This is an excellent promotion strategy as many people in the target market are likely to be business people who read business magazines.　　(3 marks)

Place

Place is the location where the product can be purchased. It includes the way the product gets from the manufacturer to the consumer.　　(3 marks)

Mercedes-Benz – Roadster

The main Mercedes dealers offer a nationwide sales and service network. Cars are purchased from Mercedes Imports in Dublin. Mercedes cars are sold worldwide.
　　(3 marks)

Evaluation

Mercedes-Benz cars are well distributed throughout the country through its network of main dealerships so that it is available to the target market. Service is reliable and dependable and convenient.　　(2 marks)

Marking scheme

Marketing Mix: Product	9 marks	3 + 3 + 3
Price	9 marks	3 + 3 + 3
Promotion	9 marks	3 + 3 + 3
Place	8 marks	3 + 3 + 2

Break-even chart

Motor Manufacturing Ltd is considering the introduction of a new product. The business has provided the following figures:

- Fixed costs – €200,000
- Variable costs – €5
- Selling price – €15
- Forecast output (sales) – 30,000 units

(i) Illustrate by means of a break-even chart:

  (A) The break-even point

  (B) The profit at forecast output

  (C) The margin of safety at forecast output

(ii) Explain 'margin of safety'.

(30 marks)

Source: 2008 Higher Level Section 3

Suggested solutions

(i)

(A) Break-even point

$$\frac{\text{Fixed Costs}}{\text{Contribution per unit}}$$

Formula: Contribution per Unit = Selling Price per Unit − Variable Cost per Unit

€15 − €5 = €10

Break-even in units

- $\dfrac{200,000}{10}$ = 20,000 units

- Break-even in € = 20,000 units × €15

$$= €300,000$$

(B) Profit at forecast output

	€
Sales (30,000 units × €15)	450,000
Less variable costs 30,000 units × €5	150,000
Contribution	300,000
Less fixed cost	200,000
Profit	100,000

(C) The margin of safety at forecast output

Formula: Sales − Break Even = Margin of Safety

30,000 units − 20,000 units = 10,000 units

Break-even Chart

(A) Break-even point 20,000 units   €300,000

(B) Profit at forecast output   €100,000

(C) Margin of Safety   10,000 units

Workings for total cost and total revenue lines

Units	S/P	V/costs	F/costs	T/costs	Revenue	Profit
0	15	0	200,000	200,000	0	0
20,000	15	100,000	200,000	300,000	300,000	0
30,000	15	150,000	200,000	350,000	450,000	100,000

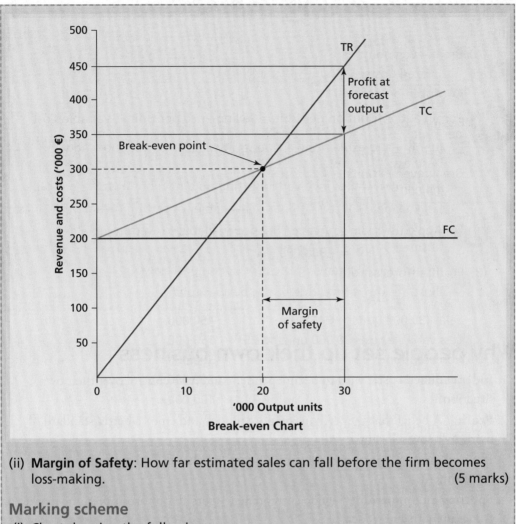

Break-even Chart

(ii) **Margin of Safety**: How far estimated sales can fall before the firm becomes loss-making. (5 marks)

Marking scheme

(i) Chart showing the following:

- Fixed cost line (2 marks)
- Total cost line (2 marks)
- Total revenue line (2 marks)
- Break-even point (5 marks)
- Forecasted profit (5 marks)
- Margin of safety (5 marks)
- Output (Axis) in units (2 marks)
- Cost and revenue (axis) (2 marks)

 25 marks

(ii) Margin of safety explanation (5 marks)

17 **Getting Started**

Why people set up their own business

1. **Independence** – The wish to be independent and have control over their own situation.
2. **Profit** – A belief that they will make more money and enjoy a better standard of living by being self-employed.
3. **Redundancy** – A person is made redundant and has difficulty finding employment.
4. **Spotting an opportunity** – The entrepreneur spots an opportunity in the market or comes up with a new idea.
5. **Ambition** – They want to fulfil a life-long ambition.

Important start-up decisions
When starting up a business an entrepreneur must make decisions on:

- Finance
- Ownership
- Production

Finance options

The entrepreneur must decide where to get the money from to set up the business. Sources of finance can be divided into three categories, depending on the length of time for which the money is required.

Sources of finance

- Short-term sources – Due for repayment within one year.
- Medium-term sources – Due to be repaid between one and five years.
- Long-term sources – Available for longer than five years.

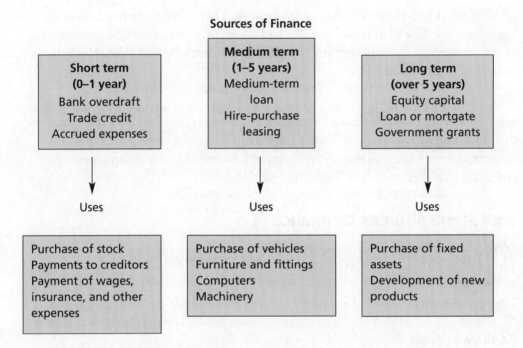

Sources of Finance

Short term (0–1 year)	Medium term (1–5 years)	Long term (over 5 years)
Bank overdraft Trade credit Accrued expenses	Medium-term loan Hire-purchase leasing	Equity capital Loan or mortgate Government grants

Uses	Uses	Uses
Purchase of stock Payments to creditors Payment of wages, insurance, and other expenses	Purchase of vehicles Furniture and fittings Computers Machinery	Purchase of fixed assets Development of new products

Factors that should be considered before choosing between different sources of finance

Cost

A business should try to obtain the cheapest source of finance available. The rate of interest is of great importance. All loans advertised by financial institutions should quote the **APR**. Close examination of the **APR** attached to each type of loan finance is needed when making the choice.

Purpose/correct match

Sources of finance must be matched with uses (e.g. a long-term business expansion plan should not be financed by a bank overdraft). Assets which are going to last a long time are paid for with long-term finance. Day-to-day expenses are financed or paid for with short-term finance.

Amount

Large amounts of money are not available through some sources. Some sources of finance may not offer flexibility for smaller amounts.

Control

Issuing new voting shares in a company could lead to a change of power. The use of loan capital will not affect voting control, but financial institutions such as the bank may take control of fixed assets or impose conditions as part of the loan agreement.

Collateral

Lenders often seek security before giving finance. This restricts the freedom of the borrower regarding what it wishes to do with these particular assets. Sometimes the borrower may not have enough assets to give as security, which can then limit the sources of finance available.

Risk

A business which has less chance of making to a profit is deemed more risky than one that does. Potential sources of finance (especially external sources) takes this into account and may not lend money to higher-risk businesses, unless there is some guarantee that their money will be returned.

Short-term sources of finance

These are sources that must be repaid within one year.

The principal sources of short-term finance include bank overdraft, trade credit and accrued expenses.

They are used to buy stock, pay wages, pay creditors and pay day-to-day expenses.

Bank overdraft

- A bank overdraft is a short-term source of finance.
- The bank allows current account holders to withdraw more money from the account than the amount in the account.
- A limit is set for the overdraft.

Cost: Interest is charged on overdrawn funds.

Risk: Bank can demand full repayment at any time.

Security: No security is required to obtain a bank overdraft.

Control: The owner keeps full control of the business.

Trade credit

- This involves buying goods on credit and paying for them later.
- It is provided by suppliers rather than by financial institutions.

Cost: It is a free source of finance but interest may be charged on overdue accounts.

Risk: Failure to repay will damage a business's credit rating and make it difficult to buy on credit in the future.

Security: No security required to buy goods on credit.

Control: The owner keeps full control of the business.

Accrued expenses

- Expenses/services incurred by a business but not yet paid for (e.g. telephone and electricity charges).
- By delaying payment the money can be used for other purposes.

Cost: It is a free source of finance – No interest is charged.

Risk: Failure to repay will damage a business's credit rating and reputation.

Security: No security required.

Control: The owner keeps full control of the business.

Medium-term sources of finance

These are sources that must be repaid between one and five years.

The principal sources of medium-term finance are medium-term loans, leasing and hire purchase. They are used to purchase vehicles, machinery, office equipment, etc.

Medium-term loan

- A medium-term loan is negotiated with the bank and repaid in agreed instalments over an agreed period between one and five years.
- The interest on the loan is tax deductible and large amounts of finance can be raised.
- Repayment can be arranged to suit ability to pay.
- The bank may require security or personal guarantees to ensure the loan is repaid.

Cost: Interest is charged on the loan.

Risk: Failure to repay the loan will damage the business's credit rating and may result in the security provided being sold to repay the loan.

Security: Security may be required depending on the amount of the loan.

Control: The owner keeps full control of the business.

Leasing

- Leasing is a medium-term source of finance and involves the renting of an asset from a finance company.
- The business will never own the asset.
- The business has possession and use of the asset during the period of the lease.
- The business does not have to use a cash lump sum to buy the asset.
- No security is required.
- Lease repayments can be set off against profits to reduce tax liability.
- The business may have the option to replace the asset if it becomes obsolete.

Cost: Monthly rentals may be expensive. Rentals are tax deductible.

Risk: Failure to repay rental will damage the business's credit rating and may result in the asset being repossessed.

Security: No security is required to obtain leasing finance.

Control: The owner keeps full control of the business.

Hire purchase

- Purchasing an asset by paying a deposit and paying the balance with interest by regular instalments over an agreed period.
- The asset remains the property of the hire-purchase company until the final payment is made.

Cost: The interest charged on hire-purchase finance is high.

Risk: Failure to repay will damage the business's credit rating and may result in the asset being repossessed.

Security: No security is required to get hire-purchase finance.

Control: The owner keeps full control of the business.

Long-term sources of finance

These are sources that must be repaid after five years.

The principal sources of long-term finance are equity capital, long-term loans and government grants.

Long-term finance should be used to finance the permanent assets of the business.

Equity capital

- A source of long-term finance.
- It is the permanent capital of a company used to finance the permanent assets of the business.
- The money is provided by the shareholders who receive dividends from company profits.
- There is no commitment to equity shareholders that they will receive a dividend each year.

Cost: Dividend paid to shareholder every year.

Risk: Loss of capital if business fails.

Security: No security is required to obtain equity capital.

Control: The owner loses some control to new shareholders. Shareholders must be given shares and votes in return for their investment.

Long-term loans

- These are loans for five years or longer.
- They are provided by financial institutions and repaid by instalments.
- Finance is used for large capital expenditure (fixed assets).

Cost: High interest payments.

Risk: Failure to repay the loan will damage the business's credit rating and may result in the security provided being sold to repay the loan.

Security: Fixed assets are required as security. If the start-up business does not own fixed assets, the owner may be asked to sign a personal guarantee that the loan will be repaid.

Control: The owner keeps full control of the business.

Government grants

- Money from the government which does not have to be repaid.
- There are usually specific conditions attached.
- The grants are expected to create employment and are only given for potentially viable projects.
- Grants are available from Enterprise Ireland and country and city enterprise boards.

Cost: No interest or repayments have to be made.

Risk: If the conditions attached are not fulfilled, the grant may be recalled.

Security: No security required to get a government grant.

Control: The owner keeps full control of the business.

Management of working capital

Management of working capital is essential for start-up businesses.

Working Capital is the finance used for the day-to-day running and payment of immediate debts of the business. It is the excess of current assets over current liabilities.

If working capital is positive, the business is said to be liquid. If working capital is negative, the business is not liquid and said to be overtrading.

Liquidity is the ability of the business to pay short-term debts as they arise.

If working capital is negative (current liabilities are greater than current assets), the business is said to be **overtrading**.

Overtrading arises when a firm increases production and sales too much or too quickly and runs short of cash.

How to manage working capital

To manage working capital a business must exercise:

- Credit control
- Stock control
- Cash flow management

Credit control

Credit control is exercised over trade debtors to ensure customers who buy goods on credit pay their debts on time to minimise the risk of bad debts.

Good working capital management involves good credit control, which improves cash flow.

Stock control

Stock control is an important part of working capital management.

It ensures that the firm has the correct amount of stock at all times to satisfy customer demand – never too much, never too little.

Cash flow management

Management of cash flow is another vital element of working capital management.

A cash flow forecast is an estimate of a firm's future cash inflow and cash outflows.

It draws attention to periods of negative cash flow so that arrangements can be made to ensure that finance is available.

It also draws attention to periods of surplus when excess funds can be invested.

Ownership options

When starting a business an entrepreneur has a choice of many different types of business structures through which to conduct business.

There are three basic structures to choose from:

- Sole trader
- Partnership
- Private limited company

Sole trader

A sole trader is a person who owns and runs his/her own business.

The key features of a sole trader are:

- Owner makes all the decisions – complete control
- Owner keeps all the profits
- Easily set up – few regulations
- Unlimited liability – sole trader is responsible for all debts of the business and may have to sell personal assets to pay business debts
- A lot of pressure and work for one person

Partnership

A partnership is when between 2 and 20 people form a business together in order to make profit.

The key features of a partnership are:

- Risks and responsibilities and decision-making are shared.
- More capital available to run the business
- Different skills and expertise of partners
- Easy and inexpensive to form
- Profits and losses are shared
- Unlimited liability

Private limited company

A private limited company is a business set up by between 1 and 99 people called shareholders.

The key features of a private limited company are:

- Shareholders have limited liability – this means that if the business fails, the shareholders can only lose the amount they have invested in the business. They cannot lose their private property to pay business debts.
- Shareholders buy shares in the company and this forms its share capital. Profits are divided among shareholders through dividends.
- A limited company is a legal entity separate from its owners.
- A board of directors is elected by shareholders to run the company.

Production options

Having decided what products to produce, a firm must choose a method of production. There are three main methods of production:

- Job production
- Batch production
- Mass production

Job production

- This is the production of a product to a specific customer order.
- It is a one-off production unit – a unique product.
- It is not produced to be held in stock.
- Highly skilled, direct labour is required.
- The product is expensive.

Examples of job production products include:

- Customised kitchen
- Wedding dress
- Specially produced pieces of crystal for presentations
- Hand-crafted furniture
- Shipbuilding

Batch production

- This is the production of certain quantities of identical products in one production run and then production switches to a different batch.
- Skilled or semi-skilled labour is used.
- Uses a lot of flexible machines (e.g. ovens).
- The products produced are of average price and held in stock in anticipation of a customer's demand.

Examples of products produced using batch production:

- Bread baked in different sizes
- Production of clothing in different sizes, colours and designs
- School textbooks
- Paint and wallpaper manufacturing
- Carpet manufacturing

Mass production

- This is the production of large numbers of identical products.
- There is non-stop, continuous production.
- Items are produced for stock and then sold – large demand is essential.
- High degree of automation, resulting in low labour costs.
- Unit costs are reduced as the firm benefits from large-scale production.

Examples of products produced using mass production:

- Golf balls
- Ball-point pens
- Cars
- Toilet paper
- Cornflakes
- Chocolate bars

Business plan

A good business plan is essential for all start-up businesses.

Benefits for a business of preparing a business plan

Guide to Future Action

A plan provides a focus for the business and guides the actions of individuals.

A **business plan** sets out how a business is going to achieve its aims and objectives. It outlines the marketing, production and financial plans for the proposed business.

Finance/Grants

A business plan can be used when seeking finance for a business venture from a financial institution or grants from government agencies.

No financial institution/government agency will give finance to a business without being convinced that the investment has a good chance of being recovered.

Assessing performance

A plan provides a benchmark against which performance can be measured. If targets are not reached, then action to fix the problem can be implemented.

Viability

In preparing a business plan, all aspects of a business are analysed. A SWOT analysis may be carried out, problem areas can be identified and steps taken to deal with them.

By planning ahead, the business can foresee difficulties and take steps to address the problems.

Example of a Business Plan

MICHELLE MORAN CATERING SERVICE LTD

Company ownership and management structure

Name of company: Michelle Moran Catering Service Ltd
Formed: 1 January 2011
Shareholders: Michelle Moran, Audrey Griffin
Registered office: 45 O'Connell Street, Killarney, Co. Kerry
Solicitors: Keane and Irwin, Killarney
Accountants: Ferguson and Keegan Ltd, Killarney
Bankers: Allied Irish Bank, Main Street, Killarney
Managing director: Michelle Moran
Education: Business studies degree, University of Limerick
Work experience: Ten years' experience in catering industry

Product or service

Salad rolls, sandwiches, sausage rolls, soup, scones, cakes
Unique selling points: Homemade products, prompt delivery, personal service and quality

Marketing and marketing strategy

Target market: 300 small businesses, including factories and schools
                        without canteen facilities requiring supplies
Market niche: Schools, colleges, and factories
Competition: Confectioners, bakeries and delicatessens
Targets: 100 customers after six months
Pricing policy: 10 per cent lower than competitors

Sales and distribution

Advertising and promotion: Brochures, newspapers, leaflets, local radio
Distribution: Local morning delivery service

Financing

Requirements: Ten-year lease of premises   €20,000
                    Equipment   €10,000
                    Motor vehicle   €15,000
                    Working capital   €5,000
                                                        €50,000

Finance available: Own investment (equity)   €10,000
                    Grant (CEB)   €5,000   €15,000
                    Finance required: €35,000

Financial projections

See projected profit and loss accounts and balance sheet (three years), cash flow forecast and break-even charts (three years) enclosed.

Michelle Moran

Michelle Moran

Business plan

HL

Paula and Thomas have recently returned to Ireland having worked with transnational companies for ten years. They wish to set up in business together in Ireland to manufacture a range of new organic breakfast cereals. Paula has particular expertise in production and finance and Thomas in marketing and human resources.

Draft a business plan for this proposed new business using **five** main headings, outlining the contents under each heading.

(40 marks)

Source: 2006 Higher Level Section 3

Suggested solution

Business Plan – Paula and Thomas

1. Description of Business

Name of company:	P&T Ltd
Address:	Main Street, Limerick
Telephone:	067-21931250
E-mail:	PandT@eircom.com
Type of business organisation:	Private limited company
Main activity of enterprise:	Manufacturing range of breakfast cereals
Owners:	Paula and Thomas
Advisers:	Limerick Enterprise Board
Bankers:	Bank of Ireland Limerick
Goals of Enterprise:	To become the biggest organic cereal producer in Ireland and to export into the EU.

2. Organisation and Management

Management Team:	Paula and Thomas
Age:	Both 35 years old
Qualifications:	Paula – Degree in Finance, C.I.T.
	Thomas – Degree in Marketing, L.I.T.
Experience:	Paula – Experience in production and finance with transnational company
	Thomas – Experience in marketing and human resources with transnational company
Staffing:	In addition to Paula and Thomas, the enterprise will have five full-time employees in the first year of operation.

3. Marketing and Marketing Strategies

Target market:	Health-conscious consumers
Market research:	Large and growing Irish market for breakfast cereals

Marketing mix:

Product:	Organic breakfast cereals
Price:	High quality; relatively high price aimed at customers with high disposable income
Promotion:	Advertising: Newspapers, radio and television
	Sales promotion: Special introductory promotional price – free samples
Place:	Distribution through supermarkets and specialist health shops
Unique selling point:	Cereals with high fruit content, organic ingredients, superior taste – no fat

4. Manufacturing Operations and Premises

Product manufacturing process:	Batch production using Irish-sourced ingredients to make a variety of breakfast cereals.
Premises:	Factory in Limerick
Plant and Equipment:	Computer-aided manufacturing
Research and Development:	Two years research into organic ingredients, design, packaging, etc.
Quality Control:	Application for ISO 9000 certification to ensure high quality standards
Experience:	Paula – experience in production

5. Financial Analysis and Investment Proposal

Finance Requirements

Cost of factory	250,000
Manufacturing equipment	600,000
Motor vehicles	50,000
Working capital	100,000
	1,000,000

Finance Available

Equity Investment

Paula	50,000	
Thomas	50,000	
Grant – Enterprise Board	100,000	200,000
Finance required		800,000

Financial Projections

Projected profit and loss and balance sheet for three years.
Cash flow forecast showing inflows and outflows of cash for three years.

Paula & Thomas

Marking scheme

5 Heading @ 8 marks each

   2 marks – Heading
   3 marks – Contents under each heading
   3 marks – Details of Paula and Thomas enterprise

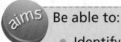

18 Business Expansion

Reasons for expansion

1. Economies of scale

The general cost of running a large enterprise rather that a smaller one may be reduced due to rationalisation and cutting down expenses. Large-scale production arising from expansion reduces the unit cost of production.

2. Increased financial strength and security

A large business enterprise commands prestige influence and power with banks, other businesses and government departments. A larger business will survive better in a recession.

3. Eliminate competition

Competition can be eliminated by a merger or takeover of a competitor that is a threat to the business.

4. Protect sources of raw materials

A business might want to control a source of raw materials on which its future depends by taking over the supplier.

5. Diversification

Growth allows a business to branch into different product ranges. This reduces risk since it a diversified business does not depend on any one product type.

6. Synergy

This is the theory that the sum of two amalgamated businesses is higher than the sum of the two enterprises if they remained separate. It allows for the closure of the inefficient plant and the sale of the assets that may not be required.

Finance for expansion

Expansion is a long-term activity, so appropriate long-term finance should be sought for it.

key point

There are three long-term sources of finance for expansion:

- Equity capital
- Retained earnings
- Debt capital

Equity capital

The company raises finance by selling ordinary shares.

Shareholders receive a share of the profit of the business in the form of a dividend.

Shareholders have voting rights and a say in policy-making.

In the event of the business being wound up, ordinary shareholders only get what remains after all other debts are paid.

Benefits of using equity capital to finance expansion

Equity finance allows a business to obtain finance without incurring debt.

Equity capital is a cheap source of finance as there is no guarantee to equity shareholders that they will receive a dividend each year.

Share capital does not have to be repaid to shareholders except on the winding up of the company.

Equity capital does not create any cost for the business except the payment of dividends.

Disadvantages of using equity capital to finance expansion

Issuing shares to new shareholders reduces the control of the existing shareholders in the decision-making process.

Issuing shares is expensive as there are various legal formalities and professional fees to be met.

Retained earnings

This is the amount of profit re-invested in the business for expansion rather than distributed as dividends.

The use of retained earnings is very suitable to finance expansion as there is no cost involved and there is no loss of control.

Debt capital

This is a long-term loan from a financial institution to finance expansion.

Interest on the loan must be repaid to the lender irrespective of profitability.

Taking out a loan does not affect the control of the owners in the decision-making process in the business.

Benefits of using debt capital to finance expansion

Debt capital is easy to get. There are many different types of business loans available from banks.

Interest payments are an allowable expense in the profit and loss account, reducing the tax liability of the business.

Disadvantages of using debt capital to finance expansion

All loan interest and capital repayments must be made to the bank, irrespective of business performance.

Repayments of interest and capital may affect the liquidity of the business.

Debt and equity capital as sources of finance for expansion

Evaluate debt and equity capital as sources of finance for business expansion.

(20 marks)

Source: 2009 Higher Level Section 3

Suggested solution

Equity Capital = Ordinary Share Capital + Reserves

Debt Capital = Long-term Loans

Debt Capital and Equity Capital may be compared as follows:

	Equity Capital	Debt Capital
1. Cost/Interest/Dividends	There is no obligation to pay dividends to shareholders.	Interest payments must be made.
2. Risk	Low – The business is lowly geared. The business has no long-term debt and no interest repayments.	High – The business is highly geared. Interest payments must be made regardless of profitability.
3. Control	The issue of shares may dilute the control of the existing shareholders.	Debt capital will not impact on control of business.
4. Security	No security required.	Security is required.
5. Tax implications	Dividends to ordinary shareholders are not tax deductible.	Interest payments are tax deductible.

Evaluation

Generally companies will use a combination of both debt capital and equity capital to finance their business.

Equity capital is low risk and does not require security. However, current loss of confidence in the stock market is a challenge to raising equity capital.

Debt capital is high risk – Interest must be paid, irrespective of profitably. However, the current economic climate poses challenges in obtaining finance from financial institutions.

Marking scheme

3 pts @ 5 marks (2+3) =   15

Evaluation required – 5 marks (2+3) =   5

                    TOTAL   20 marks

Implications of business expansion

For	Short Term	Long Term
Share Price	Share price should increase because of increased demand for shares in a bigger company.	Successful expansion will lead to an increase in the value of the business in the long term, leading to an increase in share price.
Products	Larger businesses will have a wider range of products.	Because of continuing market research and product development, there will be a wider range of products in the long term.
Company structure	A formal management structure with a clear chain of command must be set up to deal with a wider range of activities.	As business grows larger, more delegation is necessary to successfully manage the business.
Finance	Finance in the form of equity capital and debt capital must be raised to finance expansion.	As the business grows, it should be easier to raise equity capital and debt capital in the future.
Profits and dividends	The high cost of expansion and possible redundancy payments may lead to a reduction in profit and dividends in the short term.	Increased efficiency and the success of expansion will lead to increased profits and dividends in the long term.
Employees	Expansion may lead to uncertainty about the future, poor motivation, cost cutting and possible job losses.	As business grows, employees can be provided with better wages, better working conditions, training and promotion opportunities.
Customers	Economies of scale should provide customers with more competitively priced products.	Customers benefit from a wider range of products and lower prices, but lose personal contact with the owner.

Methods of expansion

Internal growth (organic growth)

This is growth generated from within the business using its own resources.
Internal growth occurs when a firm:

- Retains its profits
- Uses it to invest in additional fixed assets and resources

Internal growth is achieved by:

- Increasing sales in existing home markets
- Developing new markets – new markets can be entered by:
  - **Exporting** – Selling products into foreign markets.
  - **Franchising** – The granting of a licence by the franchiser to the franchisee allowing the sale of their product or service (e.g. McDonald's, Subway, Domino's Pizza, Supermac's, Eddie Rocket's).

External growth (inorganic growth)

Business alliance

An agreement between two or more businesses to pool resources and expertise to work together over a specified period of time or to complete a specified project while all parties maintain their separate identities.

The partners benefit from the sharing of:

A business can expand externally by:
- Business alliance
- Merger
- Takeover

- Expertise/skills
- Business networks and markets
- Increased resources

The **advantages of an alliance** as a form of business expansion are that it:

- Is a cost-effective method of expansion. Resources are shared and costs are divided between partners.
- Reduces the risks associated with expansion for each partner as risks are shared.
- Provides access to extended business network and markets.

Example: North Cork Business Alliance

A group consisting of sole traders, small businesses and companies who 'share knowledge and expertise to better serve their customers and to develop and enhance business by exchanging quality referrals'.

Merger

A merger occurs when two companies voluntarily agree to come together to run their business as one single company.

'A merger is an agreement between two companies to bring both firms together under a common board of directors.'

Example: British Airways and the Spanish carrier Iberia merged to create the world's third largest airline.

Takeover

A takeover is the purchase of one company by another with or without its consent.

Example: The Pfizer pharmaceutical takeover of rival drug maker Wyeth. The value of the takeover (€51.5 billion) was paid using equal amounts of cash, equity and debt.

Advantages of mergers and takeovers

- Economies of scale – They can make savings from being bigger.
- They can compete better with larger firms.
- They can invest more finance in research and development, leading to better quality goods for consumers.

Importance of business expansion

Importance of business expansion in Ireland

- Employment is created, which reduces numbers unemployed.
- Increased tax revenue for government.
- Better quality goods and services as more money is spent on research and development by bigger businesses.
- Bigger firms can compete better on international markets.

Importance of Irish business expansion in foreign markets

- Economies of scale – Selling into foreign markets means large-scale production, reducing unit cost.
- Increased sales and profit for firms exporting into foreign markets.
- Expanding into foreign markets means the business is less dependent on home market.
- Exporting improves balance of payments. Money comes into the country.

Applied Business Question (ABQ) (Higher Level)

Based on Units 3, 4 and 5
This is a compulsory question for Leaving Certificate 2016/2021

HL Stylish Décor Ltd

Ruth Cavanagh became Managing Director of Stylish Décor Ltd, a retail and wholesale business, one year ago. She took over the paint, wallpaper and tiling business when her father Paddy retired. Paddy had been a popular employer locally but the business had not grown and kept pace with developments in technology, marketing or human resource management. The company's premises are based in an expanding town within a one-hour commuting distance of Dublin and are in need of modernisation.

The town has seen a large increase in new house building over the last few years and its development plan provides for further housing and industrial units. Ruth is ambitious. Her aim is to become a market leader. Research has convinced her of the benefits of adding a 'Do-It-Yourself' (DIY) department to the existing business and setting up a second shop in a town less than twenty-kilometres away. These initiatives will require an increase in staff, a retraining programme for existing staff, incentives, and capital investment, if the business is to succeed.

Ruth is a Business graduate and understands the importance of marketing for the success of a business. Her enterprise's market share and turnover are below those of comparable businesses. Ruth intends to penetrate the market by a further 50 per cent within the next five years, to improve the expertise of staff, the quality of customer service and the product range. The fact that a major multiple is due to open a new hardware and gardening outlet with good parking just four kilometres away has concentrated her mind. Stylish Décor Ltd has not, up to now, invested in marketing activities. She also intends to introduce clearly defined lines of responsibility for staff in the areas of purchasing and sales/marketing and offer employees rewards for achieving targets. She wants to make changes and respond to customer needs quickly, but she is facing strong opposition from her staff.

(A) Discuss how management activities can help Ruth improve the performance of the business. (30 marks)

(B) Advise Ruth on the strategies that will help her manage the changes that have to take place if the business is to succeed. (20 marks)

(C) Illustrate, using the above text, how applying the price and promotion elements of the marketing mix can contribute to achieving Ruth's ambitions. (30 marks)

(80 marks)

Suggested solution

(A) Management activities

Planning – Involves selecting organisational goals or objectives and seeking out ways to achieve them. Plans reduce risk and uncertainty and give an organisation purpose and direction. These may include:

1. **SWOT analysis** – Analyse the present situation by carrying out a SWOT analysis:
   - **Strengths** – 'Ruth is an ambitious business graduate.'
   - **Weaknesses** – 'Business is in need of modernisation'; 'market share and turnover are below those of comparable businesses.'
   - **Opportunities** – 'Business is based in an expanding town within one hour of Dublin'; 'Large increase in new houses over the last few years and plans for further housing and industrial units.'
   - **Threats** – 'A major multiple is due to open a new outlet nearby.'

2. **Objectives** – These are the goals to be achieved.
   Link to text
   Ruth's aim is to become a market leader

3. **Strategic plans** – Strategic plans are developed over the long term (one to five years into the future).
   Link to text
   Market share and turnover low – penetrate the market by a further 50% within next five years.

4. **Tactical planning** – Applies to periods of one or two years (i.e. the short-term, day-to-day operations of the business).
   Link to text
   She wishes to add a Do-it-Yourself Department to the existing business
   Set up a second shop in a new town
   Planning can help Ruth improve the performance of the business and so achieve the goals of the organisation.

Organising

Organising involves getting things done through some form of organised structure so that a business, with its activities coordinated, has the best chance of reaching its objectives. Possible structures are line organisation and matrix structure.

Line organisation – An organisation that is divided into departments made up of line activities (i.e. activities are essential for the survival of the organisation, such as finance, production, sales, and research and development department).

Link to text

Introduce clearly defined lines of responsibility for staff in the areas of purchasing, sales/marketing

Retraining programme for existing staff

Matrix organisation (project team structure) – a team-based approach to problem-solving. The emphasis is on joining together many disciplines in the interest of completing the project.

The performance of the business can be improved through organising the business so it has the best chance of achieving its objectives.

Controlling

This is the process of comparing the firm's performance against the targets set, measuring deviations and taking action to correct them.

Link to text

Rewards for achieving targets

Ruth needs to consider the following types of control to improve the performance of the business:

- **Quality control** involves examining everything about a product or service which satisfies customers' requirements in as cheap and efficient a way as possible.

  Link to text

  Ruth intends to improve the quality of customer service.

- **Stock control** – Ensures that stocks are maintained at a level which meets customer demand, but which at the same time are kept to a minimum.

  Link to text

  Ruth intends to improve the product range

- **Credit control** – Goods are sold and payment is not made until some time into the future. A trade debtor is created; risk of bad debts.

- **Budgetary control** – A financial plan that sets out the expected income and expenditure of the enterprise for a future period of time. A comparison is made between actual financial performance and the budget figures. The cause of the variance would be investigated.

  Link to text

  Ruth needs to check cash flow to ensure that there is enough finance for 'a retraining programme for existing staff and the capital investment in the business'.

Marking scheme

(A)	Management Activities Illustration from text of the ABQ	(3 @ 10 marks) (2 + 6(3 + 3) + 2)	**30 marks**

(B) Strategies that will help to manage the changes

1. **Total commitment by senior management** (2 marks)

   There is total **senior management commitment** to the changes proposed. If this commitment is not present, then the staff concerned will immediately become aware of the half-hearted effort and the change will not progress. (2 marks)

   Link to text

   She wants to make changes but she is facing strong opposition from her staff (1 mark)

2. **Involvement and participation in the change process by employees** (2 marks)

   Genuine **involvement and participation** in the change process by employees will generate ideas that improve the proposal and create a willingness to adapt. Morale will improve and the staff will feel ownership of the change. Ruth could do this through **Empowerment** and increased responsibility of the individual and the group for all aspects of the job, including quality, can make the change more attractive and acceptable. (2 marks)

   Link to text

   Ruth intends to improve the quality of customer service (1 mark)

3. **Communications between all the parties** (2 marks)

   There must be effective **communications** between all the parties throughout the change process. This requires honesty on both sides. A constant two-way communication approach will help to reduce insecurity and ignorance and dispel fear. (2 marks)

   Link to text

   Ruth intends to introduce clearly defined lines of responsibility (1 mark)

4. **Consultation with trade unions/employee representatives**

   Consultation with trade unions/employee representatives is essential (and as early as possible) concerning the changes and the effects of the changes on them. Employees must be provided with the opportunity to understand and appreciate fully the implications of the change.

5. **Adequate funding for all stages of the change process** (2 marks)

   There is adequate **funding** for all stages of the change process. Money is needed for training and retraining in new skills, especially at the initial stages of the change. (2 marks)

   Link to text

   A retraining programme for existing staff
   To improve the expertise of staff (1 mark)

6. **Negotiation**

   The idea that the change is good for the business and good for staff security and reward must be explained. Remuneration packages, productivity agreements, and general improvement in working conditions may all be part of the change process. This is so that all parties to the process gain.

Link to text

Incentives

and employees' rewards for achieving targets

Marking scheme

(B)	Strategies to manage change Must have reference to text of ABQ	4 points @ 5 m each (2 + 2 + 1)	**20 marks**

(C) How price and promotion elements of the marketing mix can contribute to achieving Ruth's ambitions

Ruth's ambitions are:

1. To add a DIY department to the existing shop, set up a second shop in another town, employ more staff retrain existing staff, and capital investment.
2. Penetrate the market by a further fifty percent within the next five years.
3. Respond to new competition in the market.

Price and promotion elements of the marketing mix can contribute to the achievement of these ambitions.

Price – The amount of money charged for the product or service pricing policies, including cost plus pricing, penetration pricing and competitive pricing.

Promotion – Used by business enterprises to let existing and possible future customers know about the products on offer and to get them interested in buying the goods. The essential promotional methods are advertising, sales promotion, public relations, personal selling.

The purpose of all four elements of promotion is to inform the market that the enterprise has something for sale and to convince someone to actually purchase it.

Ambition 1: Business expansion through capital investment and staff increases

Expansion increases have a cost, so to survive the business must increase sales.

Price and promotion can help achieve this objective.

Price – The selling price of product can be determined by cost plus pricing: All the product costs involved in research and development, production and distribution and a margin for profit are added and the total cost determined.

Link to text

Market share and price

Purchasing

Promotion (advertising) – The use of communications to influence customers towards a particular product or service. To inform, persuade and remind customers. By advertising in newspapers or radio, Ruth can increase sales.

Link to text

Her enterprise's market share and turnover are below those of comparable businesses

Ambition 2: Penetrate the market by a further fifty per cent within five years.

Price and promotion can help achieve this objective.

Price (penetration pricing): This involves setting prices lower than the competition in order to gain and keep market share.

Link to text

Penetrate the market by fifty percent within the next five years

Promotion (sales promotion): The use of attention-seeking to attract customers to the product or services on offer. Used in addition to normal advertising, add to the attractiveness of the product. Offer to customers a bonus/incentive directly related to the product (e.g. buy one and get one free). This should increase market share.

Link to text

Penetrate the market

Ambition 3: Respond to new competition in the market

Price (competitive pricing): To compete in the market, prices must be set at the same level as those of the competition.

Link to text

Competition close by

Promotion (public relations): The provision of details of the enterprise's policies and plans to customers and the public (e.g. promoting the name of the enterprise in the public mind, generating goodwill for the enterprise's products). Publicity through sponsorship/relations with local community.

Link to text

Has not up to now invested in marketing activities
'Do It Yourself' dept.
New shop

Marking scheme

(C)	Price Promotion Relevant to the text of the ABQ	15 marks (6 (3 + 3) + 6 (3 + 3) + 3) 15 marks (6 (3 + 3) + 6 (3 + 3) + 3)	**30 marks**

UNIT 6

Domestic Environment

Business does not operate in a vacuum. It is part of the wider economic system. This unit looks at the different types of industry and business in the local and national economy. It also examines the relationship between business and the government.

Objective

To enable pupils to understand the interaction between businesses, the local community, the government and the economy.

- **Chapter 19:** Categories of Industry
- **Chapter 20:** Types of Business Organisation
- **Chapter 21:** Community Development
- **Chapter 22:** Business and the Economy
- **Chapter 23:** Government and Business
- **Chapter 24:** The Social Responsibility of Business

19 Categories of Industry

Categories of industry

- Primary Sector – extractive industries (agriculture, forestry, fishing, mining)
- Secondary Sector – manufacturing and construction
- Tertiary Sector – service industries

 key point

Primary Sector – extractive industries are:
- Agriculture
- Forestry
- Fishing
- Mining

The primary sector

The importance of the primary sector to the economy

1. Employment

Many people are employed directly and indirectly in agriculture, fishing, forestry and mining.

2. Raw materials for industry

The primary sector supplies raw materials for much of the manufacturing and construction sectors:

- Ingredients for the food-processing industry
- Timber, sand and gravel for the building and construction industry
- Energy (coal, gas, turf), which is very important in the economy.

3. Food for the country

Agriculture supplies meat, milk, fruit and vegetables. Fish is an important source of protein, vitamins and fats.

4. The market for products

Farmers buy farm machinery, fertilisers and farm chemicals. Fishermen and foresters buy equipment and materials.

5. Exports

Exports from the primary sector bring money into the country, which improves the standard of living for those involved in the primary sector and improves our balance of payments. This also reduces the country's need to import goods and services.

6. Development of natural resources

This includes mining, quarrying, etc.

Trends in the primary sector

1. Diversification

Because of falling farm incomes and production quotas, many farmers are moving away from traditional farming to enterprises such as organic farming, production of biofuels, agri-tourism. They are also changing land use to tree production, where there is a grant scheme in operation.

2. Declining numbers in the primary sector

The number of people employed in the primary sector has declined due to fluctuating prices and mechanisation. Many farms are too small to be viable, forcing many farmers to take part-time employment to increase income.

3. Declining EU payments

Traditionally, farmers received many EU grants and payments. Farmers now receive a single EU payment per annum, regardless of output.

4. Consumer confidence

Consumer confidence and concerns about the quality of food – particularly the issues of animal disease and chemical and pesticide residues in food – has led to a growth in the demand for organically produced food.

The secondary sector

The secondary sector includes the manufacturing industry and construction businesses. They take raw materials produced by the primary sector and process them into finished products.

Manufacturing industry

Pfizer

PFIZER IRELAND
PHARMACEUTICALS

exam focus

Manufacturing industry in Ireland is carried out by:

- Indigenous firms
- Transnational companies
- Agri-businesses

1. Indigenous Firms

- Indigenous firm are set up, owned and managed by Irish people, with their principal place of business in Ireland.
- The state body Enterprise Ireland has the responsibility for developing indigenous Irish industry.
- Examples of indigenous Irish industries: Blarney Woollen Mills, Roadstone Wood and Superquinn.

2. Transnational Companies

- Transnational companies are foreign firms with manufacturing plants in Ireland.
- Example: Pfizer is an American pharmaceutical company with plants in Ireland.

3. Agri-businesses

- Agri-business refers to those firms involved in food production.
- They use agriculture materials in the production of finished goods.
- Example: The Kerry Group is a major food company.

Construction industry

The construction industry is involved in building the country's infrastructure (roads, schools, hospitals) and industrial buildings and private housing.

The importance of the secondary sector to the economy

1. Employment

Manufacturing and construction provide a great deal of employment, increasing the wealth of Irish people and contributing tax revenue to the government.

2. Uses Irish raw materials

Manufacturing and construction use Irish raw materials and natural resources in helping build the country's infrastructure.

3. Exports

Much of the output of manufacturing industry is exported, which contributes positively to the balance of payments.

Trends in the secondary sector

1. Decline in employment

Downsizing and firm closures have resulted in an increase in unemployment, particularly in manufacturing and construction.

2. Increased competition

Challenges faced by the agri-business sector in food markets for foreign retailers (e.g. Aldi and Lidl).

3. Increased wages

Increased wages over the last few years have resulted in a loss of competitiveness, forcing the relocation of some manufacturing businesses to low-cost economies (e.g. some manufacturing businesses such as Dell have relocated to lower-cost economies, such as Poland).

The tertiary sector

The tertiary sector (or **services sector**) provides services to individuals and to other businesses.

Examples: financial, communication, distribution, leisure, tourism, professional and personal services, educational.

The importance of the tertiary sector to the economy

1. Employment

The sector is labour intensive and creates many jobs.

2. Support services

The sector provides support services for the efficient running of all other sectors of the economy.

3. Tax revenue

Many small, indigenous businesses are involved in providing services, contributing large amounts of tax to the government through pay, VAT and corporation tax.

4. Tourism

Tourism is a very important service industry and a big employer.

Tourists spend large amounts of money in Ireland.

Trends in the tertiary sector

1. Exporter of services

Ireland is now one of the world's leading exporters of software-related goods and services. This brings money into the country.

2. E-commerce

In relation to information communication technology (ICT) infrastructure – firms in Ireland now generate almost one-third of their turnover from e-commerce.

3. Job losses

Banks have reduced the number of staff they need. Banks and building societies have merged to form much more efficient businesses. (For example, Ulster Bank merged with First Active with the loss of 750 jobs.)

4. Information communication technology (ICT)

The sector is expanding due to developments in ICT.

20 Types of Business Organisation

Types of business organisation

There are ten main forms of business organisation:

1. Sole trader
2. Partnership
3. Private limited company
4. Public limited company
5. Business alliance
6. Franchise
7. Transnational company
8. Co-operative
9. State-owned enterprise
10. Indigenous firm

1. Sole trader

A sole trader is a business owned and controlled by one person.

Advantages and Disadvantages of Being a Sole Trader

Advantages	Disadvantages
1. Owner keeps all profit.	1. Unlimited liability – if the business fails, the owner could be sued for personal assets.
2. Owner makes all decisions – complete control.	2. Lack of capital for expansion.
3. Independence – freedom and flexibility.	3. Lack of continuity of existence.
4. Confidentiality of accounts.	4. Difficulty of raising finance.
5. Personal service to customers.	5. One person responsible for a range of tasks and decisions.
6. Easy to set up – few regulations.	6. Suffers all losses if made.
	7. A lot of pressure and work on one person.

2. Partnership

- A partnership is an agreement between two or more people to conduct business with a view to making a profit.
- Membership of a partnership is between 2 and 20.
- Partnerships are common among doctors, solicitors and accountants.

- Partners draw up a Deed of Partnership, which is a legal agreement setting out the rights, responsibilities and duties of each partner.
- A business must register its name with the Companies Registration Office if the name is different from the names of the partners.

Advantages and Disadvantages of a Partnership

Advantages	Disadvantages
1. Extra capital is available.	1. Partners have unlimited liability.
2. Shared decision-making.	2. Disagreements among partners.
3. Risk and responsibility is shared.	3. Profit shared among partners.
4. Different skills and expertise of partners.	4. Decision-making is slow.
5. Confidentiality of accounts.	5. Business does not have a separate legal existence distinct from partners.
6. Easy to form.	

3. Private limited company

- A private limited company is a business owned by between 1 and 99 shareholders.
- Shareholders contribute capital to the company.
- Shareholders appoint a board of directors to run the company.
- Shareholders have limited liability – this means that if the business fails, shareholders can lose only the amount they have invested in the business. They cannot lose their private property to pay for the debts of the business.
- The company has the word 'Limited' after its name.
- Companies are regulated by the Companies Act.
- Profits are distributed to shareholders in the form of dividends.

Steps in the formation of a private limited company

To form a private limited company, the following steps must be taken:

1. Prepare the following documents:

   - Memorandum of Association
   - Articles of Association
   - Form A1

2. Send the documents plus the appropriate fee to the Companies Registration Office (CRO).

3. The Registrar of Companies checks the documents to ensure everything is OK. The Registrar issues a Certificate of Incorporation. This is the birth certificate of a private limited company. It can then start trading.

4. The company must then hold its first meeting or statutory meeting.

Documents Needed to Form a Private Limited Company

Memorandum of Association	Articles of Association	Form A1
This document gives information about the company to outsiders It contains: • Name of company with 'Ltd' • Objectives of company • Statement of limited liability • Share capital of company	This document sets out the internal rules and regulations for the running of the company. It contains: • Details of share capital (the different classes of shares) • Details of shares (voting rights of shares, issue of shares, transfer of shares) • Regulations regarding meetings (procedures at meetings, procedure for calling meetings) • Signature of each subscriber • Details regarding directors (how directors are to be elected, powers and duties of directors) • Procedure for winding up company	This document is the application for registration. It contains: • Company name • Company's registered address • Details of secretary and directors • Declaration of compliance with Companies Acts • Statement of capital authorised and issued

Advantages and Disadvantages of a Private Limited Company

Advantages	Disadvantages
1. Shareholders have limited liability. 2. The company is a separate legal entity from the shareholders. 3. More capital can be raised from up to 99 shareholders. 4. Better credit rating with lenders. 5. Continuity of existence. 6. Risk and responsibility are shared.	1. Difficult to set up as there are many regulations to be followed. 2. Expensive formation and running costs. 3. Business affairs are public in that the annual accounts are sent to the Registrar. The books are audited and presented to the AGM. 4. Profits are shared among shareholders in the form of dividends. 5. The law is very strict on the operation and control of companies.

4. Public limited company

- A public limited company is a business owned by at least seven shareholders with no maximum requirement.
- Shares are quoted on the stock exchange so they can be brought and sold by members of the public.
- Shareholders have limited liability.

- A public limited company has the initials PLC after its name.
- Before a public limited company commences business it must hold a Trading Certificate issued by the Registrar.
- All accounts and an annual report must be published and audited each year and returns made to the Registrar for filing and access to the public.

Advantages and Disadvantages of a Public Limited Company

Advantages	Disadvantages
1. Shareholders have limited liability.	1. High formation expenses.
2. Access to large amounts of capital.	2. Accounts must be audited and published.
3. Higher credit rating with financial institutions – easier to borrow money.	3. Many legal requirements to be followed.
4. Continuity of existence.	4. Owners may have little say in the running of the company as most decisions are made by management.
5. Top-quality management can be recruited.	

People involved in a public limited company

Shareholders

- They are the individuals or institutions who invest money in a company in return for shares.
- They are the owners of the business.
- They provide the capital of the company.
- They receive dividends if the firm makes profit.
- Ordinary shareholders have one vote per share and they elect a board of directors at the AGM.

Board of Directors

- A board of directors is elected by the shareholders at the company AGM to run the business.
- The board elects a managing director to run the business on a day-to-day basis.

Managing Director

- Elected by the board of directors to run the company.
- Manages the company on a day-to-day basis on behalf of the shareholders and the board of directors.
- The managing director delegates areas of responsibility to departmental managers.

Auditors

- Auditors are accountants who are appointed to check the accuracy of the company accounts.
- They present an annual report to the shareholders on whether the accounts present a true and fair view of the company.

Company Secretary

A company secretary is an officer of a company with responsibility for:

- Notifying shareholders of the AGM.
- Organising the AGM of the company and keeping the minutes of the meeting.
- Sending annual returns to the Registrar of Companies.
- Maintaining an up-to-date register of shareholders.

5. Business alliance

- A business alliance is an agreement formed between two or more businesses to work together in particular commercial matters while at the same time remaining their separate identities independent of each other.
- The alliance involves sharing of expertise and skills, shared costs and risk and improved service for the customer. (For example, 'oneworld' is one of the world's large airline alliances and has among its members American Airlines, British Airways and Quantas.)

Advantages and Disadvantages of a Business Alliance

Advantages	Disadvantages
1. Easy to establish – few legal formalities.	1. Agreement must be negotiated between the businesses on how the alliance will work.
2. Each firm benefits from the skills and expertise of the other.	2. Ownership and control is shared – any conflict between the firms could lead to the alliance closing.
3. Firms can develop new markets for their products and services.	3. A legal contract may be difficult to get out of, should one firm wish to withdraw.
4. Economies of scale – bigger is cheaper, costs are reduced.	

6. Franchise

- This is the granting of a licence by the franchisor (existing business) to the franchisee (person setting up the business), allowing the right to use the franchisor's trade name, logo and business system, and to sell their product or service.
- The licence is expensive and a percentage of sales/royalties must be paid annually.
- Examples of franchises: McDonald's, Supermac's, Kentucky Fried Chicken, Pizza Hut, Subway, Dunkin' Donuts.

Advantages and Disadvantages of a Franchise

Advantages	Disadvantages
1. Business has the use of an established trade name, logo and style.	1. Little freedom for franchisee to be creative – must observe rules in contract.
2. Product/service will have public acceptance.	2. Cost – the initial franchise fee and ongoing royalties make franchising a costly business operation.
3. Franchisee has lower costs and so benefits from economies of scale.	
4. Faster start – support provided in start-up by franchisor.	
5. Low-risk business name and idea is proven.	
6. National advertising is undertaken by franchisor.	

7. Transnational company

A company with its headquarters in one country and branches in a number of different countries. Examples include the Smurfit Kappa Group, Ford, Intel, Coca-Cola, Nestlé, Toyota, Nokia.

Advantages and Disadvantages of Transnational Companies

Advantages	Disadvantages
1. They provide employment – employees spend their income locally.	1. Lack of loyalty – they may close a plant causing local unemployment and move to a developing country to avail of cheaper raw materials and labour.
2. They provide revenue for the government in the form of corporation tax and VAT.	2. They provide intense competition for local firms, forcing closure of some firms with job losses.
3. Much of transnational output is exported, contributing favourably to the balance of payments.	3. Most of the profits made are repatriated to their head office in another country.
4. They buy their raw materials and supplies from local Irish businesses.	4. Some transnationals have great size and power and may exert pressure on governments in host countries to achieve their objectives.

8. Co-operative

- A co-operative is a business owned and controlled by its members, all of whom share a common interest.
- They are democratically run – one person/one vote.
- They are run by an elected management committee.

Advantages and Disadvantages of a Co-operative

Advantages	Disadvantages
1. Members have limited liability.	1. Difficulty of obtaining external finance.
2. Each member has an equal say in the running of the business – one member/one vote.	2. Rules and regulations place a large burden on smaller co-operatives.
3. There is a great incentive for members to do business with the co-operative, as the amount of dividend depends on the business transacted.	3. Co-operative must submit audited accounts annually.
4. Producer co-operatives provide a market for the output of the agricultural and fishing industries.	4. Limited management expertise.
	5. Members receive a limited return on their investment.

9. State-owned enterprise

- State enterprises are set up, owned, financed and controlled by the government.
- Capital to finance the enterprise is provided by the government.
- Commercial state enterprises produce goods and services that are sold to the public (e.g. CIE, Bord na Móna).
- Non-commercial state enterprises are state funded (e.g. Environmental Protection Agency [EPA]).

Advantages and Disadvantages of a State-Owned Enterprise

Advantages	Disadvantages
1. Employment – they employ large numbers of people.	1. Some state firms suffer losses, which are borne by the taxpayer.
2. Provide essential services including, non-profitable services (e.g. Bus Éireann).	2. The absence of a profit motive may lead to inefficiency.
3. Promote industrial development (e.g. IDA, Enterprise Ireland).	3. Many state enterprises lack adequate capital, which may lead to heavy borrowing.
4. Development of the country's natural resources (e.g. Bord na Móna, Bord Gáis).	4. Directors may lack management expertise.
5. Provide important infrastructure for the development of the country.	

10. Indigenous firm

- Indigenous firms are firms that are set up in Ireland and owned and managed by Irish people.
- They produce goods and/or provide services in Ireland. Their principal place of business is in Ireland.
- Enterprise Ireland is the state agency responsible for the development of indigenous firms in Ireland.
- Examples of indigenous firms: O'Flynn Construction, based in Cork, is one of the biggest construction companies in Ireland. Other are *The Irish Times*, Supermac's and Eason's.

Advantages and Disadvantages of Indigenous Firms

Advantages	Disadvantages
1. Employment – provide a lot of employment.	1. Many indigenous firms are heavily assisted by grants.
2. Profits remain in Ireland and may be re-invested here.	2. They must have an internationally recognised brand to sell abroad.
3. They export much of their output, which has a positive effect on balance of payments.	3. It is difficult for them to compete with transnationals and competition from abroad.
4. They purchase materials and other goods and services from Irish suppliers.	
5. They contribute a great deal of revenue to the government in the form of PAYE, VAT and corporation tax.	

Reasons why a business enterprise might change its organisational structure

Businesses change their structure over time to adapt to changing circumstances and market demands.

1. Business Wants to Increase in Size

The business may wish to grow larger, and growing larger requires more people with skills and expertise. Specialisation is necessary in areas such as finance, marketing and production.

Examples:

- Changing from sole trader to a partnership or to a private limited company will mean the inclusion of new partners/shareholders who bring new skills, experience and expertise to the company.
- A private company converting to a public limited company will attract top management with new skills and expertise.

2. Limited Liability

The desire for the protection of limited liability is another reason for changing structure. A business person may wish to protect family members and personal assets from business risks.

Example: If a sole trader or partnership converts to a private limited company, all the owners get the protection of limited liability.

3. Raising Finance

If more capital is needed for the development of the business, then changing the business's status will bring in extra finance.

Examples:

- A sole trader changing to a partnership will allow the business to raise finance from new partners.
- A sole trader changing to a private limited company will allow capital to be raised from up to 99 shareholders.
- A private limited company or a co-operative converting to a public limited company can raise large amounts of finance by selling shares on the stock exchange. (Some producer co-operatives in the agricultural sector have become public limited companies, such as Kerry Group PLC.)

4. Privatisation

The state may wish to sell some of its businesses. It could therefore convert its state-owned enterprises into public limited companies.

Example: Aer Lingus was privatised in 2006.

5. Marketing

The expansion of markets may be better served by joining a business alliance with another enterprise, either abroad or in Ireland. Forming an alliance allows the firm to share skills and resources.

Example: An Irish firm forming an alliance with a foreign firm allows the Irish firm to market and distribute goods abroad.

Contrast a private limited company with a partnership as desirable forms of business organisation. (15 marks)

Source: 2001 Higher Level Section 3

Suggested solution

1. Finance for Expansion (1 mark)

A private limited company can have up to 99 shareholders, whereas a partnership can only have a maximum of 20 partners. (2 marks)

Companies therefore can raise more capital and fund it easier to expand than a partnership. (2 marks)

2. Limited/Unlimited Liability (1 mark)

All shareholders in private limited companies have the benefit of limited liability, which protects their private assets (2 marks), whereas partners in a partnership have unlimited liability, which means they could lose everything should the business fail (2 marks).

3. Continuity of Existence (1 mark)

Companies have the benefit of continuity of existence, which makes it easier to pass the company on to other people (2 marks), whereas partnerships legally end on the death or retirement of a partner (2 marks).

21 Community Development

Community development

Benefits/importance of community development

1. Employment

Creates employment and thereby increases spending in the local economy; 'spin-off jobs' are also created among suppliers and support services (e.g. transport, entertainment, etc.).

2. Promotes a culture of enterprise

Promotes an enterprise culture, encourages new ideas and attracts new businesses – and motivates entrepreneurs to set up business in the area.

3. Empowering the local community

Empowers local community and generates a sense of pride within the community. A community spirit is created, which generates growth and prosperity in the local area.

4. Skills development

Creates opportunities for personal and skills development (e.g. youth training, training for long-term unemployed).

5. Improves physical appearance of the area

(e.g. Tidy Towns Initiative).

Community initiatives

There are many agencies available to assist communities with community development projects.

exam focus

Community development is 'a voluntary effect to support and develop the social and economic activity of a local community for the benefit of the local community'.

exam focus

The agencies available to assist communities with community development projects are:

- County and city enterprise boards
- Rural development (Leader) programme
- FÁS
- Area partnership companies

County and city enterprise boards

℮° ENTERPRISE IRELAND

The 35 county and city enterprise boards were established to provide support for small businesses with ten employees or less.

CEBs provide direct grant support to new and existing enterprises and promote entrepreneurship.

Functions/services of county and city enterprise boards

1. Advice

Provide information and advice on how to go about setting up or expanding a small business venture.

2. Mentoring programmes

A mentor is an experienced business practitioner who provides advice to help decision-making and planning but does not become involved in the day-to-day management of the business.

The mentor's role is to listen, help identify problems and suggest solutions, and assist in drawing up a business plan.

The mentor advises in areas such as general management, production planning, marketing and distribution.

3. Financial supports

Priming grant – A priming grant is a business start-up grant available to micro enterprises within the first 18 months of start-up. The grant must not exceed 50% of the investment.

Feasibility study grant – Feasibility grants are designed to assist the promoter with researching market demand for a product or service and examining its sustainability.

4. Training programmes

To assist small business in meeting the challenges of starting a business, CEBs provide a range of training programmes, including sales/marketing courses, financial management training, management development courses, and e-commerce and IT skills training.

Rural development (leader) programme

Leader is a rural development programme funded by the EU and by the Irish government

Leader funding is administered by local companies who distribute grants within their areas.

The overall objective of the programme is to improve the quality of life in rural areas. This will be achieved by providing funding for the following types of projects:

- Creation of micro enterprises in rural community (e.g. food and craft enterprises).
- Encouraging rural tourism activities (e.g. marine tourism, development of walking routes).
- Village renewal and development (e.g. creation of amenity areas).

- Basic services for economy and rural population (e.g. youth cafes, community centres).
- Diversification into non-agricultural activities (e.g. waste tyre recycling services).

FÁS

FÁS is Ireland's national training and employment authority.

It provides a number of programmes to assist local community development.

FÁS Community Employment Programme

This is an employment and training programme which helps long-term unemployed re-enter the workforce.

The programme offers participants an opportunity to engage in useful work within their communities.

Voluntary organisations and public bodies may sponsor projects which are for community and public benefit.

The sponsor is provided with the finance to employ unemployed people.

Other functions of FÁS

- Training of skilled personnel for industry
- Recruitment service for job seekers
- Employers can find staff and list vacancies with FÁS
- Training programmes for apprentices to quality as craft people

Area partnership companies

There are 38 area partnership companies in the country. Their mission is to tackle social exclusion and disadvantage in urban areas. They offer a range of programmes, including:

- **Community Development Programme** – This programme supports people to come together to develop projects to tackle problems in their communities.
- **Enterprise Support Programme** – Provides a range of services to people who are long-term unemployed and interested in setting up their own business. These services include:
  - Advice and support on business planning and setting up business
  - Start your own business courses
  - Information and advice for all entrepreneurs

Examples of partnership companies include:

- Ballymun area partnership
- Bray area partnership
- Waterford area partnership

22 Business and the Economy

Economy

An economy is a system that uses the four factors of production to produce goods and services demanded by consumers.

Factors of production

Land – Natural resources available for production (e.g. land, forests, rivers, etc.). The payment for land is rent.

Labour – The human input in the production process. The payment for labour is wages/salaries.

Capital – Anything which is man-made and used in the production process (e.g. machinery buildings, factories used to produce goods and services). The payment for capital is interest.

Enterprise – Entrepreneurs organise the other factors of production to produce goods and services. Entrepreneurs are risk takers who set up a business. The payment for enterprise is profit.

Impact of economy on business

The performance of the economy affects business. The economy is affected by a number of economic variables.

Inflation

Inflation is defined as the 'sustained' increase in the general level of prices of goods and services in the economy as measured by the consumer price index.

exam focus

Important **economic variables** include:

- Inflation
- Interest rates
- Taxation
- Unemployment
- Exchange rates
- Grants/subsidies

Impact of High Inflation on Business	Benefits of Low Inflation on Business
1. Increase in the cost of production (e.g. raw materials).	1. Improved competitive position on international trade – more goods sold abroad.
2. Increased wage demands to keep up with rate of inflation.	2. Costs and wages will be more stable – lower wage demands.
3. Increase in selling price of goods/ services may lead to a fall in demand. Decline in sales/reduction in profit.	3. Higher consumer spending, increasing sales and profits.
4. Exports become less competitive because of increase in prices. Exports decrease.	4. Increased tax revenue for government – more VAT from increased spending.

Interest rates

The interest rate charged by a financial institution for a loan is the price that has to be paid for the use of the money by the borrower.

Impact of Increasing/High Interest Rates on Irish Business	Impact of Low Interest Rates on Irish Business
1. Increased cost of borrowing – expensive for people and business to borrow.	1. Businesses can borrow more easily – economic activity will increase.
2. Less investment/borrowing for expansion will be more expensive.	2. Encourages new investment as borrowing for expansion will be cheaper.
3. Reduced consumer spending means reduced sales and reduced profits.	3. Increased consumer spending means increased sales and increased profits.

Taxation

Tax is a compulsory contribution of money to the government and is paid by individuals and businesses.

Impact of High Taxes on Business	How Low Taxation Rates Can Help Business
1. Income tax (PAYE) has the effect of reducing wages/salaries – people have less disposable income, Leaving them with less incentive to work.	1. Lower PAYE/PRSI rates – employees have more incentive to work/more take lesser pay.
2. An indirect tax such as VAT increases the cost of goods and services business sales/profits fall.	2. Lower VAT rates – selling prices will be lower – more demand/more sales/more profits.

3. Corporation tax reduces company profit. Company has less money for investment/expansion. Less money for dividends to shareholders.	3. Lower corporation tax rates – companies will make more profit/more money for expansion/investment.
4. PRSI increases the cost of employing staff for business.	4. Lower PRSI rates/cost of employing staff is reduced.

Unemployment

Unemployment is the percentage of people in the labour force who are unable to find employment.

Impact of Rising Unemployment on Irish Economy	Impact of Low Unemployment on Irish Economy
1. More social welfare to be paid out by the government.	1. Wealth creation – more people have jobs and income.
2. Government revenue from taxation decreases, less PAYE/VAT.	2. Increased demand for goods and services – increased consumer spending.
3. Decrease in consumer spending/reduced sales/reduced profit.	3. More tax revenue for the government – PAYE, PRSI, VAT.
4. Possible higher taxes in the future to pay for increased government spending on social welfare.	4. Demand for labour may push up wages as firms must compete to attract skilled staff.
5. Workers become de-skilled if unemployed for a long time.	5. Greater immigration into the country.
6. Easier for businesses to find employees to fill job vacancies – wages will be lower.	

Exchange rates

The exchange rate is the price at which a currency can be exchanged for another (i.e. the price of the currency of one country in terms of the currency of another).

Impact of Exchange Rate on Business

Exchange rates have a significant impact on companies that export large amounts of their output and on companies that import large quantities of raw materials.

Impact of Increasing Value of Euro Against Other Currencies (If Euro increases against other currencies)	Impact of Decreasing Value of Euro Against Other Currencies (If Euro decreases against other currencies)
(A) EXPORTS Irish exports abroad will be more expensive and less competitive. Irish exporters will find it more difficult to sell goods abroad. Sales and profits decrease.	**(A) EXPORTS** Irish exports abroad will be cheaper. Irish exporters will find it easier to sell goods abroad. Sales and profits increase.
(B) IMPORTS Price of imported goods will decrease. Irish people will buy more foreign goods. Irish firms will pay less for raw materials from abroad – reducing business costs.	**(B) IMPORTS** Price paid for imports will increase. Irish people will buy more Irish goods. Irish firm will pay more for raw materials from abroad.

Grants and subsidies

Grants

Grants are non-repayable amounts of finance provided by the government and the EU to a business to promote enterprise and expansion.

Grants are often given to businesses to encourage them to locate in areas of greatest need (e.g. Gaeltacht areas or particularly underdeveloped areas with high unemployment).

Subsidies

A subsidy is a price support given by the government to a business to allow it to sell it products at a price below the market price.

Subsidies are designed to increase the production of (or reduce the price of) goods or services that are deemed to be essential.

Example: A subsidy to CIE to help provide a reasonably-priced public transport system.

Impact of business activity on the development of the Irish economy

Business by providing goods and services affects the economy at local and national level. It affects employment, tax revenue and the environment.

Employment

Business creates jobs in all sectors of the economy, which means less unemployment and reduced social welfare payments.

Tax revenue

There will be an increase in tax revenue:

- PAYE – because more people are employed
- VAT – because extra goods and services are purchased
- Corporation tax – because increased business leads to increased profit

Environmental costs

An increase in business may have a negative impact on the environment, including industrial pollution, illegal dumping, water and air pollution.

Creation of wealth

Business activities create profit for entrepreneurs and wages for employees. This wealth builds up into assets over time and living standards are greatly improved.

Profit re-invested

Much of the profit of business is re-invested for expansion, eventually leading to more jobs and increased output. New premises, plant and machinery are provided for the future development of the business.

23 Government and Business

Why does the government intervene in business?

The government intervenes in business for a number of reasons:

1. Essential services

Provides essential services to all parts of the country irrespective of profitability (e.g. health, education, security).

2. Government regulations

Sets down rules and regulations to be observed by business and society (e.g. Companies Act) and regulates the formation and operation of companies.

3. Protects consumers and employees

Through legislation the government protects consumers (e.g. Sale of Goods and Supply of Services Act 1980) and employees (e.g. Employment Equality Act 1998).

4. Provides infrastructure

Government capital expenditure provides the state's infrastructure (roads, railways, airports) so that the economy can operate efficiently.

5. Promotes enterprise and employment

Government promotes enterprise and employment through state agencies (e.g. Enterprise Ireland is responsible for the development of indigenous industry).

6. Develops natural resources

State companies have been set up to develop the natural resources of the country (e.g. Bord na Móna, Bord Gáis).

Government's role in creating a suitable climate for business

Businesses in the economy need a suitable climate in which they can operate. It is the role of the government to create this climate by providing the right conditions.

1. Taxation system

The tax system could be used to create a positive climate for business.

PAYE

- Reduction in PAYE rates should increase spending and stimulate demand for goods and services.
- An increase in PAYE rates could fund business supports (e.g. grants or a reduction in employers PRSI).

Tax credits

- An increase in tax credits will reduce people's tax liability and may stimulate demand for goods and services.

VAT/excise duties

- Reduction in VAT, reduces cost of goods and services, stimulates demand – makes the Irish economy more competitive.

Corporation tax

- A reduction in corporation tax may improve company profits and the ability to fund future growth of business.

Stamp duty

- Changes may re-stimulate demand in the construction sector.

2. Government expenditure

- **Capital spending** on roads, hospitals, communications improves the infrastructure of the country, boosts the construction sectors and allows business to function more efficiently.
- **Current spending** on goods and services creates business for firms supplying these goods and services.

3. Government agencies

Government agencies play an important role in encouraging a climate for business through the many services they provide. These agencies include:

- **County and city enterprise boards** – provide grants and supports to micro enterprises.
- **Enterprise Ireland** – provides grants and incentives to indigenous firms.
- **IDA Ireland** – provides grants and incentives to encourage foreign firms to locate in Ireland.
- **FÁS** – Provides training to ensure a skilled workforce is available to meet the future needs of business.

4. Government planning

National pay deals agreed between the government and the social partners create a suitable climate for business in the following ways:

- **Reasonable wages** – increases ensures that business costs are controlled.
- **Industrial relations** in the country is improved.

Businesses can plan ahead because they know their future wage costs.

5. Economic policies

- **Low interest rates** will allow business and individuals to borrow more easily. Demand for goods and services will increase.
- **Low inflation** keeps prices down, leading to increased demand for goods and services.
- **Low unemployment** will increase demand for goods and services.

Government's role in regulating business

The government must regulate business in order to ensure that employees and consumers' rights are safeguarded and the environment is protected. It regulates business through legislation and state agencies, including:

1. Health and Safety Authority (HSA)

Responsible for ensuring health and safety at work.

2. National Consumer Agency

Ensures that all businesses obey consumer legislation.

Informs consumers of their rights.

3. Data Protection Agency

Protects the public against misuse of data in manual or electronic format.

4. Environmental Protection Agency (EPA)

Monitors businesses to ensure that they do not damage the environment and prosecutes offenders.

5. Companies Act 1990

Governs the operation of all companies in Ireland.

The Irish government and the labour force in Ireland

The Irish government affects the labour force in Ireland in a number of ways:

- **As an employer** – The Irish government is the single largest employer, employing 250,000 public servant workers (civil service, state bodies). Pay cuts of 5% to 15% introduced in the budget in 2010 led to industrial unrest/disputes. There is currently an embargo on recruitment.
- **Taxation policies** – Low rates of **income tax** will result in consumers having more disposable income, therefore spending more money on goods and services. This creates a demand for these goods and services, leading to increased production and job creation.
- **Corporation tax** – Corporation tax remaining at 12.5% means that more foreign companies may locate/remain in Ireland and offer employment. It also encourages Irish entrepreneurs to set up in Ireland and create jobs.
- **Infrastructure** – Government investment in the country's infrastructure (building of new motorways, schools, hospitals, etc.) leads to an increase in the number of

workers employed in the construction industry. It encourages other businesses to operate here in Ireland and thereby increases employment.

- **Increased spending on education/training** – Government investments in the education of the Irish labour force through training schemes, short-term courses, and upskilling programmes will result in a more skilled, educated and employable work force.
- **Grants and incentives** – Given to foreign companies to locate in Ireland will result in foreign industry providing employment to the Irish labour force.
- **Entrepreneurship** – The Irish government encourages the development of enterprise through supports provided by CEBs, Business Innovation Centres, etc.

Privatisation

Privatisation is the sale of shares in a state-owned enterprise to the private sector (i.e. selling state businesses to private investors on the stock exchange)
The business would then be owned and controlled by shareholders, just like any other business enterprise.
Example: Aer Lingus was privatised in 2006.

Arguments in favour of privatisation of state enterprises

1. Government revenue
Selling off a state company provides the government with a large amount of money (e.g. Aer Lingus privatised in 2006).

2. Reduced government expenditure
The sale of a loss-making enterprise means it will no longer have to be subsidised on a yearly basis by the government, which means less borrowing.

3. Access to finance
Privatised firms are able to take out loans and sell shares and generally have greater access to sources of finance than state enterprises. This makes it easier to finance expansion.

4. Efficiency
State-owned firms are often perceived as being inefficient because they can rely on government funding and have little competition. Private firms are driven by profit motive and should therefore be more efficiently run.

5. Competition
The elimination of a state monopoly can result in open market competition and can lead to greater choice and lower prices for consumers.

Arguments against privatisation of state enterprises

1. Loss of state assets

Privatisation results in a loss of state assets and a loss of future profit to the state.

2. Increased unemployment

There may be a loss of jobs through rationalisation of services leading to higher social welfare spending.

3. Loss of essential services

Non-profit-making essential services may be discontinued by the private business in an effort to reduce costs (e.g. postal, electricity, gas and water, and transport services to remote areas).

4. Profit motive

Privatised companies must maximise returns to shareholders and this could result in increased prices for consumers.

5. Loss of control

The share of privatised firms may end up with foreign investors. Profit from successful enterprises may end up in foreign hands instead of being available to the citizens of Ireland.

 **The Social Responsibility of Business**

 Be able to:

- Identify important environmental issues in business.
- Define ethical business practice.
- Describe the characteristics of an environmentally conscious company.
- Analyse the impact of environmental issues on business.
- Discuss the social responsibilities of business.
- Evaluate the effects on a firm's costs of meeting its ethical, social and environmental responsibilities.

Business ethics

Business ethics are moral principles that govern the actions of individuals or groups of business people. They are the guiding principles like honesty and fairness on how to act in business situations.

Ethical business practice involves conducting business guided by a set of moral principles that govern the actions of an individual or group in certain circumstances.

A **code of ethics** is a formal written statement setting out the behaviour expected from a business in its dealings with employees, customers and the community in which it operates.

Social responsibility of business

The social responsibility of a business is its duty and obligation to treat all those with whom it comes into contact with justice, fairness and honesty.

Social responsibilities of business
'Business is not only about doing things right, it is also about doing the right things.'
Discuss the social responsibilities that a business has to its various stakeholders.

(20 marks)

Source: 2009 Higher Level Section 3

Suggested solution
Business has an obligation to act ethically in its interaction with its various stakeholders and the wider community.

All business practice with shareholders, employees, customers, government, suppliers and the general public should be guided by the principles of honesty, equity, transparency and environmental consciousness.

Social Responsibility to Shareholders/Investors (1 Mark)	Social Responsible to Customers (1 Mark)
Provide a fair return on the investment by shareholders. (2 marks)	Provide goods of merchantable quality and fit for purpose. (2 marks)
Present a true and fair view of the financial performance of the business. (2 marks)	Deal with customers complaints seriously. (2 marks) Use fair and honesty advertising. Abide by health and safety regulations.
To act in accordance with the memorandum and articles of association.	Produce safe and reliable products at reasonable prices.
Social Responsibility to Employees (1 mark)	**Social Responsibility to Government (1 mark)**
Pay fair wages to all employees. (2 marks)	Adhere to all relevant legislation, company law, equality legislation. (2 marks)
Provide a safe working environment. (2 marks)	Pay taxes due, VAT income tax, corporation tax. (2 marks)
Treat all employees with dignity and respect – no discrimination.	Be co-operative with government, agencies (e.g. EPA).
Provide equal opportunities for promotion to all employees.	
Adhere to employment and health and safety regulations.	
	Social Responsibility to Suppliers
	Treat all suppliers fairly. Pay amounts agree within the time agreed. Honouring contracts.

Marking scheme
- 4 stakeholders @ 5 marks each
- 1 mark – Stakeholder
- 2 marks – Point of information
- 2 marks – Point of information

How business can be socially responsible

1. Making it an objective

Business should make social responsibility an objective when preparing their mission statement.

2. Code of ethics

Develop and promote a code of ethics within the company, setting out guidelines to management and staff the standards of behaviour expected of them when acting on behalf of the company.

3. Obeying legislation

Working closely with the EPA and obeying regulations regarding pollution, etc.

4. Consultation with stakeholders

When developing policies that affect the environment.

5. Community involvement:

Getting involved in the community (e.g. by sponsoring clubs, providing facilities for schools, etc.)

Environmental issues facing businesses

1. Pollution

Pollution means introducing into the environment chemical substances that endanger human health and form the environment.

Business must minimise polluting the air and water.

2. Climate change

The burning of fossil fuels in factories and businesses and emissions from vehicles causes greenhouse gases such as carbon dioxide being released into the atmosphere. This traps heat and causes the Earth's temperature to rise, leading to hurricanes, melting glaciers, rising sea levels, floods and drought.

Businesses and individuals can contribute to the solution of this problem by using cleaner fuels, recycling waste, reducing car emissions and using renewable forms of energy to reduce 'greenhouse gases'.

3. Waste management

Business has a responsibility to minimise the amount of waste it produces.

Business and individuals must find ways to reduce, reuse and recycle as much of their waste as possible.

Example: A company in County Cork recycles waste rubber tyres into shredded rubber for use in a variety of markets, including equestrian surfaces, garden/landscaping markets, playgrounds, sports facilities.

4. Sustainable development

This refers to a form of development that meets present-day needs without compromising the ability of future generations to satisfy their own needs.

Example: Using renewable energy resources (such as wind and solar power) instead of fossil fuels (such as coal, oil, and gas), which are not renewable.

HL

Environmentally responsible business

'As global warming becomes a reality for the world there is an increasing concern for the protection of the environment.'

Illustrate how businesses in Ireland today could become more environmentally responsible.

(20 marks)

Source: 2008 Higher Level Section 3

Suggested solution

1. **Control/reduce pollution**

   Control/reduce pollution – by implementing cleaner policies.

   Air Pollution – ensuring that factory emissions do not pollute the air.

   Example: Burning less fossil fuel, replacing CFCs with alternatives.

   Water Pollution – No effluent or chemicals discharged into water systems.

   Noise Pollution – Keeping noise levels to a minimum.

2. **Proper disposal methods**

   Developing environmentally acceptable disposal methods – no illegal dumping.

   Example: Encouraging the use of sorting systems for paper, clothes, plastic, etc. and recycling whenever possible.

3. **Consultation**

   Consult with local community groups and environmental bodies to ensure consensus.

   Example: Set up environmental consulting committee to listen to the concerns of local people.

4. **Cleaner machinery**

   Invest in machinery that reduces discharges into the environment.

   Example: Buy only energy-efficient equipment /machinery.

5. **Environmental impact assessment**

   Business should prepare an environmental impact assessment before commencing any new developments. This assesses the impact of the project or development on the environment and identifies steps that can be taken to minimise any negative impacts.

Marking scheme

- 4 points @ 5 marks (2 + 3)

Characteristics of an environmentally conscious business

Consultation

Engages in consultation with all the interested parties when developing and implementing policies that affect the environment.

Honesty

Tells the truth and is above-board in all matters affecting the environment. Environmentally conscious businesses are not afraid to have their affairs examined, as they generally have nothing to hide (e.g. it does not hide industrial accidents).

Awareness of environmental issues

Promotes environmental issues among its employees, customers and the business community and spends money on these issues. Regular communication and engagement with staff to increase awareness and promoting positive behaviours with regard to the environment.

Openness to development of new product design/clean manufacturing processes/recycling

Designs products that are durable and capable of maximum possible lifespan/helps to reduce energy consumption/waste.

Uses parts that can be recycled/safely disposed/avoiding environmentally sensitive materials/pollution prevention. Continually reducing the impact of its products on the environment through improved recycling and reuse programmes.

Sensitive to all environmental considerations in its policy-making

Conducts environmental audits (environmental impact statements) to assess the impact of their business on the environment.

Compliant with the law

Conducts business with integrity and complies with the environmental laws and regulations. Seeks advice from the EPA to ensure compliance.

Engages in sustainable development

Takes into account the needs of future generations when using national resources. Businesses should adopt an environmentally-friendly approach when using natural resources. This is especially important because of the potential for climate change. Greater use could be made of wind and sunshine to create energy, and businesses should use this energy more efficiently (e.g. CFC bulbs).

Effects of meeting ethical, social and environmental responsibilities on a firm's revenue and costs

Effects on revenue

- A firm's revenues should increase as a result of being socially responsible.
- Environmentally-conscious customers will always support businesses that are socially responsible, so sales and profits will increase.
- Firms that market their products using ethical business practices as their unique selling point are likely to attract more customers, increasing sales and profits.

Two examples:

- The Body Shop's unique selling point is that its products are not tested on animals.
- Food companies that sell *'organic' products* attract more customers, thereby increasing sales and profits. Glenisk Ltd, Tullamore, Co Offaly, produce a range of organic dairy products where raw materials are processed without the use of pesticides or synthetic fertilizers.

Effects on costs

Costs may be **increased** initially due to:

- Higher wages and better conditions for employees – proper training, etc. will increase labour costs.
- Using environmentally-friendly raw materials and packaging may be more expensive, leading to increases in the cost of production.
- The cost of installing special equipment to reduce noise, pollution and emissions will increase costs.
- Developing codes of practice and compliance with legislative requirements will increase costs.
- The safe disposal of dangerous and toxic waste has a cost.

In the long term, costs may be **reduced** due to:

- Using cleaner technologies and systems will reduce costs and insurance premiums.
- Using renewable energy rather than non-renewable energy may reduce costs over time.

Applied Business Question (ABQ) (Higher Level)

Based on Units 4, 5 and 6
This is a compulsory question for Leaving Certificate 2012/2017

McGComputers

(HL)

McGComputers was founded in 1986 by Jason McGinley. It is an independent firm specialising in the sale and repair of computers, operating from a premises fronting onto the main street of a large town. Jason had worked a standard five-day week in his previous job, as a qualified engineer, with a transnational computer company. The new venture forced him to adjust to working long and irregular hours, and to manage with limited financial resources. The change also meant a review of his commitments to health and life plans, and the provision of his home as security. While his formal bookkeeping skills were limited, he maintained details of all customers and their transactions.

Responding to published official forecasts and trade publications, Jason recruited sales people and qualified technicians to serve the client base and expand the product range of the firm. He encouraged the staff to engage with customers and to note their reactions to new ideas and products. His reliance on trust in the staff has been successful in that only one employee has had to be dismissed for theft. McGComputers is now well established with twelve full-time employees and five service vehicles on the road. It regularly hosts product presentations and demonstrations on its premises for representative sections of its customer base.

Siobhán, Jason's daughter and a recent business graduate, has joined the firm. Siobhán would like to add other services such as website design and maintenance, training and consultancy, and has held focused discussions with groups of customers. This has led Jason to consider reorganising the firm and leaving the day-to-day running with Siobhán. Overall policy control would rest with him, supported by a limited number of reward-seeking investors.

(A) Discuss the methods of market research currently used in the business and how these could be developed. (20 marks)

(B) Describe the types of insurance appropriate to the context described above. (30 marks)

(C) Evaluate McGComputers as a type of business organisation with appropriate recommendations. (30 marks)

(80 marks)

Suggested solution

(A) Market research techniques currently used and development of methods to achieve sales

Market research is the gathering, in a systematic way, of important and relevant information about specific market features and trends. Market research gathers information on:

- The number of customers in the market, their spending patterns etc.
- Customer likes and dislikes, opinions on why a product is preferred etc.

It reduces risk for a business and allows the business to plan for the future with reasonable confidence.

Methods of market research are desk research and field research.

- ***Desk Research*** – Desk (Secondary) research involves using information that is already available within a business or from outside sources.
  - **Internal sources** – Information from within a business includes: sales figures and salespersons' reports on file. The study of these sources from the firm's files will help to locate the most and least successful products, any changes that have taken place and trends for the future. The research will reveal the nature of the problem.

Link to text

He maintained details of all customers and their transactions.

- **External sources** – Information from outside sources includes: magazines, reports, government statistics/publications, Internet, newspapers, trade directories/publications.

Link to text

Responding to published official forecasts and trade publications.

How it could be developed

Desk research could be developed by using the Internet and online surveys to obtain information on the market and their competitors.

Link to text

website design.

Field research – Field (primary) research involves making contact with people in the market, mainly by means of interview and the use of questionnaires. Methods of field research include interviews, surveys, customer panels and observation.

- Surveys – The main purpose of surveys is to determine from the responses how consumers in general will react to new products. The survey is usually conducted by telephone or by post. They require that potential customers are actually interviewed by researchers and the responses recorded.

- Customer panels – questionnaires must be prepared in such a way that the information acquired is useful and relevant. The questionnaires are completed by members of the public at large, randomly selected or by certain sections of the public who are specially selected.
- Observation – Observe and watching the reactions of individuals.

Link to text

He encouraged staff to engage with customers and to note their reactions to new ideas and products.

How it could be developed

Field research could be developed by seeking feedback from customers.

Link to text

McGComputers regularly hosts product presentations and demonstrations on its premises for representative sections of its customer base.

If they conduct surveys using questionnaires they will get valuable information from customers.

Link to text

Siobhán has held focused discussions with groups of customers.

Marking scheme

(A)	Methods of market research Relevant to the text of ABQ	2 @ 10 marks (2 + 6 (3 + 3) +2)	20 marks

(B) Types of appropriate insurance

Appropriate types of insurance include:

   (i) **Motor insurance** (2 marks)

     Motor insurance commercial policies include third party and comprehensive. (2 marks)

     Link to text

     five service vehicles on the road (2 marks)

  (ii) **Property insurance** (2 marks)

     Fire is covered by fire policies on both premises and stock, smoke and water damage. (2 marks)

     Link to text

     operating from a premises fronting onto the main street of a large town (2 marks)

 (iii) **Fidelity guarantee** (2 marks)

     Covers dishonesty of employees. Against theft of cash or stock. (2 marks)

     Link to text

     one employee has had to be dismissed for theft (2 marks)

(iv) **Public liability** (2 marks)

Protects company in the event of accidents to members of the public on company premises. (2 marks)

Link to text

hosts product presentations and demonstrations on its premises. (2 marks)

(v) **Employers liability** (2 marks)

Protects company against claims by employees due to accidents at work. (2 marks)

Jason recruited sales people and qualified technicians (2 marks)

Marking scheme

(B)	Types of insurance Must have reference to text of ABQ	5 @ 6 m each (2 + 2 + 2)	30 marks

(C) Evaluation of the type of business organisation

Sole Trader

A **Sole Trader** is a person who owns and runs his own business.

(i) **Ownership/management**

A Sole Trader is a person who owns and runs a business enterprise under his/her own name or under a business name.

Link to text

McGComputers was founded in 1986 by Jason McGinley, independent firm.

(ii) **Lack of capital**

There is limited capital available for expansion in the future.

Link to text

new venture, manage with limited financial resources

(iii) **Unlimited liability**

The owner must bear all the risk of possible business losses and is personally liable for all debts of the enterprise in the event of it having to close down.

Link to text

provision of his home as security.

(iv) **Long working hours**

The owner usually works full-time in the business.

Link to text

The new venture forced him to adjust to working long and irregular hours

(v) **Owner makes all the decisions**

The owner can make quick business decisions, however, there are limited skills to draw on.

Link to text

His formal bookkeeping skills were limited

(C)	Type of business organisation Sole Trader Relevant to text of ABQ	15 marks – 5 @ 3 m each (3 + 3 + 3 + 3 + 3)	**15 marks**

Recommendation: Private limited company

A **private limited company** is a business enterprise with 1 to 99 shareholders.

(i) Ownership/management

By converting to a private limited company, the business can have up to 99 shareholders.

Link to text

Supported by limited number of reward-seeking investors.

(ii) Availability of capital

A private limited company will give Jason access to additional capital. It is often easier to raise finance from financial institutions. Companies in general are given a higher credit rating by suppliers of finance.

Link to text

Limited number of investors

(iii) Limited liability

Shareholders are extended the status of limited liability. His private assets are protected. This is particularly important to the small investor who may stand to lose all if things go wrong (e.g. if the enterprise was a sole trader).

Link to text

This has led Jason to consider reorganising the firm

(iv) Shared workload

The tasks of managing and controlling the operations of the company can be divided among a team of personnel.

Link to text

Overall policy control would rest with Jason while leaving day-to-day running with Siobhán

Marking scheme

Recommendation Private limited company Relevant to the text of ABQ	15 marks – 5 @ 3 m each (3 + 3 + 3 + 3 + 3)	**15 marks**

UNIT 7

International Environment

Ireland is open to economic, social and cultural trends from abroad, and the international environment has a significant impact on Irish business. This unit introduces the international trading environment and describes developments in international business. It also deals with Ireland's membership of the European Union.

Objective

To enable students to understand the opportunities and challenges facing Irish business in the international environment.

- **Chapter 25:** Introduction to the International Trading Environment
- **Chapter 26:** The European Union
- **Chapter 27:** International Business

Introduction to the International Trading Environment

Be able to:

- Explain the significance of international trade to the Irish economy.
- Discuss the changing nature of the international economy and its effects on Irish business.
- Discuss the opportunities and challenges facing Irish business in developed and developing markets.

Ireland as an open economy

An open economy is an economy that engages in international trade and is importing and exporting. Ireland has a small open economy that engages in international trade. Nearly 80% of what is produced in Ireland is exported.

This impacts on Ireland's economic development as follows:

- Creates employment.
- Earns foreign currency for the country.
- Generates revenue for the government.
- Helps economic growth.
- Enables essential raw materials and finished goods to be imported.
- Offers wider choice and lower prices to consumers.

International trade

This is trade between countries. It involves exporting and importing goods and services.

Exporting

Exporting is producing goods and services in one country and selling them to another country.

- **Visible exports** are **physical goods** sold to other countries and resulting in an inflow of cash (e.g. agricultural products produced in Ireland and sold abroad, such as beef exported to the UK and lamb exported to France).
- **Invisible exports** are **services** sold by one country to other countries. This includes activities that bring money into the country. In the case of Ireland, this includes:
  - Foreign students coming to Ireland to learn English during the summer.
  - Irish musicians performing abroad.

Importing

Importing is buying goods and services from a foreign country, which means money goes out of the country.

- **Visible imports** are **physical goods** bought from other countries, such as:
  - Cars from Germany.
  - Wine from South Africa.
  - Leather shoes from Italy.
- **Invisible imports** are **services** bought from other countries, which means that Irish money goes to a foreign country:
  - Irish people going on holiday to Spain.
  - Foreign musicians performing in Ireland.

International trade is measured by:

- Balance of trade
- Balance of payments

Measuring international trade

- **Balance of trade**
  - If visible exports are greater than visible imports, there is a **surplus** in balance of trade.
  - If visible exports are less than visible imports, there is a **deficit** in the balance of trade.

Balance of trade = visible exports − visible imports

- **Balance of payments**
  - The balance of payments is the difference between the value of **total exports** (visible and invisible) and the value of **total imports** (visible and invisible). It is expressed as a surplus or deficit.

Balance of payments = total exports − total imports

  - It is the amount of money coming into a country minus money going out of a country during the course of a year.

Using the following information, calculate:

(i) Balance of trade

(ii) Balance of payments

Total imports	€16 billion
Invisible exports	€11 billion
Total exports	€19 billion
Invisible imports	€9 billion

(8 marks)

Source: 2006 Higher Level Section A

Suggested solution
(i) Balance of trade: **€1 billion**
(ii) Balance of payments: **€3 billion**

Workings
Visible exports = €19B − €11B = €8 billion
Visible imports = €16B − €9B = €7 billion
Balance of trade = visible exports − visible imports
= €8 billion (2) − €7 billion (2)
= €1 billion (1)
Balance of Payments = Total exports − Total imports
= 19 billion (1) − €16 billion (1)
= €3 billion (1)

Reasons for exporting

1. Domestic market is too small; Irish firms have to export to expand, to increase sales and profits and survive.
2. To spread the business risk by not relying on local markets only.
3. Irish firms can avail of economies of scale from large-scale production by going on to the export market. This means a lower cost of production and a more competitive price, resulting in increased sales and more profits.

Reasons for importing

1. There is a lack of raw materials for industry (e.g. oil).
2. The climate is unsuitable for the production of certain products (e.g. bananas).
3. Customers want choice and variety (e.g. Italian shoes, French wines).
4. Certain finished goods demanded by consumers cannot be produced here (e.g. Japanese cars).

The significance of international trade to Irish economy

1. **Comparative advantage**: Some countries have an advantage and a tradition of certain skills in producing goods and services (e.g. food production in Ireland). Surpluses of these products can be exported in exchange for imports of essential raw materials required for production (e.g. oil).
2. **Variety and choice**: Trade allows consumers to enjoy a wide choice and variety of goods that cannot be produced here because of climate or lack of essential factors of production (e.g. fruit, food products).

3. **Economies of scale**: Large-scale production through exporting allows for economies of scale. This means lower costs of production and a more competitive price with increased sales and profit.

4. **Economic growth**: International trade allows countries like Ireland with small home markets to achieve growth through exports. It provides foreign markets for Irish produce. By selling abroad, foreign currency is earned, which is used to pay for the imports people in Ireland need.

5. **Increased efficiency**: International trade increases competition. Production is more efficient, which means lower prices for consumers.

Free trade and protectionism

Free trade

This means there are no barriers to the movement of goods and services between countries. Free trade exists between EU member countries.

Protectionism

This is setting up **barriers to trade** to reduce imports to the country, to protect home industry from foreign competition, and to protect jobs. Barriers to trade include:

- **Tariffs** – Taxes or duties on imported goods to make them more expensive and they will be less competitive on the domestic market.
  - They encourage consumers to buy more home-produced goods.
- **Quotas** – A limit on the quantity of goods that can be imported/exported.
  - Quotas discourage imports and/or encourage sales of domestically-produced goods.
- **Embargos** – A ban on importing of specified goods from particular countries.
- **Subsidies**, which are payments by governments to firms to reduce cost of production, allow them to sell goods at a more competitive price on export markets.

Changing trends in the international economy and their impact on Irish businesses

1. **Global recession**: Here and internationally, the financial system remains crippled in the wake of the credit crunch and, in our case, write-offs relating to property loans.

Impact: Dell, like most major companies, has been hit by the international recession and is looking for ways to make the company more competitive. It can manufacture computers more cheaply in Poland.

2. **The International Banking Crisis** has triggered a worldwide recession. Irish businesses' confidence about future prospects for business has fallen. The worldwide banking crisis has had a broad impact on Irish businesses as they face higher financing costs.

Impact: Difficulty in getting credit (e.g. bank overdrafts and loans).

3. **Deregulation** has increased competition in the market place and reduced protectionism i.e. removal of trade barriers. Irish businesses now need to be more competitive as they face competition from larger foreign companies. They need to produce top quality goods and services at competitive prices in order to survive. In Ireland deregulation allows new business to enter the market place and offer Irish consumers value for their money.

Impact: Deregulation of the **electricity** and **airline** sectors has offered choices and value for money for Irish businesses.

4. **The growth in trading blocs and agreements:** The EU is an example of a trading bloc which allows free trade among its members. Being a member, Ireland can trade freely with other countries in the EU without any barriers or restrictions.

Impact: This offers a wider market place (495 million) for Irish foods and services due to the growth in membership.

5. **The World Trade Organisation** is the body responsible for promoting fair trade between countries. It negotiates between member states by encouraging deregulation and the removal of barriers to trade.

Impact: This allows for huge sales opportunities abroad for Irish businesses.

6. **The European Union/enlarging the European Union:** As countries in Eastern Europe join the EU, opportunities arise for Irish business to promote their goods and services abroad.

Impact: There is a huge population in these countries and a demand for Irish products and services.

7. **Emerging countries/new market opportunities:** Due to the growth of economies in the Pacific Rim (South Korea, China, Japan, Taiwan, Singapore, Thailand, Malaysia, Indonesia), new markets have emerged. These economies are developing rapidly; the Pacific Rim is the fastest-growing economic region in the world.

Impact: The Pacific Rim countries have provided both markets and competition for Irish businesses.

8. **The influence of transnational corporations (TNCs):** Some TNCs are more powerful than the country in which they operate. Ireland attracts these companies by offering tax incentives. (Ireland has a very low corporation tax rate of 12.5%.) TNCs often lobby governments and the EU to accept their conditions of trade. This enables them to trade with fewer restrictions.

Impact: There could be major consequences for the Irish economy if TNCs choose not to locate in Ireland as they are very large and employ significant numbers of workers (e.g. Pfizer, Boston Scientific).

9. **Technology**: The information and communications technology (ICT) sector has shown remarkable growth in recent years. ICT companies in Ireland are engaged in a range of activities (networks, software development, etc.)

Impact: E-commerce/business has enabled Irish businesses to advertise what they do worldwide. Developments in technology have allowed this to take place. Businesses are now in constant contact with companies around the globe.

10. **Competition**: Eastern Europe countries such as the Czech Republic, Hungary and Slovakia have opened up their economies to market forces.

Impact: This presents a particular challenge for Ireland as these countries are excellent producers of agricultural products and can offer quality at a lower price to the European consumer.

11. **Growth in globalisation**: Treating the world as one single market place for standardised products is seen in Ireland today. The use of the Internet and TV has helped businesses to develop global brands by advertising and promoting them around the world (e.g. Sony, McDonald's, Toyota, Coca-Cola).

Impact: Irish firms need to be able to compete in the world markets.

Opportunities and challenges in international trade

International trade – opportunities for Irish businesses

1. **Access to larger markets**

   EU membership gives Irish firms access to a market of 500 million consumers. This large market allows Irish firms to expand and grow, which would not be possible with the small Irish home market.

2. **Economies of scale**

   Because of large-scale production for many markets, Irish firms can benefit from economies of scale, which allow us to compete with products from low-cost economies.

3. **Earn foreign currency**

   International trade allows Irish businesses to export into foreign countries and earn foreign currency. This money can be used to pay for imports of essential raw materials and finished goods required by the Irish economy.

4. **Highly-skilled workforce**

Ireland possesses a well-educated and highly-skilled workforce. Many Irish people have obtained valuable experience through engaging in international trade. This creates opportunities for Irish businesses as they have a pool of experienced people from which to recruit.

5. **Ireland's green image**

Ireland's image abroad as a green, healthy and environmentally-friendly country is particularly helpful when marketing abroad, particularly in relation to Ireland's tourism and food industries.

6. **English – a language of trade**

English is an important international trading language and gives Ireland an advantage when doing business internationally.

7. **Free trade and markets**

As trade restrictions are abolished and as access to new and existing markets emerges, Ireland is finding that international trade provides huge opportunities for increased sales and profit.

International trade – challenges faced by Irish businesses

1. **Competition**

International competition requires companies to acquire greater efficiency and to improve quality and standards in order to survive in domestic and export markets.

2. **High cost base**

Ireland is an economy with a high cost base for raw materials, labour and insurance. This makes it difficult for Irish firms to compete against businesses from low-cost economies. Irish firms must produce high-quality products in order to compete on international markets.

3. **Distribution costs**

Because of Ireland's location on the edge of Europe, distribution costs for exports are high, making Irish products less competitive. A similar problem exists in relation to raw materials imported into Ireland.

4. **Different language, customs, cultures in other countries**

Possessing competency in multiple languages is important for firms that want to successfully engage in international trade. Firms must also consider the customs and cultures of different countries when marketing products abroad.

5. **Payment difficulties**

There may be problems getting paid for exports. Problems collecting debts are more difficult when dealing in foreign markets.

6. **Cost of adapting products to meet international standards and regulations**

Products being exported from Ireland may have to be adapted to satisfy safety laws and other international standards and regulations in foreign markets. Different climates around the world may require products to be adapted before being exported.

The role of information and communication technology (ICT) in international trade

1. **Marketing and access to global markets**

   The Internet allows Irish firms to market and sell their products through their websites to customers worldwide. For example, customers can place orders and make payments by credit card. This is called e-commerce.

2. **Instant communication**

   Instant communication with customers all over the world is made possible through the use of e-mail and mobile phones.

3. **Market research**

   The Internet allows Irish firms to carry out research and acquire up-to-date information on markets, size of populations, which helps them to make decisions regarding individual markets.

4. **Reduced costs – videoconferencing**

   Videoconferencing allows managers of international businesses to be in touch with people in different locations around the world in order to hold meetings and exchange up-to-date information to aid their decision-making. Videoconferencing is one tool that eliminates the need for staff to make expensive and time-consuming trips to attend meetings around the world.

Be able to:

- Name and describe the main institutions of the EU.
- Describe the decision-making process of the EU.
- Explain the role of special interest groups in the EU decision-making process.
- Explain the purpose of the main EU policies and directives.
- Identify the effects of the Single Market on Irish business.

Importance of European Union membership to Ireland

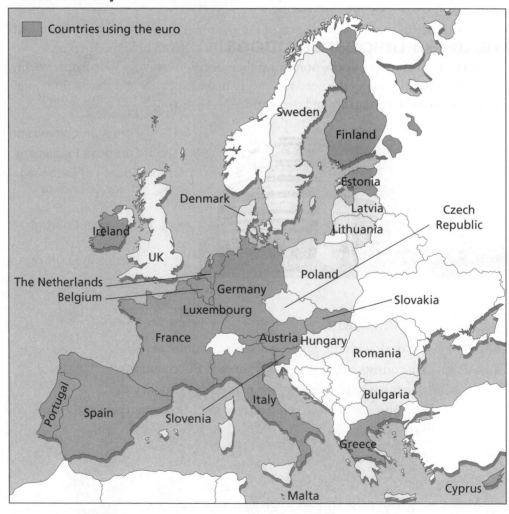

1. Large market
The EU is a trading bloc made up of 27 countries with a population of half a billion people. Irish firms have huge opportunities for exporting and expansion.

2. Free-trade area
The EU is a free-trade area where there is free movement of goods, services, capital and labour.

3. Economies of scale
The EU provides a huge market for the products of Irish firms. Economies of scale can be achieved through expansion into these markets.

4. EU grants and supports
The EU has given Ireland many grants to build infrastructure such as roads, airports, etc. Supports to Irish agriculture under the Common Agricultural Policy have increased farm incomes and improved living standards in Ireland.

5. Common currency
Countries in the Eurozone – including Ireland – have a single international currency, the Euro. This has made trade and travel easier and has eliminated the cost of currency conversion.

European Union institutions

exam focus

The main institutions of the EU are:

- European Commission
- European Parliament
- Council of European Union/Council of Ministers
- European Court of Auditors
- European Court of Justice

European Commission
The Commission deals with the day-to-day administration of the EU.

The Commission consists of one member from each EU country.

Each Commissioner has responsibility for a particular EU policy area.

The Commission must act in the best interests of the EU and independently of member states.

Functions of the European Commission
- Drafts proposals for new EU laws.
- Makes sure existing EU laws are implemented and obeyed.

- Implements agreed policies of EU (e.g. Common Agriculture Policy, Competition Policy).
- Manages and supervises the EU budget.
- Represents the EU internationally.

European Parliament

Members of European Parliament (MEPs) are elected by the citizens of the EU to represent their interests.

The parliament has 785 members from all 27 countries.

Functions of the European Parliament

- Discusses proposed new laws and proposes amendments.
- Approves the annual EU budget and monitors spending.
- Supervisory powers over other European institutions – vets members of the European Commission and votes on whether to accept the new Commission or not.

Council of European Union/Council of Ministers

The EU's main decision-making body – The Council must adopt all legislation before it becomes law.

The Council is comprised of ministers from the governments of each EU member state. The topic on the agenda determines which minister attends.

Most decisions are made by majority voting. However, unanimous agreement is required for certain issues (e.g. decisions affecting taxation or the entrance of new countries to join the EU).

Functions of the Council of Ministers

- To decide on legislation/to pass European laws – Most EU laws are passed jointly by the Council and the Parliament. (This is called 'co-decision'.)
- To approve the EU's budget – The EU annual budget is approved or rejected jointly by the Council and the Parliament.
- Officially signs a number of international agreements with international organisations.

European Court of Auditors

The Court of Auditors is based in Luxembourg. It has one member from each country appointed for a term of six years.

Functions of European Court of Auditors

- Checks that the EU budget is spent according to the regulations of the EU and for the purpose intended.
- Carries out spot checks on the budget to ensure that no fraud is taking place.
- Prepares an annual report certifying that the accounts are reliable and that the money has been properly used.

European Court of Justice

The Court of Justice is based in Luxembourg. It has one judge per member state.

Functions of the European Court of Justice

- Ensures that EU legislation is interpreted and applied in the same way in all EU countries so that the law is equal for everyone.
- Ensures that EU member state and institutions obey the law. It can impose fines on member states if they break the laws.
- Rules on disputes that come before it.

The decision-making process in the European Union

PROPOSAL STAGE

Proposals for a new law are drafted by the Commission.

CONSULTATION STAGE

Parliament debates the proposed new law and may propose amendments. The proposal is returned to the Commission for consideration.

REDRAFTING STAGE

If the Commission accepts these amendments it will send the redrafted law to the Council of Ministers and the Parliament.

APPROVAL STAGE

The Council of Ministers and Parliament jointly decide whether the proposal will become law. This is called 'co-decision'. If both accept the proposal, it becomes an EU law.

IMPLEMENTATION STAGE

EU laws are implemented by:
- Regulation
- Directive
- Decision

The decision-making process in the European Union

EU regulations

A regulation is an EU law which becomes immediately enforceable as law in all member states.

They take precedence over national laws.

They are self-executing and do not need any implementing measures.

Example: Regulation on single member private limited company formation.

EU directives

A directive provides an outline to member states of legislation to be achieved in a specific area by a given date.

It obliges member states to change their natural laws to allow for EU rules within a time limit.

The directive is binding on each state but the choice as to how to incorporate it into national legislation is left to the authorities in the member states.

Some directives that have on impact on business in Ireland include:

- The Nitrates Directive – directing the levels of fertilizer to be used on land by Irish farmers.
- The Waste Electrical and Electronic Equipment Directive – this directive states that retailers when supplying a new product, must accept back waste electrical and electronic equipment from households free of charge.

Decisions

Decisions are directed at specific member states' organisations or individuals. They are binding and must be carried out by the party involved.

The role of interest groups in EU decision-making

Interest group or pressure groups who protect the interests of their members and try to influence the decision-making of the EU.

They are not part of the EU's political framework but they use methods such as lobbying information campaigns and public protests in an attempt to influence EU decisions.

Example: The IFA has an office in Brussels to promote and defend the interests of Irish farmers in Europe.

European Union policies and their impact on business

Common policies have been adopted by the EU in many different areas:

Common Agricultural Policy

The common agricultural policy was introduced to make the European Union self sufficient in food and to improve farm incomes.

Since Ireland joined the EU, the Common Agricultural Policy has had a huge impact on Irish farming and agriculture and through those industries it had a massive influence on the Irish economy.

exam focus

The most important policies are:

- Common Agricultural Policy (CAP)
- Common Fisheries Policy (CFP)
- Competition Policy
- European Union Social Charter
- Economic and Monetary Union (EMU)
- Single European Market (SEM)

Impact of Common Agricultural Policy on Ireland

The objectives of the common agricultural policy were:

1. To make the EU self-sufficient in food

CAP aids the provision of safe, traceable food and ensures farmers continually improve their production standards.

> **Impact on Ireland**: Because of CAP, food production has been assured. Ireland is self-sufficient in food products and it is also a major exporter of food products to world markets. This also makes an important contribution to the balance of payments because of the big export market.

2. To improve farm incomes and to ensure a fair standard of living for the agricultural community

> **Impact on Ireland**: Through a series of payments to Irish farmers CAP has supported the Irish agricultural industry. There are about 130,000 farmers in Ireland. CAP introduced a system of direct payments to farmers through an annual single payment called the 'single payment scheme'. This provides income stability for members of the Irish farming community.

3. To increase productivity

> **Impact on Ireland**: CAP provided an opportunity for Irish farmers to Increase productivity. By providing grants for investment in new technology and farm improvements, agricultural productivity and efficiency has improved.

4. To stabilise markets and regulate prices

CAP stabilises agricultural markets and regulates prices so that farmers can be assured that there will not be huge fluctuations in prices they receive for their output.

> **Impact on Ireland**: Since joining the EU, Irish farmers have benefited from major funding from CAP.

5. To ensure reasonable prices for consumers

> **Impact on Ireland**: Irish consumers have a regular supply and choice of high quality products at reasonable prices, produced to the highest food safety and traceability standards.

6. To provide access to a large EU market

Thanks to the CAP Irish farmers have open access to one of the largest markets in the world. Agriculture makes a big contribution to Ireland's overall exports.

> **Impact on Ireland**: Access to EU markets has brought a lot of sales and profits to Irish farmers.

7. To preserve and restore rural infrastructure and villages

Impact on Ireland: This supports Ireland's tourism industry.

8. To benefit Irish agriculture from money from the structural funds.

Common Fisheries Policy (CFP)

The Common Fisheries Policy is an EU policy covering all aspects of fishing in the EU. The main provisions of the policy are:

1. **To support the incomes of those involved in the fishing industry**
   CFP aims to achieve this by:

   - Reserving access to Irish coastal waters to fishermen from local ports to a distance of 12 miles offshore. This prevents foreign boats from fishing in these areas.
   - Setting the price of fish at the start of each year, which guarantees Irish fishermen a decent income.
   - Providing grants for the modernisation of fishing boats and improving technology, which helps to increase catches and improves sales and profit.

   Impact on Ireland: The restructuring of the fishing industry in the EU has ensured better prices for efficient Irish fishermen and improves their income.

2. **To promote the conservation of Irish fish stocks**
   This policy is designed to protect fish stocks from overfishing.
   CFP aims to achieve this by:

   - Setting maximum quantities (quotas) of fish that can be caught each year.
   - Regulating the mesh size of nets to limit the catching of small fish.
   - Restricting fishing in certain areas to protect fish breeding grounds.

   Impact on Ireland: CFP protects the marine environment and helps conserve and improve fish stocks.

3. **To promote the marketing of fisheries products**
   CFP aims to achieve this by:

   - Implementing a marketing fisheries policy designed to stabilise markets, guarantee a steady supply of quality fish products at reasonable prices to Irish consumers, and support Irish fishermen.

   Impact on Ireland: This policy provides good quality food for Irish and EU consumers.

4. **To monitor fishing activity**
   The responsibility to ensure that all rules are applied rests with each member state (Ireland in this case).

Impact on Ireland: The EU provides aid to Ireland for the purchase of fishery protection vessels and aircraft for the authorities.

Competition Policy

The aim of the Competition Policy is to ensure that there is fair competition among businesses in the EU so that consumers get a choice of quality goods and services at reasonable prices (i.e. the existence of competition among suppliers).

It ensures that Irish businesses operate on a fair basis and that customers benefit.

The main areas of competition policy are:

1. **Cartels**

   This restricts Irish businesses from forming anti-competitive cartels which:

   - Fix prices or keep prices artificially high
   - Divide up the market
   - Prevent new firms entering the market

   Example: In 2007 members of the Irish Ford Dealers Association established a cartel to fix the selling price of motor vehicles which was in breach of competition law.

   Impact on Ireland:

   - Irish Consumers are assured of better choice, quality and prices of goods and services.
   - It is easier for new Irish firms to set up and compete in the market.

2. **Dominant position**

   Firms in a dominant position in the market cannot abuse that position to charge excessively high prices, restrict smaller competitors, or drive firms out of the market.

   Example: A dominant firm selling at low cost with the aim of eliminating competitors or making market entry more difficult.

   Impact on Ireland:

   - Abuse of dominant position by firms is eliminated.
   - Irish consumers are protected against firms that abuse their dominant position.
   - Smaller Irish firms cannot be forced out of the market by larger businesses.

3. **Mergers and takeovers**

   The European Commission has the power to control mergers and takeovers if it believes they would restrict competition or create a dominant position.

   Example: July 2010 Ryanair had their application to take over Aer Lingus in 2007 blocked by the European Court of Justice. The Court said the takeover would give Ryanair a dominant position, which would represent a monopoly adversely affecting consumers.

> **Impact on Ireland:** It protects consumers and the general public against mergers and takeovers that restrict competition, or create a monopoly or dominant position.

4. Monopolies

All monopolies must be deregulated to allow firms into the market. They must be open to competition.

Examples: The electricity market in Ireland has been open for competition. Prior to this, ESB operated a state-owned monopoly. At present, independent suppliers such as Airtricity and Energia are gaining a foothold in the Irish electricity market. The Irish telecommunications industry was also deregulated – the telecoms market was opened to competition.

> **Impact on Ireland:**
> - A number of Irish consumers have switched their service provider to avail of cheaper prices.
> - Competition in these sectors should ensure more choice, a better service and cheaper prices for consumers.

European Union social charter

The aim of the social charter is to protect the rights of workers in the European Union. It leads to better employment legislation and an improvement in workers' rights and protects them. The social charter proclaims the following rights:

1. The right to freedom of movement/the right to work in the EU country of one's choice

> **Impact on Ireland:**
> - Irish workers can live and work anywhere in the EU.
> - Irish firms can recruit workers from other EU countries.

2. The right to a fair wage

> **Impact on Ireland:**
> - All Irish workers must be paid the minimum wage. This provides employees with a reasonable standard of living.
> - Payment of the minimum wage increases business costs.

3. The right to equal treatment for men and women

Impact on Ireland: The policy has ensured greater equality of treatment for Irish men and women in the workplace.

4. The right to health protection, safety at work and improved working conditions

Impact on Ireland: The policy has improved working conditions for Irish workers through the introduction of a standard working week, holiday entitlements, health protection and safety of all employees at work.

5. The right to consultation and participation for workers

The right to participate and be consulted in decision-making.

Impact on Ireland: Irish employers must consult their workers about issues of concern to them in relation to their employment.

6. The right to vocational training

Impact on Ireland: The European Social Fund provides finance to train workers who are unemployed in order to provide them with opportunities to rejoin the workforce.

Economic and Monetary Union (EMU)

The policy of the Economic and Monetary Union is designed to meet two objectives:

- The introduction of a single currency – the Euro.
- The creation of a single monetary policy for the European Union to be implemented by the European Central Bank.

Benefits of EMU for Ireland

1. Reduced business costs

Irish firms will not have to pay bank charges for currency conversion when Irish firms deal with customers in Eurozone countries.

2. No exchange rate risks in the Eurozone

Irish firms exporting and importing within the Eurozone don't have to worry about changes in the exchange rate as all transactions are in Euro. This should lead to more trade between countries.

3. Price transparency

All goods and services are priced in Euro. Price comparisons between different countries have become easier for Irish consumers to make.

4. Lower interest rates

The ECB sets interest rates in the Eurozone. The ECB has kept interest rates low to reduce the cost of borrowing for individuals and businesses. This reduces costs and increases profit for businesses and reduces loan and mortgage repayments for individuals.

5. Lower inflation

The primary objective of the European Central Bank is maintaining a regime of price stability and low inflation.

6. Tourism and travel

Travel within the Eurozone is easier as people don't have to change currency when travelling within it.

Disadvantages of the EMU for Ireland

1. UK does not use the Euro

The UK is not a member of the single currency, and a large part of Ireland's international trade is with the UK. Sterling may go up or down in value relative to the Euro. Fluctuating exchange rates can lead to exchange rate losses for Irish firms.

2. Irish interest rates are set by the ECB

The ECB controls interest rates in the Eurozone. The rates are set for Europe as a whole and do not always suit the Irish economy.

The Single European Market

The Single European Market removed barriers to trade among member states in order to provide full and open competition in both goods and labour within the EU.

Single European Market

Discuss the impact of the Single European Market on Irish business.   (25 marks)

Source: 2008 Higher Level Section 3

Suggested solution

Base your answer on the highlighted sections entitled 'Impact on Irish Business' presented below.

Marking scheme

- 5 points @ 5 marks (2 + 3) = 25 marks.

Impact of the Single European Market on Irish business

1. Free trade between member states

The elimination of barriers or tariffs allows the free movement of goods/services throughout the European Union.

Impact on Irish Business

- Irish firms have free access to EU market for exports.
- However, it puts pressure on Irish firms to become more competitive in order to compete with foreign goods coming into Ireland.

2. Free movement of capital

Firms can move capital from one country to another.

Impact on Irish Business

Individuals/businesses can invest in shares in companies throughout Europe.

3. Free movement of people

European citizens are allowed move freely between member states.

Impact on Irish Business

- Free movement may lead to competition for local jobs by non-nationals.
- It may lead to a scarcity of skilled staff in Ireland as workers may move to other countries.

4. Economies of Scale

Larger market could result in large-scale production, resulting in economies of scale and possible lowering of costs. Open borders allow firms to expand.

Impact on Irish Business

This should increase the competitiveness of Irish businesses.

5. Common external tariffs

The EU has a common system of barriers on goods imported from outside the EU.

Impact on Irish Business

Irish industry is protected from goods from outside the EU.

6. Public procurement

Governments are required to put public contracts up for tender from firms throughout the European Union.

Impact on Irish Business

This could result in the loss of large contracts for Irish firms.

7. Documentation simplified

The introduction of a single administration document has eliminated a vast number of administrative forms.

> **Impact on Irish Business**
> This has resulted in the lowering of administration costs for Irish Businesses.

Opportunities and challenges for Irish business in the EU market

Evaluate the opportunities and challenges for Irish business in the EU market.

(30 marks)

Source: 2009 Higher Level Section 3

Suggested solution

Base your answer on the highlighted sections entitled 'Evaluation' presented below.

Marking scheme
- Present three opportunities and two challenges (or vice versa).
- 5 points @ 5 marks (3 + 2)   = 25
- Evaluation − 5 marks 3 + 2   5
- Total   30

Opportunities in the EU market for Irish business

1. Free access to EU market for Irish exports

The EU market is the third largest in the world.

> **Evaluation**
> Business risks are reduced because of reduced dependence on the Irish domestic market.

2. Free movement of services, labour and capital

There is free movement of services, labour and capital throughout the EU.

> **Evaluation**
> - The Irish construction sector benefited hugely from availability of Polish and other EU workers during the boom years.
> - Businesses may source the best/investment/borrowing opportunities in EU.

3. Economies of scale

Economies of scale are made possible by the creation of a huge EU market.

> **Evaluation**
> This should increase the competitiveness of Irish businesses when selling abroad.

4. EU financial assistance

Funds from the EU are available for infrastructural development – improved infrastructure in Ireland.

> **Evaluation**
> Improved infrastructure in Ireland (e.g. better roads have benefited Irish business).

5. Lower transport/distribution costs

Free movement of goods and lower administration costs.

> **Evaluation**
> It has become easier and cheaper for Irish firms to do business in the EU.

6. Public procurement

Irish firms are eligible to tender for government contracts in EU states.

> **Evaluation**
> Irish companies can quote for government contracts in any EU member state.

Challenges in the EU market for Irish business

1. High distribution costs

Ireland is a small island on the periphery of Europe.

> **Evaluation**
> Distribution costs for exports are high, making Irish products less competitive.

2. Competition

Increased competition from other EU countries.

> **Evaluation**
> Some Irish firms may have difficulty surviving against foreign competition and imports from other EU countries.

3. Public procurement

EU companies are eligible to tender for Irish government contracts.

> **Evaluation**
> Irish firms are no longer guaranteed to get Irish government contracts.

4. High cost base

Ireland has high labour costs.

> **Evaluation**
> Some multinationals (e.g. Dell) have transferred production to lower-cost economies like Poland.

27 International Business

aims Be able to:

- Explain the role of global marketing in international business.
- Explain the role of information technology in globalisation.
- Describe the reasons for the development of transnational companies.

Global marketing

Global business

A global business sells the same product worldwide
It sees the whole world as its market and produces
a product for that market.
Examples: Toyota, Microsoft, Intel, Google,
Nokia, Dell.

Global product

A global product is designed to appeal to
consumers all over the world. It may
have to be adapted to suit different
markets.
Examples: Coca-Cola, Nike Runners.

Global marketing

Global marketing involves marketing a firm's
products and identity throughout the world as
if the world is one market.

A global firm must develop a global marketing mix in relation to the 4P's (product,
price, promotion, place). Global marketing uses either a standardised (same) marketing
mix or an adapted marketing mix to take account of differences in markets.

Role of global marketing in international business

1. **Activities planned and organised on a global basis**

   Business decisions are based on what is happening in world markets rather than
   national markets.

2. **Product standardisation of brand and product**

   Global companies do not consider the differences between countries and culture as
   being important. They attempt to sell one product in the same way worldwide,

focusing all the time on the similarities in the markets and attempting to satisfy the common desires of people everywhere.

3. **Reduction in costs and economies of scale**

Global marketing allows firms to expand globally, availing of the elimination of trade barriers, improvements in transport and advances in ICT, resulting in the achievement of economies of scale, reduction in costs and increasing profit.

4. **Facilities in many different locations**

Global companies set up assembly and manufacturing facilities in a number of different countries and export their products worldwide.

They seek out the most cost-effective locations and most cost-effective methods of production. They may manufacture the products in one country and assemble them in another country.

5. **Availability of high-quality products at lower prices**

Because of economies of scale, consumers get reliable, high-quality products at lower prices.

Global marketing mix

When marketing a product to a global market, a global company will use a **standardised marketing mix** throughout the world – The product is promoted, priced, distributed and sold in exactly the same way in different markets.

However, because of social, cultural, legal and economic differences in some markets, it may have to adapt the marketing mix to suit those markets. This is called an **adapted marketing mix**.

Elements of the global marketing mix

Global product

Product is the element of the marketing that global firm try not to change.

The global business aims to sell the same product in all markets, to develop a unique selling point and global brand and to benefit from economies of scale.

However, the product may need to be adjusted to reflect technical/legal requirements (e.g. left-hand drive car, etc.).

Packaging may also need to be changed to cater for the needs of the local market (e.g. recyclable materials).

Global price

Global firms try to keep the price the same in all markets, but prices may vary in different countries due to different factors, such as:

- Cost of living/incomes in different countries
- Recognising costs of production and extra transport distribution and marketing costs
- Duties or tariffs that might have to be paid
- Local prices levels/competitors' prices

Global promotion

If a global business can use the same promotional mix globally, it will save money. However, promotion may change in different countries to take account of legislation, language and culture.

Slogans need to be checked to avoid confusion and misunderstanding.

In addition to promoting goods and services through the normal avenues for advertising and sales promotion, global firms may use other promotion methods, including:

- Attending trade fairs
- Participating in trade missions
- Using the Internet

Global place

Global channels of distribution are necessary to implement a global marketing mix. Channels include:

- Selling directly to customers.
- Using an agent – An independent person who will act on behalf of the firm, generally receiving a commission on sales.
- Forming a strategic alliance with a foreign company to produce and/or market products. Both companies work together for mutual benefit.

Role of information and communication technology (ICT) in globalisation

Advances in ICT have greatly advances the development of globalisation. Applications such as e-mail, videoconferencing and EDI allow global business to function efficiently. ICT helps global firms in several ways.

1. **Communication**

   ICT allows global firms to transmit information to remote locations around the world (e.g. e-mail).

2. **Videoconferencing**

   Managers meetings can take place in different locations around the world without the need for expensive and time-consuming travel. Face-to-face communication is no longer necessary.

3. **Decision-making**

   Management can access data from anywhere in the world, availing of up-to-date information for speedy decision-making.

4. **Responding to change**

   Management must respond quickly to changes in the global market. Advanced ICT allows firms to respond faster than competitors to avail of opportunities.

Transnational companies

HL

Transnational companies

(i) Explain the term 'transnational company (TNC)'.

(ii) Discuss the reasons for the development of transnational companies in Ireland.

(20 marks)

Source: 2008 Higher Level Section 3

Suggested solution

(i) Transnational company (TNC)

A transnational company has its controlling headquarters in one country and branches in many other countries.

It operates on a worldwide scale

A transnational produces and markets goods in many countries. It treats the world as a single market place and may move operations from one country to another in response to changing market conditions.

Examples: Ford, Intel, Nestlé, Coca-Cola, CRH.

(ii) Reason for the development of transnational companies in Ireland

- **Transport improvements**

  The availability of faster and cheaper methods of air and sea travel has made it easier to supply markets worldwide.

- **Advances in communications technology**

  Improvements in communication have made it easier and faster to send and receive information (e.g. videoconferencing allows managers in different locations to hold a meeting without having to travel).

- **Economies of scale**

  Expanding abroad allows firms to achieve economies of scale, thereby lowering costs per unit. This enables them to compete more effectively with larger competitors.

- **Larger markets**

  Many companies find that their home market is saturated and does not offer the necessary scope for expansion. By setting up operations overseas they can maximise sales and spread business risk.

- **Removal of trade barriers**

  The removal of trade barriers has opened up international markets. The World Trade Organisation (WTO) has facilitated agreements between countries, eliminating or reducing barriers and freeing up international trade.

  A transnational company can locate a branch in Ireland and sell products into the EU member states.

Positive impact of transnational companies on Ireland

Transnational companies **impact positively** on the Irish economy in the following ways:

1. **Employment**

   Transnational companies buy raw materials and services from local firms, creating local employment. They are also a major direct employer in many locations in the country.

2. **Balance of payments**

   They export much of their finished products. Also, the level of imports of manufacturing products is reduced. This has a positive effect on the balance of payments.

3. **Government revenue**

   Transnationals are a major source of revenue for the government through corporation tax on profits, VAT on purchases, and PAYE and PRSI paid by employees.

4. **Competition**

   Transnational companies create competition for indigenous Irish firms. This is good for the Irish consumer as it leads to reduced prices and increased efficiency, resulting in better quality goods and services.

Negative impact of transnational companies on Ireland

Transnational companies **impact negatively** on the Irish economy in the following ways:

1. **Possible closure**

   Transnational companies may close plants in Ireland and move abroad in an effort to cut costs and become more competitive (e.g. in 2010 Dell moved its manufacturing operation from Limerick to Poland with the loss of 1,900 jobs in Ireland).

2. **Repatriation of profits**

   Most of their profits are transferred to head office, so the profits made do not benefit the Irish economy.

3. **Size and impact**

   Because of their size, transnationals have been known to exert pressure on governments and may threaten to withdraw from a country if they do not get their own way on grants, taxes, etc.

Applied Business Question (ABQ) (Higher Level)

Based on Units 5, 6 and 7
This is a compulsory question for Leaving Certificate 2013/2018

Fruit First Ltd

Fruit First Ltd produces a range of 'smoothies', a fruit drink made from crushed fruit. Mary Ryan, a food scientist in the food industry, identified a gap in the market for an Irish supplier of natural fruit drinks. In her spare time she produced a batch of smoothies, supplying samples to local shops. Encouraged by the favourable responses, she left her job and set up Fruit First Ltd in 2001.

The business, based in the midlands, sources fresh fruit locally and from abroad. Bringing new investors on board in 2006 enabled Fruit First to invest in larger premises, doubling its production capacity. Profits are approaching €1 million and the business now employs thirty full-time workers.

The chilled drink products come in attractively-designed cartons of different sizes, supplied by a local firm. Fruit First vans deliver the products to retail outlets, nutrition shops and fitness centres nationwide. Mary's focus on producing a quality product has allowed her to command a higher price than her competitors. Annual investment in research and development has led to a widening of the product range and development of a green image for the business. Initially, Mary used local supermarkets to encourage consumers to taste the products. Over time, Fruit First's marketing strategies expanded and the brand has now become associated with 'National Healthy Heart Day'.

As the leading Irish supplier of smoothies, further expansion in the small Irish market is unlikely. Mary sees the potential to grow the business and she is considering entering the UK market initially and subsequently the wider EU market. While recognising the high cost base in Ireland and the perishable nature of the product, Mary has begun developing an export strategy. Fruit First is in discussion with a leading food retailing chain in relation to supplying shops throughout the UK. Mary views this as an opportunity and a necessary step before entering the wider EU market place.

(A) Evaluate the elements of the marketing mix for Fruit First Ltd.   (30 marks)

(B) Discuss how Fruit First Ltd benefits the local **and** national economy. Refer to the above text in your answer.   (25 marks)

(C) You have been appointed to advise Fruit First Ltd on entering international markets. Outline your analysis of the opportunities **and** challenges facing Fruit First Ltd and make an appropriate recommendation.   (25 marks)

(80 marks)

Suggested solution

(A) Evaluate the elements of the marketing mix

Product (2 marks)

The product is the physical good or service provided. The product is made up of the detailed characteristics of the good/service on offer, e.g. its distinctive features, its form, shape and colour. It includes any relevant information on the item for the customer such as its quality, after-sales service, guarantees, brand name and image, etc. Green image is a unique selling point (USP). (2 marks)

Link to text

Crushed Fruit Drink (2 marks)

Evaluation (product) – There is a commitment to R&D and this will ensure that the product will evolve. The product life cycle should be considered. (2 marks)

Price (2 marks)

Price is what one pays for a product. It is also the representation of the value of the product to the buyer. The price of a product on the market will be determined by the product's unique properties, the cost of manufacture, the competition, target market, etc. If the particular product is aimed at the luxury end or segment (niche) of the market then the price set may be high. (2 marks)

Link to text

Mary's focus on producing a quality product has allowed her command a higher price than her competitors (2 marks)

Evaluation (price) – The pricing strategy operation in Ireland may not operate in the UK as there may be more competition there. (2 marks)

Promotion (2 marks)

Promotion is concerned with letting existing and possible future customers know about the products on offer in order to increase sales. The essential promotional techniques (methods) are advertising, sales promotion, public relations (sponsorship), and personal selling. (2 marks)

Link to text

Development of a green image for the business
Brand association with National Healthy Heart Day
Attractively designed cartons
Supplying samples to local shops (2 marks)

Evaluation (promotion) – The promotion strategies include the supply of samples and the association with the 'National Healthy Heart Day'. Fruit First may have to develop their promotion mix further to include advertising and other sales promotion techniques. (2 marks)

Place (2 marks)

Firms must use the most suitable and cost-effective way of distributing their products. The channel of distribution used in the case of Fruit First Ltd is the manufacturer to the retailer to consumer. It is a perishable good which needs to get to the market quickly. The business need to stay close to the consumers to see where trends are going. (2 marks)

Link to text

Vans deliver the products to the retail outlets, nutrition centres and fitness centres nationwide. Distribute in foreign markets through leading food retailer chains. (2 marks)

Evaluation (place) – with the proposed expansion to the UK there may be channel of distribution problems.

Marking scheme

(A)	Evaluate elements of the marking mix. Must be linked to Text of ABQ.	4 elements @ 6 marks each (2 + 2 + 2) (State, Explain, Link) Evaluation @ 6 marks 3 evaluations @ 2 marks each.	30 marks

(B) The benefits of Fruit First Ltd for the local and national economy

I. Employment (3 marks)

Enterprises create jobs directly, with many of the employees drawn from the local community. Jobs are also created indirectly in supplier firms and those firms supplying services. (2 marks)

Link to text

The business employs thirty full-time workers (2 marks)

II. Increased business activity/local suppliers (2 marks)

There is increased business activity in the local area leading to more money in circulation for the benefit of other businesses. Business activity is sustained by reinvestment of surpluses in the business. (2 marks)

Possible links to text include:

Sources fresh fruit locally

Invest in larger premises doubling its production capacity. (2 marks)

III. Government revenue (2 marks)

The government receives extra revenue from VAT on the sale of goods and extra income tax from the increased number of people employed. It is also a profitable company paying corporations' profits tax. (2 marks)

Possible links to text include:

Leading Irish supplier of smoothies (high sales)

Sources fresh fruit from abroad (customs duty)

Profits are approaching €1 million (corporations, profits, tax).

30 full-time employees (Income tax). (2 marks)

IV. Foreign trade/increased exports/imports (2 marks)

If products are produced here and sold abroad they bring foreign currency into the country. This foreign currency can in turn be used to pay for imports. Favourable balance of trade/balance of payments.

Trade provides opportunities to develop good relationships with other countries. (2 marks)

Possible links to text include:

Mary has begun developing an export strategy

Sources fresh fruit from abroad' (2 marks)

Marking scheme

(B)	Discuss the benefits to local and national economy. Must be linked to text of ABQ. 2 national/2 local benefits	4 points at 7 + 6 + 6 + 6 marks (3 + 2 + 2) and (2 + 2 + 2) (State, Discuss, Link)	25 marks

(C) The opportunities and challenges for Fruit First Ltd in international markets, including recommendations

(i) The **opportunities** facing Fruit First Ltd are:

I. Access to bigger markets (2 marks)

Export markets provide a larger potential market for a firm and provide an opportunity to increase sales and profits. (2 marks)

Link to text

To sell to the UK and subsequently the wider EU market (2 marks)

II. Economies of scale (2 marks)

An economy of scale reduces cost per unit as a firm increases in size i.e. reductions in costs that come from buying, producing and selling in large quantities. (2 marks)

Link to text

While recognising the high cost base in Ireland (2 marks)

III. Reduced risk

By diversifying into a new market a firm is spreading its risk making it less dependent on one market.

Link to text

As the leading Irish supplier of smoothies further expansion in the Irish market is unlikely

(ii) The **challenges** facing Fruit First Ltd are:

    I. Competition   (2 marks)

    The UK and the EU markets are much larger than Ireland and there is likely to be large well established firms operating in those markets thereby providing more competition for Fruit First Ltd.   (2 marks)

    Possible links to text include:

    Leading Irish supplier of smoothies . . . small Irish market

    Investment in R&D. Product development and the widening of the product range have helped it to keep ahead of competitors in Ireland.   (2 marks)

    II. Currency   (2 marks)

    The UK is not a member of the Single Currency and Sterling may go up or down in value relative to the Euro. Fluctuating exchange rates can lead to exchange rate losses for Irish firms. A falling value of sterling damages the competitiveness of Irish exports.   (2 marks)

    Link to text

    UK food retailer/fluctuating exchange rate   (2 marks)

    III. Language

    Selling abroad often involves selling through a foreign language. This will affect aspects of the business including documentation, labelling, advertising etc. This will apply to most countries across Europe.

    Link to text

    Considering entering the wider EU market.   (2 marks)

(iii) The **recommendations** for the Fruit First Ltd are:

    (i) Start in the UK market – Have the language/familiarity with culture/good trade links/close to the Irish market (i.e. low transport costs) etc.   (3 marks)

Marking scheme

(C)	Analyse the opportunities and challenges on entering international markets. Must be linked to Text of ABQ. 2 Opportunities/2 Challenges. Appropriate Recommendation.	4 points at 5 marks each (2 + 2 + 1) (State, Analyse, Link) 1 @ 5 marks (2 + 3)	25 marks

Index